The Roman Frontier on the Gask Ridge Perth and Kinross

An interim report on the Roman Gask Project
1995 – 2000

D. J. Woolliscroft

with contributions by

A. T. Croom, M. H. Davies, A. C. Finnegan, M. A. Hall
K. F. Hartley, B. Hoffmann, A. J. Hughes, N. J. Lockett
and S. Ramsay

BAR British Series 335
2002

Published in 2016 by
BAR Publishing, Oxford

BAR British Series 335

The Roman Frontier on the Gask Ridge: Perth and Kinross

ISBN 978 1 84171 410 3

BAR Publishing is the trading name of British Archaeological Reports (Oxford) Ltd.
British Archaeological Reports was first incorporated in 1974 to publish the BAR
Series, International and British. In 1992 Hadrian Books Ltd became part of the BAR
group. This volume was originally published by Archaeopress in conjunction with
British Archaeological Reports (Oxford) Ltd / Hadrian Books Ltd, the Series principal
publisher, in 2002. This present volume is published by BAR Publishing, 2016.

Printed in England

BAR
PUBLISHING

BAR titles are available from:

BAR Publishing
122 Banbury Rd, Oxford, OX2 7BP, UK
EMAIL   info@barpublishing.com
PHONE   +44 (0)1865 310431
FAX   +44 (0)1865 316916
www.barpublishing.com

Ardoch Roman fort.

Contents

List of Illustrations.

Preface

The Roman Gask Project was founded in 1995 in the University of Manchester, with the writer as Director. It has since been engaged in an intensive campaign of surveys, excavation and archive work, which has included, where necessary, preparing past research by other workers for publication. Its remit was kept deliberately broad to cover all of Roman Scotland north of the Antonine Wall but, as its name suggests, its principle focus has been on the system of military works on and around the Gask Ridge in Perthshire. The Project is still very much under way and seems likely to continue for the foreseeable future. The current work is thus an interim report to describe the progress made during its first five years.

The monograph will be divided into two main sections. Chapter One will attempt to provide an overview of the current state of knowledge on the Gask, drawn together from many disparate sources, both from our own work and that of others. It will also try to give some idea of the problems still remaining and the likely thrust of future research. The remaining, much shorter, chapters will report on a series of field work programs, mostly by the Gask Project itself, but with two rescued from the archives and dating from the 1960's and 70's.

During its brief life, the Gask Project has undertaken nineteen excavations, large and small, along with numerous conventional and geophysical surveys, museum and archive work, air photographic flights and field walking tasks. None of this could have been done without a great deal of help and the writer would like to thank the small army of people without whose support and enthusiasm this book could not have been produced, most of whom gave of their time and expertise or allowed access to land unpaid. Firstly, I must thank the two other full members of the Project: my Deputy Director Dr Birgitta Hoffmann and Dr Neil Lockett, our expert on civilian activity. Both have directed field work on behalf of the Project and contributed to its publications and their unstinting hard work in often difficult conditions is very much appreciated. Over fifty students and volunteers from ten different countries have taken part in our field program to date and space does not allow me to mention every participant by name, but I would like to give special thanks to our small but dedicated team of regular trench supervisors: Mr K M Miller, Ms A J Hughes, Dr A G Keen, Mr M T Murphy, Ms S Moore and Ms A T Hamel.

Others have provided specialist services and I would particularly like to thank Dr S Ramsay for her environmental work, Ms A C Finnegan for her studies of our lithic finds, Mr P Green who has run our Web site since its inception and Dr A T Croom, Dr K Hartley, Dr V G Swan and Mrs F C Wild for their pottery analyses. Dr D Simpson has made his medical services available to our excavations and Mr W Fuller has patiently flown a nervous yet demanding archaeologist around the skies of the region on air photographic flights.

A large number of colleagues have offered valuable ideas and suggestions and, on occasions, shot down my own more fanciful interpretations. My thanks are especially due to Prof W S Hanson, Prof D J Breeze, Ms R Jones, Mr G S Maxwell, Prof L J F Keppie, Mr M A Hall, Dr T M Allan, Dr J C C Romans and to the RCAHMS.

I would also like to take the opportunity of thanking the various bodies who have funded our work. The Perth & Kinross Heritage Trust, have financed i.a. most of our scientific and air photographic program as well as providing a great deal of other vital support. The Society of Antiquaries of Scotland and The Roman Research Trust, have sponsored many of our excavations and my thanks are also due to Historic Scotland, The Derrick Riley Bursary, The University of Manchester and Ilford (UK) Ltd all of whom have given much appreciated support.

During the life of the Project we have been made more welcome than we had dared hope by the farmers and land owners on whose land we have operated. Without their support we could have achieved nothing and, to date, we have yet to be refused permission to do anything we have asked for. I am grateful to Mr R D Baird, Mr R M Smith, Mr R H B Smith, Ardoch Farming Co Ltd, Blackford Farms Ltd, The Duplin Estate, Mr A Simpson, Mr M Bullough, Mr J Christie, Mr J Guthrie, Mr I D Brown, Mr W Fotheringham, Mr W Rob, Mr R Hamilton, Mr D W Scougall, Mr A Scougall and Mr D Graham. We are also grateful to Mr and Mrs A D and E Graham for providing accommodation for our often wet and muddy dig crews.

Finally, I owe thanks to the shades of a number of colleagues now departed, notably: Dr D J Christison, Prof A S Robertson, Prof J K St Joseph, Mr E Bradley, Mrs D M Lye and, in particular, Prof G D B Jones. Some of these I have the honour to have known, some I did not, but all have inspired my interest in this area and it is to them that this book is dedicated.

David Woolliscroft   2002

1. The Roman Gask Frontier: The Current State of Research.

D J Woolliscroft

Topography and Background

The Roman Gask system consists of a chain of fortifications strung out along the Roman road between the forts of Camelon (Falkirk) and Bertha on the Tay (fig 1.1). It is made up of four basic elements, of which the first is the road itself. This is a classic, well engineered, all weather Roman road of between 6 and 8m wide and consists of a rammed gravel surface usually resting on a bed of larger stones. In damp areas the entire structure has sometimes been built up on a low turf built mound or "agger" (Chap 5) and it makes occasional use of small cuttings and embankments to smooth its gradients, especially when crossing stream valleys (Chap 7). The usual drainage ditches to either side are, however, often lacking. As befits a Roman road, it frequently runs almost perfectly straight for miles at a time and much of it can still be seen today. Quite a number of stretches are still in use, as either public roads or farm and forestry tracks. Of the rest, the great bulk has now been traced by air photography, either as parch marks, produced by the structure itself, or as parallel lines of crop marks caused by the small quarry pits from which the building material was dug (fig 7.1). For the most part, only short sections still remain to be identified, although the exact line of the last few miles before the Tay has yet to be traced.

The fortifications consist of a series of turf and timber built forts, smaller fortlets and watch towers, all of which lie close to and often right beside, the road (fig 1.2 and Appendix 2). There are three forts on the line: Ardoch, Strageath and Bertha and all three are large (up to 3.5 ha (8.6 acres)) auxiliary forts, capable of holding at least one complete unit. Only Ardoch has yet produced any evidence to identify its garrison, but this fort has yielded the tombstone of a soldier of Cohors I Hispanorum (The First Cohort of Spaniards), apparently dating to the first century AD (RIB 2213). This unit is later attested as being 1000 strong and "equitata" (part mounted), but at Ardoch the cohort seems to have been just 500 strong and its title, as given on the inscription, would suggest a purely infantry unit (Jarrett 1994, 45f).

The fortlets are much smaller installations of around 20m x 22m internally. They are broadly comparable in size with the milecastles of Hadrian's Wall, but appear far less frequently on the Gask. Three are now known with certainty, at Glenbank, Kaims Castle (fig 1.3) and Midgate (fig 1.8), with one more suspected at Raith (see below) and they may occur at a fairly regular spacing interval of six Roman miles (8.87 km).

The smallest and most common site type on the system are the towers. 18 are known at present and there are almost certainly more still awaiting discovery. These were simple timber structures (fig 1.4), perhaps originally around 10m high, and were founded on four large timber corner posts. They were surrounded by a low turf rampart (an unusual feature on Roman timber

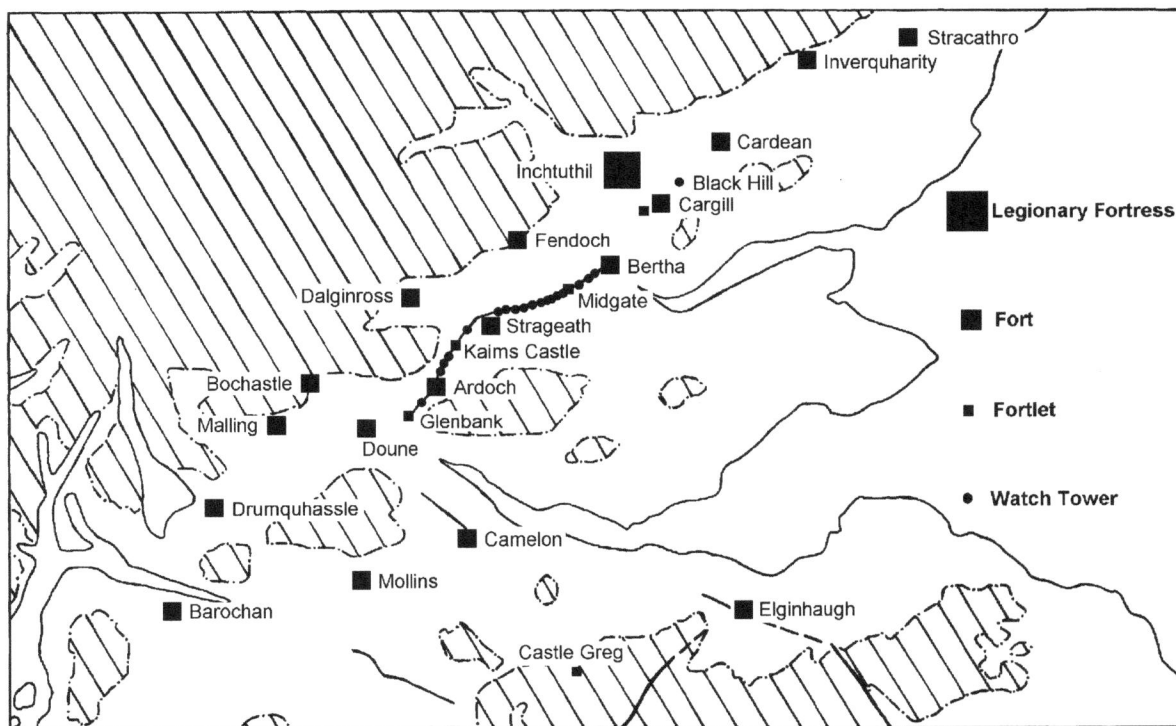

Fig 1.1 Northern Scotland in the Flavian Period.

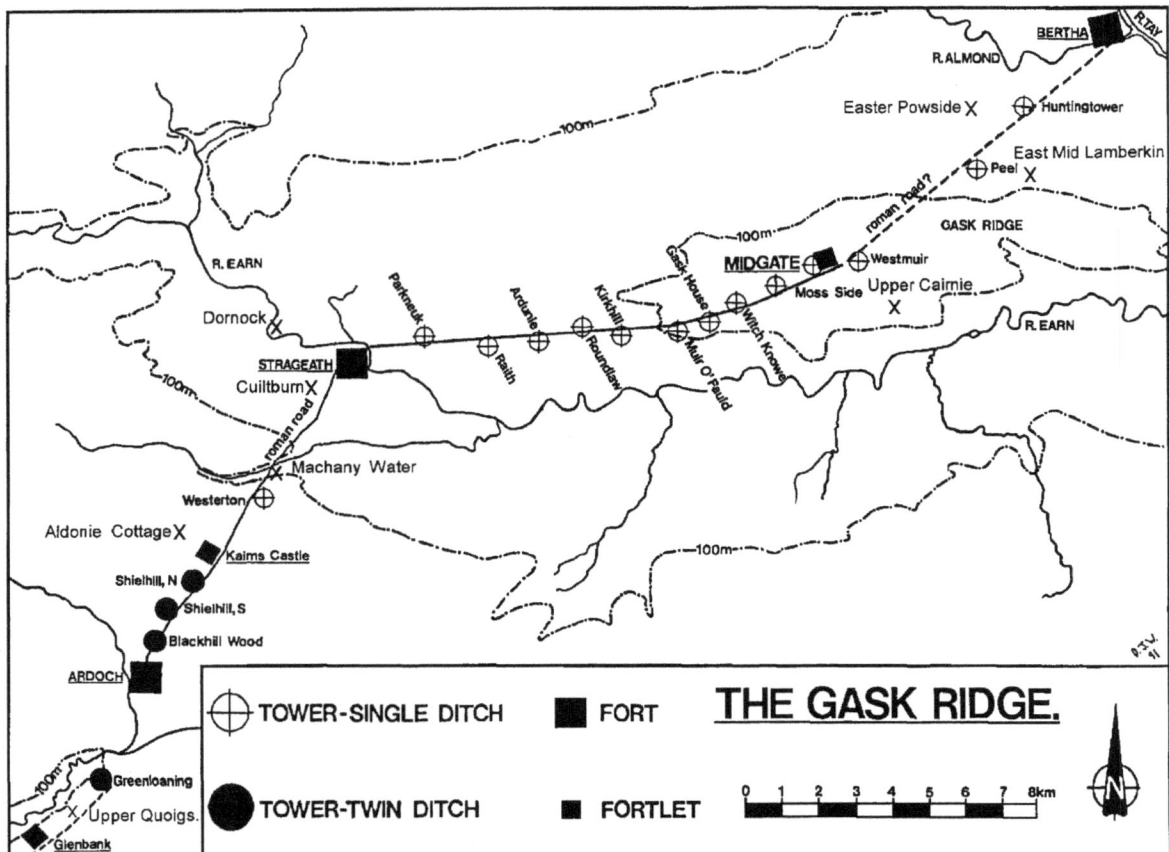

Fig 1.2 The Roman Gask Frontier.

towers elsewhere) and then by circular to sub-rectangular ring ditches, with single entrance breaks. Their entire diameter is generally less than 25m. The towers presumably acted as observation posts, although they probably also had a signalling capability, if only to allow them to transmit warnings to the principle garrison sites. Roman artistic representations, such as the opening scenes of Trajan's column (Woolliscroft 2001, fig 4), show such towers with pyramidal roofs and elevated balconies, presumably to act as observation platforms, but although the ground plans of many of the Gask towers have now been excavated in detail, we have little or no evidence with which to reconstruct their upper superstructures.

As currently known (fig 1.2), the line begins at Glenbank fortlet, some 6 km to the north of Dunblane, and runs north-east up the south side of Strathallan (see Appendix 1) as far as the hamlet of Greenloaning where the first known tower is located. Here it crosses the Allan Water and turns north to reach the fort of Ardoch (see frontispiece), just outside the modern village of Braco. It then runs slightly east of north up a long incline until it reaches Kaims Castle fortlet (fig 1.3) which marks the watershed between Strathallan and Strathearn. From here it continues on the same heading

down to cross the Earn at the fort of Strageath, having first crossed its tributary, the Machany Water, at Bishop's Bridge. The road then strikes out almost due east and climbs up to run along the southern edge of the fairly broad flat summit of the Gask Ridge, a long, low, if prominent, glacial feature from which the system as a whole takes its name. It keeps to the ridge top for roughly 10 km, during the last three of which it swings to the north-east, and then runs off down a relatively gentle incline towards the fort of Bertha which lies on the Tay/Almond confluence just upstream of Perth. The last few miles lie in rich agricultural land where the road has long been ploughed away and, although two towers are now known, at Peel and West Mains of Huntingtower, the road itself can only be traced via a few, somewhat ambiguous, air photographic features and a well defined quarry pit alignment to the west of Huntingtower Castle. It is assumed, however, to run just to the south of modern Tibbermore, past Huntingtower Castle and across the Almond valley to the fort. Hopefully much of this sector will be traced more precisely in the future, although erosion in the Almond flood plane may have removed any trace of the final 1-2km. In all the system, as currently understood, is 37 km long and has 24 known installations.

2

Fig 1.3. Kaims Castle fortlet from the air.

The Gask line was, at the very least, a fortified and carefully monitored road, but it is usually regarded as a fully fledged Roman frontier system, perhaps designed to protect Fife and, more specifically, the always strategically important, potential invasion route down Strathearn. At first sight, however, there is nothing particularly remarkable about it. It belongs to a familiar class of Roman linear land defences, which also includes, for example, the Wetterau Limes in Germany (Klee 1989). It is, though, an extremely early example. For the line has for some time been tentatively dated to the 80's AD and the reign of the last of the Flavian dynasty of Emperors, Domitian, 40 years before the construction of Hadrian's Wall. It is certainly the oldest frontier in Britain but, for many years, it was thought to be slightly later than the beginnings of the line in Germany, largely thanks to the Roman writer (and former governor of Britain) Frontinus (Strategematon II, 3,10), who refers to Domitian extending the frontier during his German wars in 83 AD. Recently, however, the Germans have announced a re-dating of their frontier to the reign of the Emperor Trajan, 15-20 years later (Körtüm 1998), which means that the Gask may now represent the very earliest of these systems: in effect the prototype limes (pronounced "Leemase") frontier. As such, it suddenly acquires a special place in Roman frontier studies, far beyond its own (albeit considerable) intrinsic interest, because the state of development of the prototype has obvious implications for any study of the later evolution of Roman frontier design.

Until recently, however, the Gask has been curiously neglected, especially when compared with the two British mural frontiers: Hadrian's Wall and the Antonine Wall. For, although the system has attracted attention from some of the great names of Roman military archaeology for over a century and much good work has been done, this has seldom been on a sustained basis and, in particular, there has been less interest than one might have liked in studying the line as an integrated system rather than as simply a collection of individual sites. Given the frontier's new importance, such a situation could no longer be accepted and it was to make some amends that the Roman Gask Project was initially founded. Its work has now made a contribution in a number of areas and much of the archaeological detail is either already in print, or dealt with in the later chapters of this book. The rest of this chapter, however, will offer a synthesis of the results obtained to date and attempt to deal with a range of more general, systemic questions.

The Date of the System

Let us start with the sometimes controversial matter of the system's date and length of occupation. Of the three main garrison forts on the line: Ardoch, Strageath and

3

Bertha, the first two have for many years been known to have both Flavian and, mid second century, Antonine occupations (Breeze 1983 and Frere and Wilkes 1989, 69f). It had always seemed likely that Bertha would show a similar pattern and the Gask Project has now been able to prove this, thanks to a collection of fieldwalking finds loaned to us for analysis by an amateur group (Chap 3). Unfortunately, there has long been a near total lack of datable material from the minor installations: the towers and fortlets, to show which (if any) of the fort occupations they accompanied. Indeed, at the time the Project was founded, the only published dating evidence from any of these sites was two sherds of pottery: one from Gask House tower on the Gask Ridge proper (Robertson 1974, 20f) and one from Westerton tower to the south of Strageath (Hanson and Friell 1995, 506f). This is hardly a great deal to build on when trying to date an entire frontier and the situation was made worse by the nature of the material. For, unfortunately, even these meagre finds are not as helpful as they might have been. The Gask House sherd is definitely a fragment of Flavian mortarium, but it was essentially unstratified since it came from the back fill of the tower's ditch and so doesn't necessarily derive from the site's occupation. Gask House sits only meters from both the Roman road and a small, undated, Roman

temporary camp and it is not difficult to imagine a pot sherd from either the camp or from road traffic being discarded on an abandoned site. The situation at Westerton is even less auspicious, for the sherd there was only described in the report as "probably Flavian" and it too came from an ambiguous context in the ditch fill. Worse still there is, as yet, no dating evidence whatever for the system's three fortlets. Despite these difficulties, however, a belief has grown up that the entire system of forts, fortlets and towers must all be Flavian in origin.

It must be admitted from the outset that the Gask Project's own work has, so far, done only a little to improve this absolute dating deficiency. For in, to date, nineteen excavations we have only been able to add four more datable finds, two of which are no more closely datable than that they are Roman. Roman timber towers are notorious for their lack of artefacts, so this should come as no great surprise and the finds do at least provide some small additional support for the traditional Flavian date, but again the material came from less than helpful contexts. The first was a sherd of late first century glass from the top of the ditch fill at Shielhill South tower (Woolliscroft and Hoffmann 1998, 451), whilst the second, a piece of decorated Flavian Samian

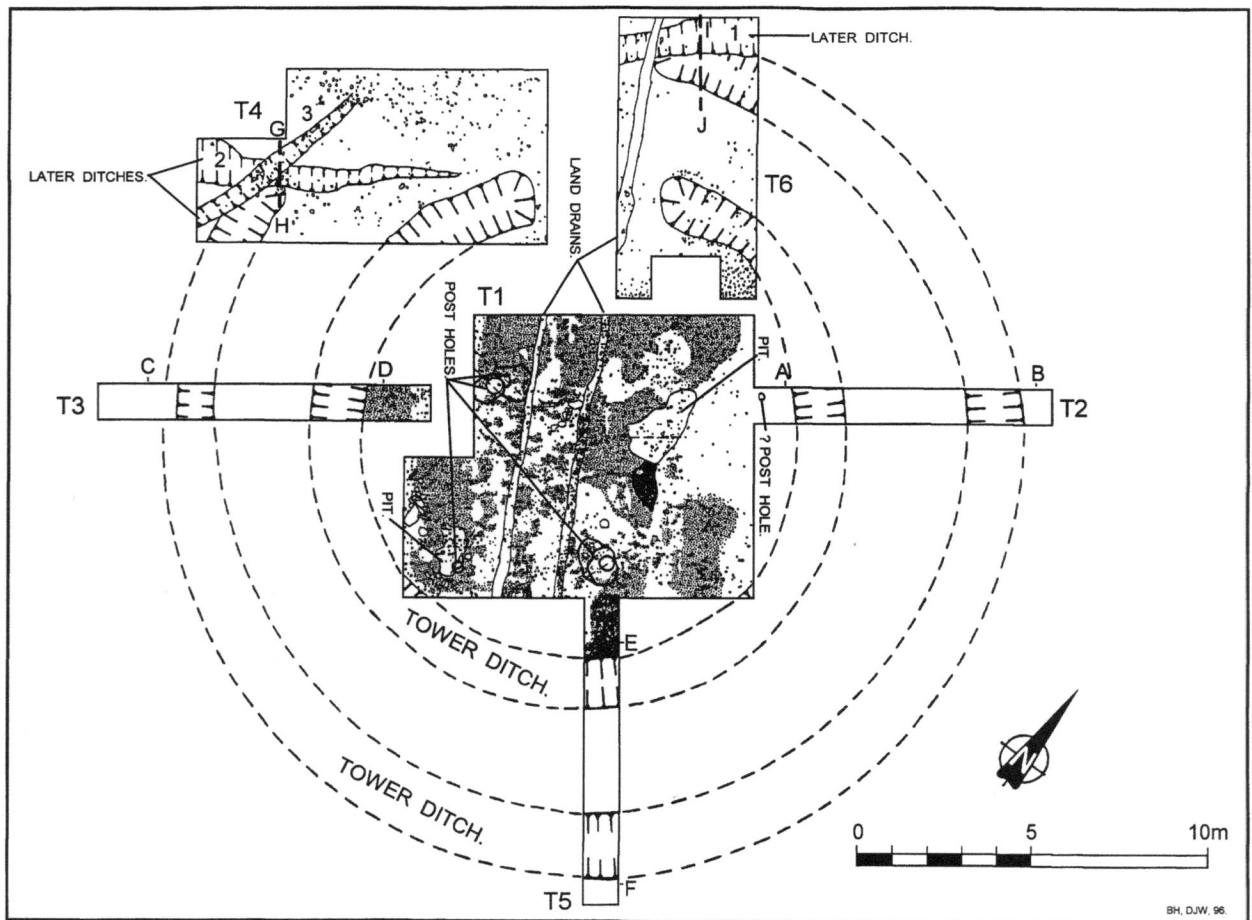

Fig 1.4 Greenloaning tower, site plan.

4

ware (fig 1.16), derives from a still rather mysterious site at Cuiltburn. Cuiltburn also produced a less closely datable fragment of Roman course ware, as did the watchtower at Huntingtower (Woolliscroft forthcoming (a)). Nevertheless, it does appear ever more likely that the tower line is first century in date, although the position regarding the fortlets still remains open to question. If nothing else, however, the lack of finds from the Gask towers may allow us to say something about the way in which they were occupied. For the absence of general refuse makes it seem unlikely that the tower crews actually lived on site. This picture is further strengthened by the fact that, despite the excellent state of preservation of some of the sites, no Gask tower has yet produced evidence for hearths, which again suggests that no cooking activities took place on site. The tower crews may, thus, have been outstationed on a shift basis from larger installations, most probably the forts. Any food eaten on duty might then have been in the nature of a cold packed lunch, or cooked and eaten from metal mess tins which would not have suffered the breakages inevitable with pottery and so will not have left archaeological remains. Cooking may have been done over braziers, which might again have left little archaeological trace, although the fact that no signs of pre-demolition fire ash have been found on any of the towers makes even this somewhat open to question. Indeed, the absence of hearths might even suggest that occupation was seasonal, for the sites would have been bitterly cold in winter without artificial heating. This does seem unlikely, however, and again braziers (perhaps used at upper floor level) might have been used without leaving much mark on the archaeological record, especially if the ash was dumped outside the ditch circuits (which usually represent the limits of excavation).

Where the Gask Project's activities have been of considerably more help is in shedding light on the system's likely life span. In the past this has usually been assumed to have been exceedingly brief, perhaps no more than a season or two (e.g. Breeze 1982, 65) and the reasons are fairly simple. For, if the Roman historian Tacitus (Agricola 22) is to be believed, the Romans did not even reach this area until the famous governor Agricola's third campaign, at the earliest, which was in 79 or 80 AD depending on which of two competing chronologies one prefers (Syme 1958, 22, A Birley 1976, and Hanson 1987, 40f). The Samian pottery, on the other hand, points to a Roman withdrawal in or before 90 AD (Hartley 1972, 13f), whilst Hobley (1989) has argued, from coin evidence, that they must have left by 86 or, more probably, 87. But many would doubt whether the system would even have lasted this long, partly through a reluctance to believe that it could have coexisted with the more northerly line of so called "glen blocking" forts (from Drumquhassle to Inchtuthil, around the southern highland fringe (fig 1.1)) and partly because of a

perceived difference between the structural histories of the towers and forts. For Ardoch and Strageath (less is known about Bertha) have shown signs of two structural phases within the Flavian period (for Ardoch: Christison and Cunningham 1898, Macdonald 1919, 122-6, Breeze 1983, 229ff, for Strageath, Frere and Wilkes 1989, 69f), suggesting either two occupations separated by a short abandonment or, simply, a long enough occupation for rebuilding to become necessary. Only a single phase had been recognised in the minor installations, however, which has led to a number of suggestions for suitable stages within the Flavian conquest and occupation where a short chronology system might be fitted. For example, Breeze (1982, 65) has proposed that the frontier may have been built right at the end of the Flavian occupation, after the abandonment of the glenblocker line and the legionary fortress of Inchtuthil. He would see this as a last ditch and ultimately unsuccessful attempt to hold onto at least some conquered territory, most notably the Fife peninsular, whose inhabitants the Venicones have sometimes been held to have been pro-Roman (e.g. Hanson 1987, 157). G.S. Maxwell (1990, 360), on the other hand, has argued for a slightly earlier date, perhaps as a temporary line of consolidation at the very end of Agricola's governorship, with at least some of the glenblockers, including Inchtuthil, being assigned to his, as yet unknown, successor. Frere (1980, 96) has proposed a foundation two years earlier still, in 80 or 81 and would again suggest that the system's role was to provide cover for a protectorate of some sort in Fife, whilst Shotter (1996, 40) has in the past argued for 79 or 80. Finally, Pitts and St.Joseph (1985, 278f) would date the line to Agricola's sixth campaigning season (82 or 83 AD) but, unlike most other scholars, they argue that the Gask and the Glenblockers do belong together, with the Gask acting as a fortified supply line for the more forward forts.

The present writer has also argued in the past that the two lines could be mutually supporting and so could usefully operate together (Woolliscroft 1993, 299f). Here it is important to note that almost all of the towers on the Gask Ridge itself were provided with excellent views south over Strathearn, even though this has often been at the expense of their having little or no view to the immediate north. It would thus be relatively easy to approach the system fairly closely from that direction without being detected, even though the towers are almost always intervisible with both of their neighbours and almost all of the road is in sight of one or more of them. Such a layout would have been potentially dangerous for such a lightly manned system if it was specifically designed to control movements across the actual line from the north. It thus presumably reflects on the frontier's intended function and suggests that this was first and foremost to monitor the valley. For the situation would have been simple to avoid, as the tower chain could easily have been run just a little further forward from where it would have gained a vastly better view to the north. Such is the shape of the flat, fairly broad topped ridge summit, however, that this his would have cost it its views of the Strath, and the line actually chosen is probably a compromise since it does allow some towers, notably Raith, Moss Side and Midgate, to retain longer distance views to the Highland line itself (especially from their full original height), whilst the bulk of the line concentrated on Strathearn, presumably to prevent any attempted flanking manoeuvres by that route.

Such a compromise might, though, be thought to depend, at least partly, on the system's relationship with the glenblockers. For if we are to see these forts in their traditionally envisaged defensive role (Ogilvie and Richmond 1967, 76), rather than as springboards for further assaults into the highland massif that never materialised (Breeze 1982, 55f), their positions are such that most would probably have received little or no prior warning of attack. They were thus also exposed to considerable danger, especially if they are regarded as standing alone. Under normal circumstances, one assumes that the Romans would have maintained

intelligence cover ahead of their lines to give advance warning of any major attack (Woolliscroft 1988, 23ff). But, in the fluid conditions that are likely to have existed for much of the Flavian period in Scotland, intelligence breakdowns could easily have placed the glenblockers in serious jeopardy. A number of the forts, notably Fendoch (Richmond and McIntyre 1936 and 1939) and Bochastle (Anderson 1956), are sited right in the mouths of their glens and have views of only a few hundred metres into them. Fendoch has long been claimed to have been screened to some degree by a watch tower set on the opposite side of the Sma' Glen (fig 1.14 and Keppie 1998, 160) which would have improved observation cover, although not to the degree that has often been claimed. But the identity of this site is open to question (see below) and certainly no such towers have been claimed at any of the other forts, even though the conditions for site survival in the rugged, unploughed glen mouths are often excellent. The glenblockers might thus expect no more than a few minutes warning of surprise attacks down their glens, so that even with garrisons of full cohort strength they could easily have become hostages to fortune. Gask

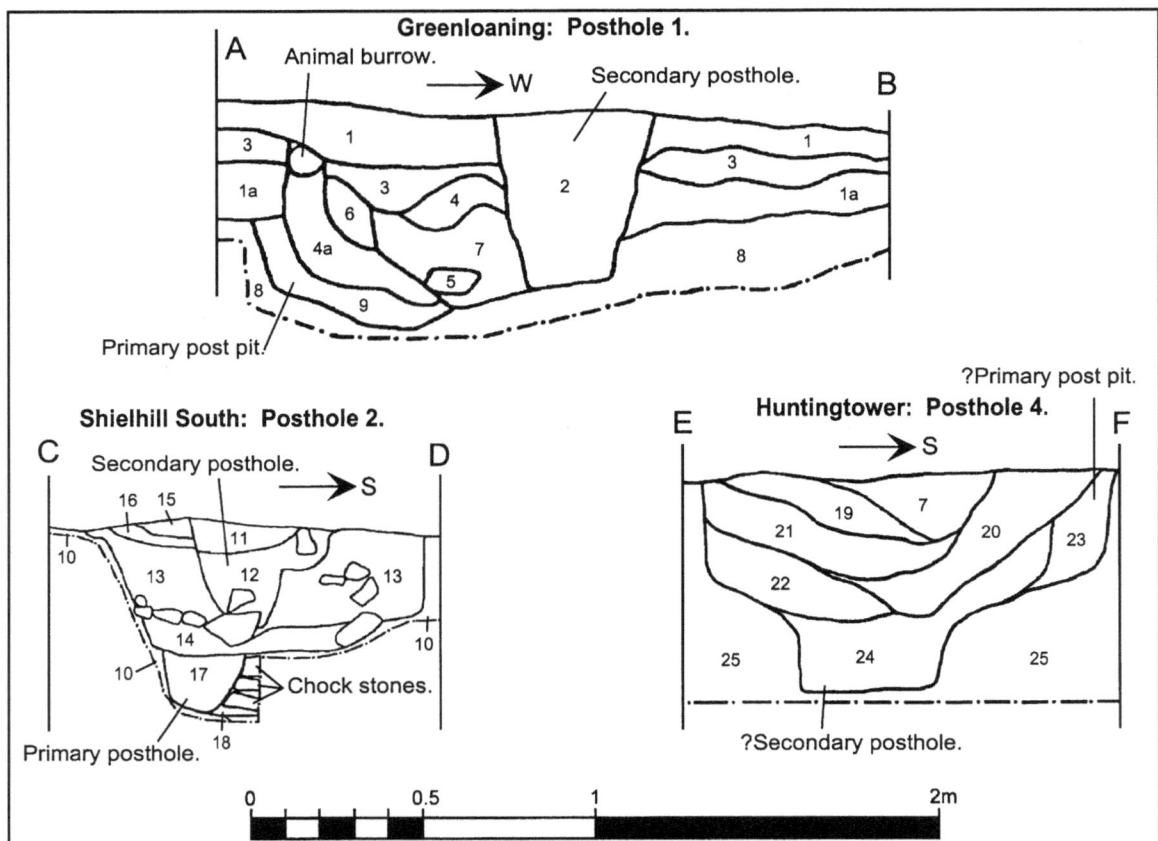

1. Gravel in brown clay. 2. Brown loam with charcoal. 3. Dark brown gritty loam. 4. Pink clay. 5. Dark brown gritty clay. 6. Brown sandy loam with gravel. 7. Brown loam with clay. 8. Natural dark brown sand. 9. Brown sandy loam. 10. Natural sand/gravel aggregate. 11. Grey loam with charcoal. 12. Pink/grey loam with charcoal. 13. Brown sandy clay with stones. 14. Grey/brown loam with gravel. 15. Burnt red sandy clay. 16. Burnt turf. 17. Loose dark brown loam. 18. Brown sand. 19. Grey/green turf. 20. Pale orange sandy clay. 21. Soft red sandy clay. 22. Orange/red sandy clay. 23. Red/brown sandy clay. 24. Red/orange clay with sand. 25. Natural red/orange clay.

Fig 1.5. Posthole sections from the towers of Greenloaning, Shielhill South and Huntingtower.

sites like Raith and Midgate, on the other hand, could, between them, have watched over many miles of the same Highland fringe, but from a safer distance of about 10km and this could have significant strategic implications. There is obviously little point in an early warning system if the warnings it provides come too late for effective counter measures to be taken. The Gask Ridge, however, is far enough back from the Highlands to give up to an hour's warning of any attack (even by horsemen) and thus allow the mobilisation of its own fort garrisons, whilst still being close enough to provide a clear view of events, at least during daylight and in reasonable weather. The Gask could thus have represented a back stop frontier and flank guard to which the glenblockers, at least to some extent, acted as outposts, positioned in the mouths of the passes from which any trouble was likely to erupt.

Again, however, many of these theories are predicated on a belief in a short, single phased, occupation for the Gask towers. But, the Gask Project's first excavation put this in immediate doubt. For it found that the corner posts of Greenloaning (the southernmost Gask tower currently known) had been replaced at some point during its occupation, suggesting signs of two, and possibly three, structural phases (Woolliscroft & Hoffmann 1997). Fig 1.5 shows sample post hole sections from each of the three Gask Project tower excavations (the full corpus for each is published in the individual site reports) and the situation at Greenloaning is typified by section A-B. Here, Layer 9 appears to represent the remains of a pit, probably an early post pit, overlain by a layer of rammed gravel, L'1a, which is presumably the primary metalled interior surface. Both layers have clearly been cut by a second pit, consisting of at least layers 3, 4, 5, 6 and 7, which are fill layers holding the pipe for a now vanished post (L'2) against the pit side. The pit has then been overlain by a second layer of metalling (L'1) which extends up to the sides of the post itself. There are thus two clear phases present. This still leaves one slight difficulty, however, for layer 4a which also cuts L's 1a and 9 appears to have been cut in its turn by the secondary post pit. It is, of course possible that this layer represents the remains of a back filled demolition pit, dug to extract the primary post, but this would imply that this hypothetical feature had then been filled in prior to the second post pit being dug. This is may be a perfectly plausible scenario, but it is equally possible that the layer represents the remains of yet another post pit, giving us no fewer than three structural phases on the site.

At first, the importance of this discovery need not have been particularly great, for the results related to only one tower out of the 18 known and it was not hard to think of circumstances in which a single installation might have required rebuilding which need have no implications for the rest of the line. There were no signs of fire associated with the end of the first phase, but any

number of factors, from poor materials to faulty initial construction, or even storm damage, could have necessitated remedial work on just this one site. Soon afterwards, however, the writer was given the opportunity publish past excavations by the late Prof J.K. St.Joseph at the nearby towers of Shielhill North (Chap 6) and South. Minor problems with the dig archives necessitated the re-excavation of one of the sites to ensure that St.Joseph's results were not misrepresented. Shielhill South was chosen as the target (Woolliscroft & Hoffmann 1998) and once again, the site produced two tower post phases. Indeed, if anything, the results were even clearer. Fig 1.5, section C-D, shows the remains of two surviving post pipes. The primary post (L'17) was heavily chocked with stones set in a sand matrix (L'18). This feature had then been dug into by a second pit (L'13) which had held a somewhat shallower set post (L'12) with no chock stones. Moreover, there were again tantalising signs of what might be a third phase, for layer 14 may represent traces of yet another pit, later dug into by layer 13, although again it might also represent an intervening demolition layer associated with the removal of the primary post. Once again there were no signs of fire damage associated with the end of the first phase and the damage to the primary post does not appear to be consistent with its being displaced, let alone torn out of the ground, by a storm. Shielhill South also showed very clear signs of a ditch re-cut (fig 1.6), something which had not been evident at Greenloaning, and an excavation by the Centre for Field Archaeology has still more recently produced similar post hole evidence for the intervening tower at Blackhill Wood (Glendinning and Dunwell 2000, 273ff).

What all of this means is that all three of these towers, which range over a 5km stretch of the line, have had to be completely rebuilt at least once and possibly twice during their operational lives, something far more difficult to explain in terms of some localised accident or construction error. Indeed, fig 1.5 shows the final post pipe at Shielhill South to be noticeably shallower than the primary, so that if anything, the primary tower was better constructed (and more storm proof) than its successor. The alternative, however, is that the towers were rebuilt simply because they had reached the end of their usable lives, and this would certainly suggest rather more than just a brief occupation. Of course it could be argued that this might indicate only that the Gask towers, like the forts, were reoccupied 60 years later in the Antonine period but, on current evidence, this does seem very unlikely. For, although Shielhill South produced one of the new first century dates, the minor installations have yet to produce a single Antonine find. Moreover at Greenloaning, where the interior surfacing survived well, there was no significant accumulation of soil or other rubbish that might have served as an indication of a prolonged abandonment between the tower phases. Instead we find only a thin band of loamy material (fig 1.5, section A-B, L'3) between the primary and secondary metalling layers, which probably reflects nothing more than dirt trampled into the site during its rebuilding. The fact that the replacement posts at all three sites were set in almost exactly the same positions as their predecessors (whose locations must thus presumably still have been known) would also suggest that there was no significant break between occupations, especially as the tower at Greenloaning is set in an unusual off centre position which was unlikely to be repeated by chance. We would, therefore, appear to have evidence for a quite prolonged, but still wholly Flavian, occupation.

At least one other site also needs to be considered here, the Flavian fort of Cargill, which lies near the Tay/Isla confluence, some 13km to the north-east of Bertha, and also well behind the highland line (fig 1.1). This site appears to continue the inner, or Gask, line of forts and it is even possible that the frontier itself might continue, for although no towers are yet known between Bertha and Cargill, there is one example a further 1.5km to the north-east at Black Hill (Abercromby 1904 and Richmond 1940). Cargill was partially excavated in the early 1980's and, although the full report remains unpublished, clear evidence for two phases was recovered (Maxwell and Wilson 1987, 16). The Gask Project's Deputy Director, Dr B.Hoffmann, is currently preparing the late Prof A.S. Robertson's larger scale excavations at the next rearward fort to the north-east, Cardean, near Meigle, and a similar pattern appears to be emerging there. But this is not the end of the Cargill story, for the fort lies only c. 300m from a large (c. 0.47ha (1.17 acre)) Flavian fortlet. There would seem to be little need for two installations of this size to be sited in such close proximity and so the fort and fortlet are unlikely to be contemporary. Cargill might thus show evidence for yet a third phase and again a prolonged occupation seems assured.

Just how prolonged, though, still remains open to question, for Hanson (1978) has pointed out that the Romans sometimes used far from ideal timber in their military structures: alder for example, which tends to rot fairly quickly when set into the ground. Environmental analyses from a number of Gask sites have suggested that virtually the only trees in this landscape in Roman times were water loving species, such as alder, around the rivers, which would have severely restricted the Romans' choice of timber if only local trees could be used. Even if such material was employed though, we might still expect tower uprights of up to 0.4m in diameter to be at least reasonably durable, and so not likely to need too frequent replacement. There is evidence, however, that timber may have been imported from elsewhere for use on the Gask, for our own analysis of wood fragments found by A.S. Robertson in the post holes of Roundlaw tower (Robertson 1974, 27 and Ramsay in Woolliscroft forthcoming (a)), coupled

to earlier evidence from Raith (Christison 1901, 28), would suggest that the structural timber actually used was good solid oak. This could have been expected to last for many years before needing to be replaced, especially if it was treated with pitch before being set into post holes, and the likely life span of the installations would increase accordingly. That said, neither Roundlaw nor Raith were published to a standard where any phasing evidence could be detected, and the excavation records from both sites appear to have disappeared. Indeed no post hole or ditch sections from any Gask tower were published until the report for Westerton (Hanson and Friell 1995, 505), the last Gask site to be excavated before our own work began. This means that the significance of these oak finds cannot be pushed too far. It is possible, for example, that any earlier phases on these sites may indeed have used substandard timber and so may still have needed rapid replacement. It is even possible that the towers were rebuilt specifically because imported oak became available. Alternatively, given the fact that Roundlaw and Raith are virtually neighbours (being separated only by Ardunie), it is possible that access to some very localised stand of oak may have made these site more durable than those elsewhere on the line so that no rebuilding became necessary and it is noteworthy in this context that some oak pollen was detected in the rampart material from the nearby fort of Strageath (Butler 1989, 272).

Nevertheless, there is other, less equivocal, evidence for prolonged occupation. In particular, it is significant that the ditches at Shielhill South were not re-cut until a considerable depth of silt had formed in their bottoms. Fig 1.6 shows the corpus of ditch sections from the site and it is readily apparent that in places the silt deposits in the primary cuts had become so deep that the re-cutting was far from a simple cleaning operation. It has in fact missed the original ditch bottom in places. Perhaps the clearest example is section K-L, which cut the inner of the two tower ditches. Here the primary cut is represented by a classic, if small, V shaped Roman military ditch which had filled (L's 7 and 11) almost to its full original depth before being cut by a second, broadly similar, ditch (L'2) which rather than simply re-emptying the original cut has been driven right through its northern side so that the two ditch bottoms lie c. 0.35m apart. This silting must have taken some time and, further to the south, the fortlet of Glenbank had needed its ditches cleaned out no less than three times. We might conclude, therefore, that we again, like the forts, have either a single extended Flavian occupation, perhaps lasting for the full seven to eight years of the known Flavian period, if not longer or, at the very least, that we have two or more distinct Flavian phases separated by such short periods of disuse that they are now all but undetectable by archaeology. In the latter case, of course, the occupations may still have been brief as the towers would then have been replaced as an act of policy, rather than through maintenance as their timbers decayed.

Which of these options is more likely is currently impossible to determine and may remain so unless precise dating evidence, such as dendro- chronological data, can be obtained, particularly from the primary tower phases (the Roundlaw fragments were unphased stratigraphically and not large enough to provide a dendro date). There are, though, a number of clues which may prove to be relevant in the future. We have already seen that layer 4a at Greenloaning and layer 14 at Shielhill South (fig 1.5, sections A-B and C-D) might represent demolition deposits. If so, this would imply that the primary post holes had been back filled once the posts themselves had been extracted, only to be reopened when the secondary post pits were dug. This would seem somewhat odd in the context of a straightforward rebuild, but makes perfect sense if the initial intent was abandonment. On the other hand, however, the same layers could also be interpreted as parts of a further tower phase and it may be significant here that, at both sites, the end of the first phase is not associated with signs of burning. For at Greenloaning and Shielhill South there were clear indications that when the sites were finally abandoned, the demolished secondary tower components were burnt on site and

St.Joseph's work at Shielhill North (Chap 7) produced signs of similar treatment. Shielhill South, in particular, yielded both fire residue and considerable evidence of scorching. Indeed the clay capping of one of the backfilled post holes had been fired to the point that it resembled a friable form of earthenware. It is possible, of course, that the primary demolition could have followed a different pattern even if the original intent was the same, and whatever the intentions of those who removed the original posts, they must have done something with the material. But it does not appear to have been burned where it had stood and, at the very least, one can better understand a reluctance to contaminate the interior tower area if it was known that it was to continue in use.

If, on the other hand, we are to imagine a really prolonged life for the Gask, extending beyond the current 79 - 87 AD limits on the Flavian period, just how long an occupation could we envisage? Hanson (1978, 296) has estimated the likely useful life of an oak timber only 4 inches (102 mm) in diameter at around thirty years, and that of a similar alder timber at a little under ten. The Gask towers used much larger posts, however, which can be expected to have had longer lives and, in fact, timber buildings can survive almost indefinitely so long as their structural timbers are

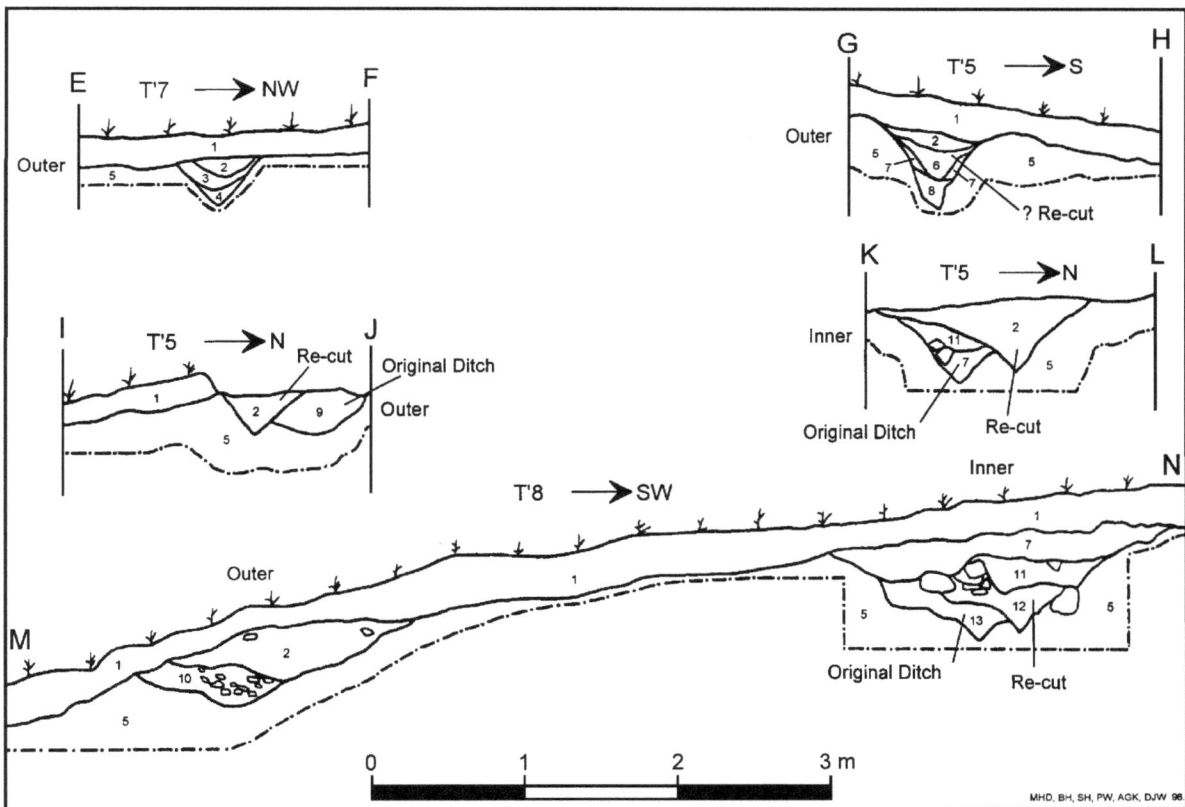

1. Turf and topsoil. 2. Dark grey loam with gravel. 3. Gravel with dark brown sand. 4. Dark brown gritty sand. 5. Natural sand, clay, gravel aggregate. 6. Buff sandy clay. 7. Pink/grey loam with pebbles. 8. Plum clay with stones. 9. Grey brown sand and pea gravel. 10. Stones with dark grey loam. 11. Beige clay with gravel. 12. Yellow/beige clay with gravel. 13. Silty grey clay with gravel.

Fig 1.6. Shielhill South: ditch sections.

9

kept dry. There is evidence from a number of sites that the Gask towers had wattle and daub side cladding (see below) which should have afforded some protection to their posts (and occupants), although how watertight they would have been is impossible to judge. Certainly the timber tower reconstruction built in 1974 at the Stanegate fort of Vindolanda, which is itself somewhat leaky, still remains stable after a life of 26 years (it was originally expected to last 15), despite not being pre-treated with preservative (pers com A Birley). It is possible that mechanical stresses due to high winds would have been more damaging to a free standing tower than to one, like the Vindolanda example which is set into a rampart, especially as some of the Gask tower post holes seem to have been rather shallow. It is also difficult to judge the extent to which the possible use of unseasoned wood might have affected matters. Nevertheless, a service life of well over a decade does not seem unreasonable, so that the full life span of two tower phases could well be over twenty or even thirty years.

Such a long occupation currently appears historically impossible, however, for it would potentially take us back to the time of Nero for a starting date, or forward into the late reign of Trajan, when there were already signs on the Tyne-Solway isthmus of the frontier development that was eventually to result in Hadrian's Wall (Jones & Woolliscroft, 2001, Chap 2). Indeed the very fact of two (or more) tower phases, given such a long potential service life, might even be taken as further evidence for two separate occupations. Again, we might cut this down somewhat by envisaging a primary phase using a shorter lived timber than oak (although there is no evidence for this) and it is certainly possible that the second phase was abandoned well before its timbers wore out, but it may also be feasible to project the life of the system both beyond its currently theorised end date and/or before its supposed earliest possible start date.

Current theory on the end of the Gask rests largely on Hobley's (1989) analysis of the coins from northern Scotland. Roman 1st century coinage did not, it seems, enter Britain in a steady flow. Instead, new coins were only provided by the central mint when they were needed for some reason, perhaps to top up a government pool usually reliant on the province's own taxation. There are thus "surge" years when large numbers of coins arrived, followed by dearth periods (which could last for many years) when new coins were rare and probably only entered through trade and other non governmental processes. 86 and 87 AD were particular surge years, so much so that it is unusual for a site of any significance occupied during those years not to produce their coins. There was then a pause in the coin supply lasting until after the death of Domitian in 96. Northern Scotland has produced a number of coins of 86, including one from the Gask fort of Strageath (Frere

and Wilkes 1989, 139) and an unusually high percentage of these were lost in mint or near mint condition. None are known with certainty from 87, however. Under these circumstances, the absence of 87 coins would suggest that the Gask went out of use at some time after the coinage of 86 arrived in the province, but before the arrival of coins of 87, which might be expected to be well into that year. At first sight this does appear to be a convincing argument and it may well prove to be right, but it does have small weaknesses which may or may not turn out to be relevant. Most importantly, we need to consider whether the current corpus of material is large enough to be statistically significant? This is sometimes doubted (J. Casey, pers com). Only eleven coins of 86 AD are known from military sites north of the Antonine Wall, seven of which come from Inchtuthil, with one more each from the forts of Stracathro, Dalginross, Strageath and Camelon. (Robertson 1983, 419). This is hardly a large sample, especially since the identity of one of these coins is disputed. The only difference between the coins of the two years is a single numeral. In 86 Domitian was Consul for the 12th time and so the coins bear the legend "COS XII". In 87, with the Emperor's 13th Consulship, this changes to "COS XIII" and one of the Inchtuthil coins was identified by its excavator, Sir Ian Richmond, as reading COS XIII. The piece now seems to have been lost and A.S. Robertson in her coin report for the fortress publication (Pitts and St.Joseph 1985, 284, No 7) leaves the matter open, although clearly preferring a date of 86. But whatever the case with this particular example, it should be remembered that a single firmly dated coin of 87 would have the potential to extend the occupation of the Gask, not by a single year, but by the decade which elapsed before coins arrived in bulk again at the start of the reign of Nerva. More realistically, it would certainly allow us to extend the occupation until around 90 AD, after which the Samian pottery also ceases to take us further (Hartley 1972).

As for an earlier start than 79/80; the current limit is imposed by Tacitus' account of the activities of his father-in-law, Agricola, which credits him with being the first Roman governor of Britain to invade Scotland and parts of northern England. This short book is our only source for this period of British history and has been studied and dissected more than almost any other non religious text. Scholars have attempted to tease out ever more subtle nuances of meaning as though this is all that is needed for some ultimate truth to be revealed. Is this necessarily so credible a work, however? Indeed, to what extent can we trust it at all? Tacitus' "Agricola" is all too often treated as a straightforward biography, or even as history, but in reality it is no such thing and was never meant to be. It is a eulogy to his late father-in-law, modelled on the orations in praise of the dead given at Roman funerals and, as such, strict historical truth may have taken a poor second place (albeit perhaps within limits) to the glorification of the subject.

Agricola's achievements can thus be expected to have been lauded to the maximum, possibly well past the point of exaggeration, whilst those of others may have been ignored or belittled, not necessarily out of malice, but simply because they were irrelevant to the writer's theme. The work is also notoriously vague when it comes to geographical detail. Certainly it is interesting, if ultimately futile, to speculate whether we might have gained a very different picture of the first century invasion of Scotland had a more objective historical account survived, and this might even apply to Tacitus' own "Histories", from which the relevant sections have been lost. Quite how far fetched such a work could become is debatable. For example one of the puzzles of Agricola's governorship has always been his unusually long seven year term of office. Interestingly both Tacitus and Cassius Dio (Histories 66, 20-21), the only other ancient writer to mention Agricola's activities, say that the last notable event of the governorship was a circumnavigation of Britain by the fleet. This allowed Agricola to be the first Roman to conclusively prove that Britain was an island, for which he was given triumphal ornaments. Dio adds one more detail, however, telling us that this took place in 79 AD and that the Emperor Titus received his 15th imperial salutation on the strength of it. If both the date and the sequence are right, then Agricola would actually have had a perfectly normal three year term in office (76-79) and would never have served under Domitian, but this would probably make the "Agricola" too tall a tale even for Tacitus.

Somewhat nebulous doubts over Tacitus' veracity are hardly new, but his credit was recently given a more concrete blow by tree ring dates for a series of timbers from the rampart of the earliest fort at Carlisle (Caruana 1997, 40f, and forthcoming, and Groves 1990). As with Scotland, Tacitus assigns the conquest of northern England to Agricola and so, not surprisingly, Carlisle had always been assumed to have been an Agricolan creation. It thus came as something of a shock that the dendro-chronological dates provided a very firm foundation date of late 72 (or just possibly early 73) AD. This installation was no temporary camp that could be assigned to some minor unrecorded military excursion, but a permanent Roman fort. Yet it had been founded five years before Agricola's tenure of office even began, by his predecessor but one as Governor, Q Petillius Cerialis (Gov. 71-73/4), under whose auspices, incidentally, Agricola served as commander of Legio XX Valeria Victrix (Tacitus Agricola 7-8). Such a serious contradiction of Tacitus' account has forced a complete re-examination of our wider accepted orthodoxy for the history of this period and evidence has now been put forward to suggest that Cerialis' activities may have extended well beyond Carlisle. Moreover, Pliny the Elder makes a reference in his Natural Histories (IV, 102) to Roman military activity against Caledonians within thirty years of the invasion, i.e. by or

before 73, whilst the poet Statius (Silvae V, II, 145) specifically refers to Cerialis' own predecessor, M. Vettius Bolanus (Gov 69-71) setting up "watch towers and strongholds" in Caledonia. Statius was a poet and his own geography may be as uncertain as Tacitus'. To him "Caledonia" may have meant little more than "up north somewhere", indeed it is even possible that he may be describing the otherwise undated line of early Roman watchtowers over the Stainmore pass between Brough and Bowes (on the modern A66) in northern England. Pliny was a very different animal, however: a scientist and friend of the Emperor Vespasian, he was a senior Roman official who knew his geography and might be expected to use political language precisely. Under normal circumstances his "within thirty years" might even then be taken as somewhat vague, with a margin for error which might be pushed as far as Tacitus' AD 79 start date for Agricola. But Pliny died in 79, in the same eruption of Mt Vesusius that destroyed Pompeii and, as the dedication on his Natural Histories suggests that it was published a year or two earlier, in 77, there can be little doubt that he is referring to operations before Agricola became governor.

Pliny's remarks might still not be enough to prove permanent occupation, rather than occasional campaigning in Scotland, but archaeology might now be bridging that gap. Caruana (1997, 46f) has recently suggested that enough Neronian and early Flavian material has been found to suggest (although not yet prove) pre or very early Flavian occupation at Camelon, at the southern end of the Gask road, and possibly even at Strageath, with further evidence from more southerly Scottish forts such as Dalswinton, Broomholm, Castledykes and Newstead. By chance the Gask Project's Deputy Director has recently been writing a book length report on the glass found during all excavation and field walking activity at the latter (Hoffmann forthcoming) and informs me that she too would now be more comfortable with a pre-Agricolan foundation date for the site. Meanwhile Shotter (2000a, 194f) has pointed to the presence of disproportionately large numbers of Neronian and early Flavian coins from a number of Scottish sites which might again point to possible Cerialian activity at Strageath and Camelon, along with the Antonine Wall forts of Mumrills and Castlecary (Cardean may also now follow this pattern). He even goes so far as to suggest a Cerialian origin for the Gask line itself, and this would certainly not seem so controversial a hypothesis as it would have been only a few years ago. It cannot be stressed too highly that the final answer to this question is still beyond our grasp. Nevertheless, a maximum life span for the Gask of around 18 years (from c.72/3 to c.90) no longer appears impossible on either archaeological or historical grounds and, at the very least, it may be time that we began to reject any need to explain away what would otherwise have been valid archaeological data simply because it conflicts with Tacitus. We should also beware of entering circular arguments by attributing Tacitean datings to artefact types found on Flavian forts in Scotland and then using these to date other sites in the area, or even (worse still) to confirm the dates of the original find sites.

The above discussion raises a number of issues without reaching concrete conclusions but, at least until recently, it could also have been somewhat premature, because there is another more immediate problem in extrapolating the results from Greenloaning, Shielhill South and Blackhill Wood to the rest of the Gask system. For these three towers are part of a clear group of four, from Greenloaning to Shielhill North (fig 1.2), at the southernmost end of the line, which all have one marked difference from the rest of the series, in that they have two ring ditches surrounding them, rather than the usual one. This may sound like a minor detail, but given the shortage of dating evidence (and it should be remembered that, to date, we have only a single sherd of loosely datable first century glass between all four of these sites), there could be no automatic guarantee that they shared exactly the same history as the rest of the line. We might, for example, envisage a situation in which the southern end of the frontier was built first and then extended using a slightly different tower design. Moreover, if that was the case, it might also be possible that the southern towers were rebuilt when this extension was added, simply so that everything was new together, even though this might not yet have been necessary on structural grounds. In other words, it remained possible that we might still be dealing with a relatively brief

chronology, especially if the extension, and with it the second structural phase in the south, was short lived. Can we then see signs of two or more phases in any of the more northerly single ditched sites, which make up the bulk of the line? In other words does the whole system show the same phasing pattern, and thus a unified history, or is this southern sector genuinely different?

In fact, there has long been at least tentative evidence that some of the northern sites were indeed rebuilt. Perhaps the strongest contender was the tower at Westerton (Hanson and Friell 1995), the most southerly single ditched site so far known. Here the one fully excavated post hole proved, like those of the double ditched sites, to have two separate posts in it. At the time, this was unparalleled and, in the absence of clear stratigraphic evidence, the excavators assumed that they were contemporary and explained one as the main structural post for the tower and the other as a support for a raised balcony close to tower top level. This never seemed a particularly satisfactory interpretation, however, for although there are near contemporary artistic representations of Roman towers with balconies, notably in the opening scenes of Trajan's column, these always show them as carried via cantilevers by the tower itself rather than by independently founded ground supports. This is certainly a more elegant engineering solution and the writer understands that at least one of the excavators is now inclined to regard the double post here as evidence for a rebuild (Pers com. W S Hanson).

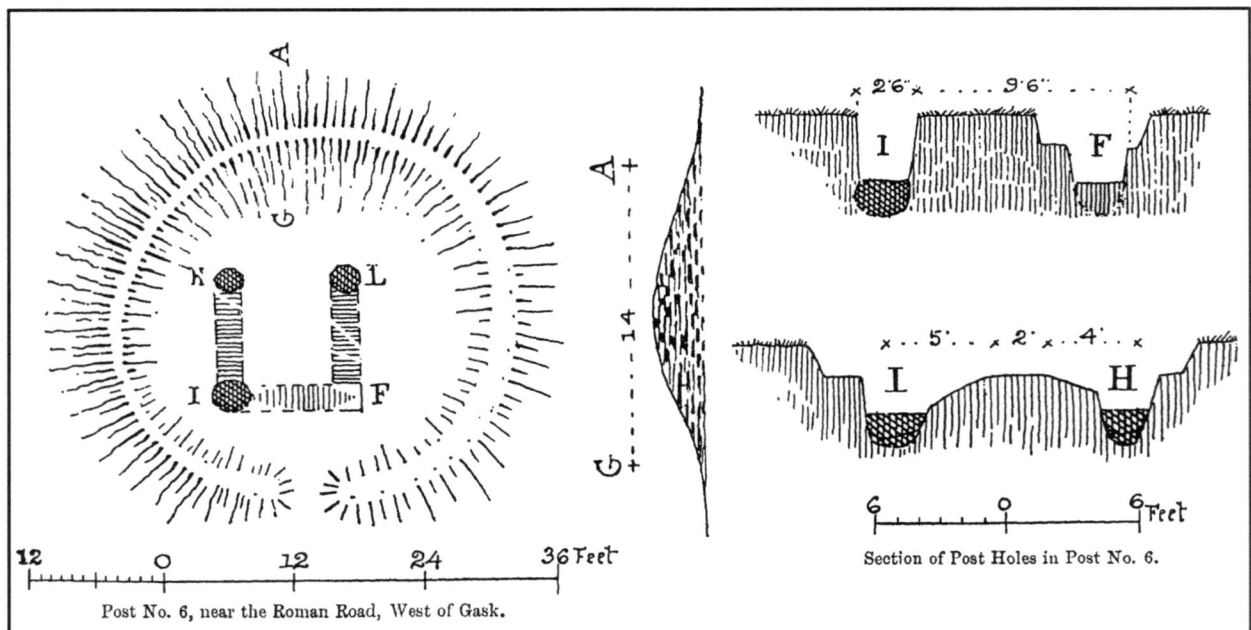

Fig 1.7 Moss Side tower, Christison's plan and section.

12

The next candidate was Moss Side, on the Gask Ridge proper. This site was excavated by Christison (1901, 29) a century ago and, as can be seen from his plan (fig 1.7), it has, uniquely amongst the Gask towers, a set of timber beams linking the four corner posts. The obvious first reaction might be to suggest that these would have formed the base for some form of side cladding, perhaps of wattle and daub panels, to create a usable space inside what would otherwise have been an open framed structure. Such a move would seem eminently sensible given the local climate and traces of either burned daub and/or carbonised hazel twigs, which may derive from wattling, have came to light at Shielhill South, Raith and Shielhill North, although as yet there are no parallels for the Moss Side beam slots. The trouble is that Christison himself appears to reject such an interpretation. His short (one paragraph) report states that at least one of the tower corner posts had been removed (fig 1.7, corner F) to allow the beams to be installed, which suggests that the posts and beams belong to two entirely different buildings, with the second period perhaps representing some form of beam founded block house. Of course archaeological technique was then in its infancy and he may well be wrong. But for the moment at least we have the statement of the excavator that this is a two period site and, as his excavation records appear to have disappeared, we have no real evidence with which to gainsay him.

Next come two potentially fascinating sites. Some years ago, a survey and small excavation by the writer (Woolliscroft 1993, 302ff) reconfirmed the presence of a fortlet at Midgate (also known as Thorny Hill), towards the eastern end of the Gask Ridge. The existence of this site had previously come to be forgotten or even denied, for some reason (Crawford 1949, 54f), despite its excavation by Christison (1901, 32ff) at the start of the 20th century and despite the fact that it is still clearly visible as a well preserved field monument. The work confirmed the site's plan and the Roman nature of its ditches (albeit it had been damaged by the insertion of a small World War II anti aircraft position into its interior) and it is interesting to note that, as can be seen from fig 1.8, the fortlet's west ditch comes to within just 13m of that of a ring feature thought to be one of the Gask towers. Obviously, therefore, the two features cannot be contemporary. There is simply no point in putting a fortlet and tower so close together. Sadly the ditches do not actually intersect and they remain just far enough apart that their upcast does not appear to overlap, so that it has proved impossible, so far, to determine which feature was built first. But, whatever the case, this duel installation should be another indication of two structural periods, except that here, instead of a simple tower rebuild, we would have one entirely different site type replacing the other. Ironically, however, it has recently been pointed

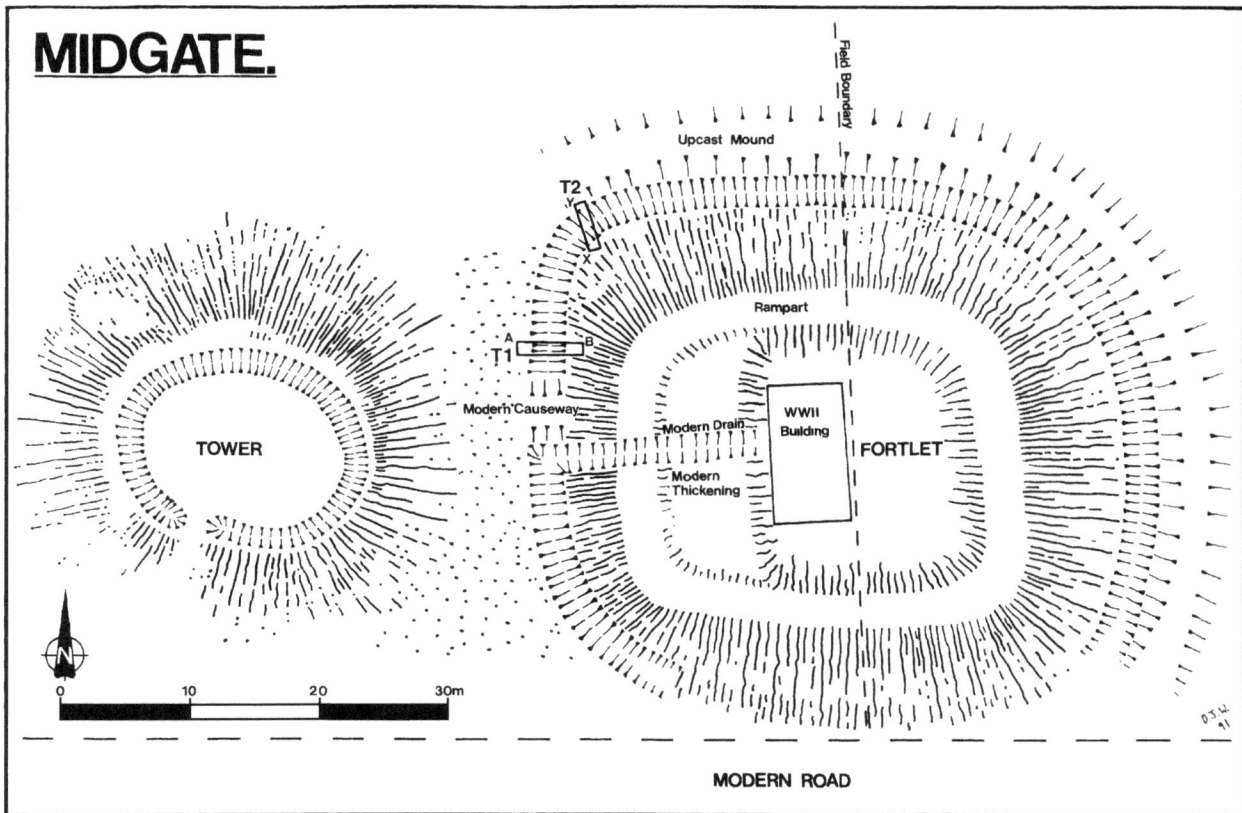

Fig 1.8. Midgate tower and fortlet.

13

out by Hanson and Friell (1995, 514) that whilst the long rejected fortlet is unquestionably there, legitimate objections could be levelled at the tower, whose identity had never before been doubted: for no post holes were found in its interior. Instead, they suggest that it might be a barrow. Like the fortlet, the tower was excavated by Christison's team in 1900, but despite their early date, these excavators were perfectly capable of finding timber features elsewhere. They had indeed pioneered timber archaeology in Scotland during their work at Ardoch only a few years before (Christison and Cunningham 1898). The writer can affirm from experience that the site's loose sandy subsoil is not the easiest material in which to see subtle, timber derived features but, even so, this particular group should have been capable of finding them. The site is in other respects perfectly in keeping with the other towers in its vicinity, however (see below). It has a penannular ring ditch with its single entrance break facing a modern road which runs on the Roman line. It has a V shaped ditch c. 3m wide and 1.5m deep (which is both abnormally large and the wrong shape for a cist barrow ditch in this area) and, although Hanson and Friell drew attention to the ditch circuit's unusual oval shape, the morphology of the narrow knoll on which it stands makes this all but inevitable. Nevertheless, the lack of internal posts is a cause for concern and, although the truth of the matter

may well be that Christison simply failed to locate them, there must be at least some residual doubt as to the site's identity, at least until further work can be done here.

The final site is Raith (fig 1.2), probably the best vantage point on the entire line. This site was partially excavated and claimed as a tower during the construction of a water tank in 1901 (Christison 1901, 28f). But, more recently, air photographs (notably CUCAP AKD96, (fig 1.9)) have shown what may be a rectangular fortlet ditch surrounding the site, along with a clear, but apparently never published, temporary camp. This again raises the possibility of a tower and fortlet on the same spot, except that in this case the two would actually be superimposed, in whichever order, rather than being kept a few metres apart as at Midgate. Indeed if this scenario can be confirmed it may be necessary to look more closely at the surroundings of the other two Gask fortlets, Kaims Castle and Glenbank, to see if all of them replaced (or were replaced by) towers. In this context it may or may not be relevant that our own excavations at Glenbank found only a single structural phase in the fortlet's gate tower although, as this stood on even larger timbers than the tower posts, these may simply have been longer lived. It is also worth mentioning that the writer was once informed by the late Prof G.D.B.Jones that he had seen

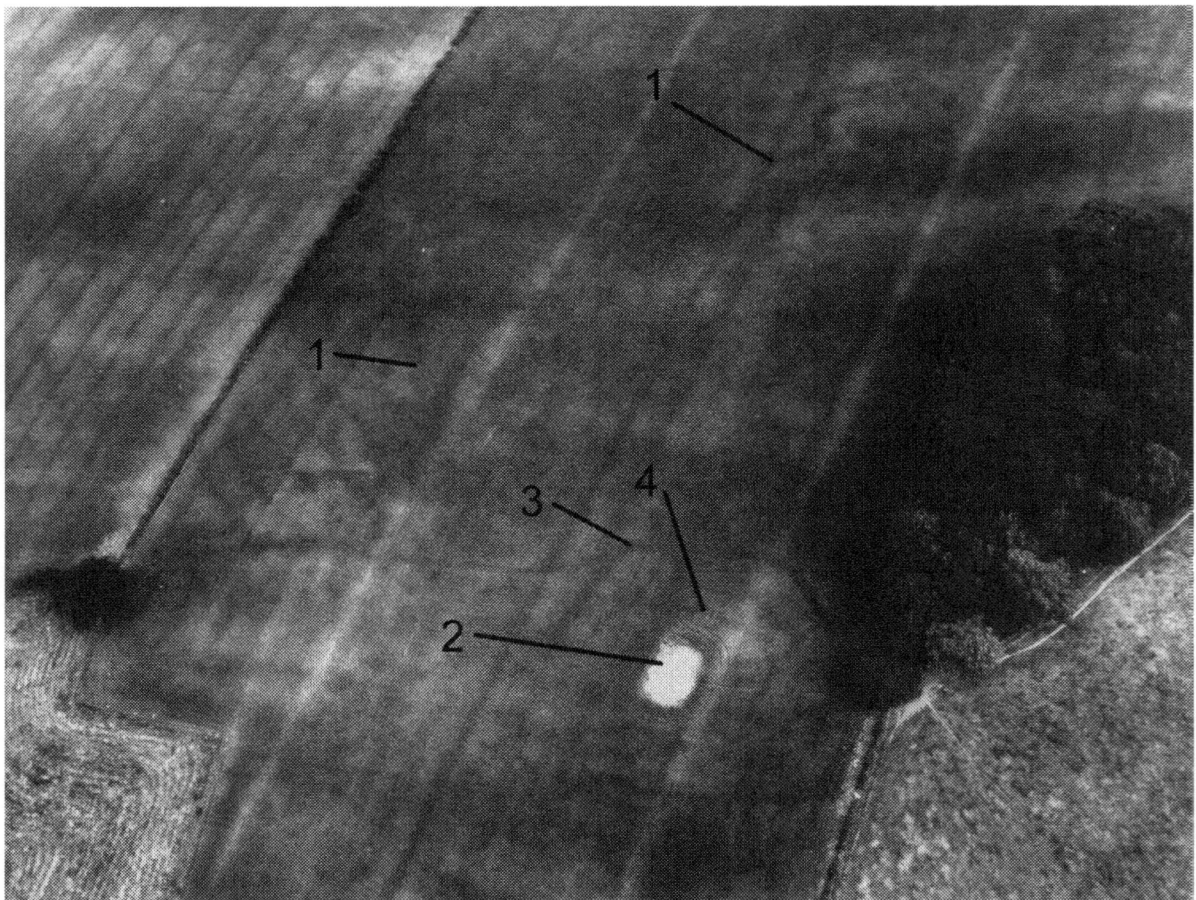

Fig 1.9. *Raith from the air (Cambridge University Collection, copyright reserved).*
1. *Roman temporary camp ditch.* 2. *1901 water tank.* 3. *Old plantation ditch.* 4. *Possible fortlet ditch.*

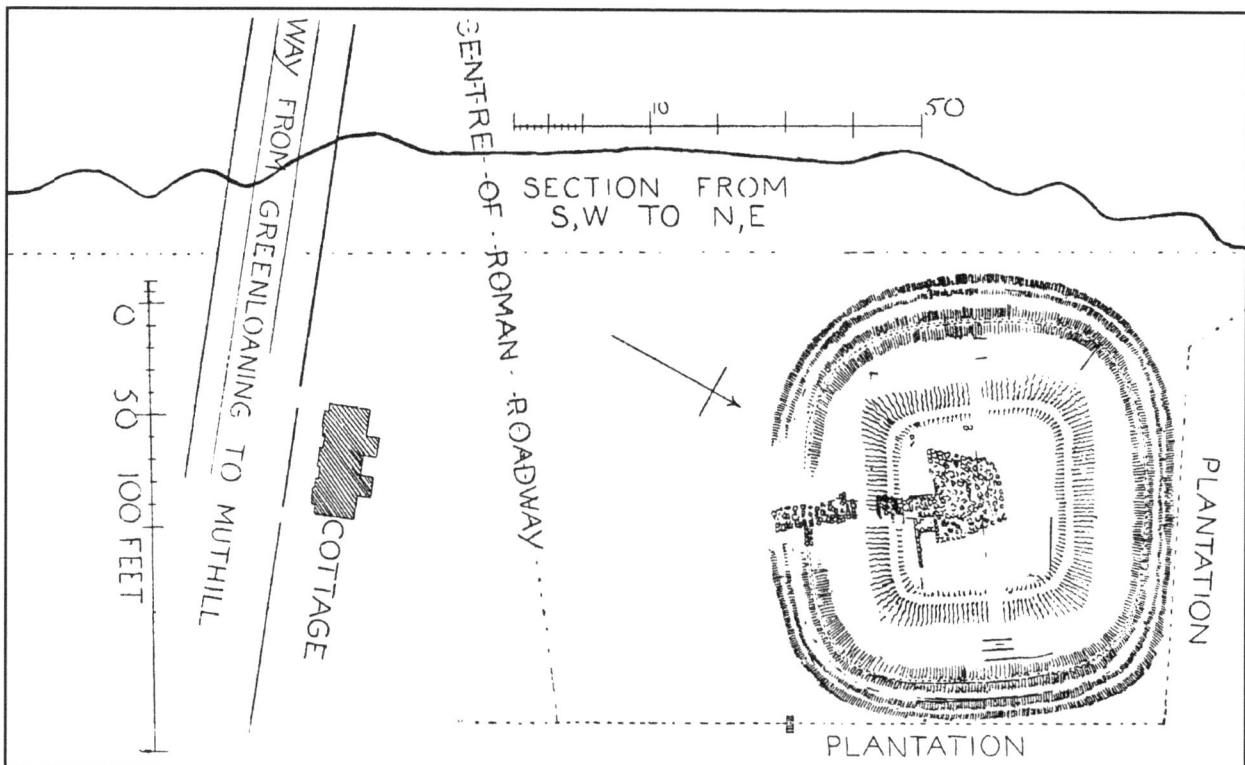

Fig 1.10. Kaims Castle fortlet: Christison's 1901 plan.

a feature from the air resembling a tower ditch on the small knoll immediately south of Kaims Castle fortlet. No such feature is visible on any of his surviving air photographs (held by the University of Manchester), but the possibility is still intriguing enough that the Gask Project is hoping to conduct geophysical work on the site at some point.

As at Midgate, however, there are problems. Aside from the fact that the Raith fortlet has yet to be confirmed by excavation, our own resistivity survey of the site failed to find any sign of a circular tower ditch in the area around the water tank and, whilst it is true that the construction of this tank must have damaged the site quite considerably, it should not have been enough to obliterate the entire circuit of a 20 - 25m diameter ring ditch. The published account of the excavation is vague in the extreme, reporting only post holes and some unidentified red pottery (with no ditch located). It may well be, therefore, that what was really found was part of a fortlet gate structure. and certainly the air photographic evidence would place the tank in approximately the right place within the possible fortlet ditch circuit. If so then there may never have been a tower on the site and so again no second period can be proven until further work can be done here.

The Gask fortlets also suffer from a more general problem for, despite our own extensive excavations at Glenbank, they have yet to produce any dating evidence. This means that there is no guarantee that they belong

with the Flavian system at all. One quite convincing indicator may be seen in the fact that Glenbank, in the south, had a double ditch, like the towers around it, whereas the northern fortlets, like their towers, had single ditches. For this does suggest integration between the two site types and thus a Flavian date for the fortlets. Nevertheless, the forts were reused in the Antonine Period, presumably as outposts for the Antonine Wall, and so, we have recently proved (Chap 3), was the former glenblocker fort at Dalginross (which has also produced a coin of Alexander Severus (222-35) (Crawford 1949, 43)). The possibility cannot yet be discounted, therefore, that we have a Flavian system of forts and towers and an Antonine one of forts and fortlets, rather than just forts as has usually been envisaged. This would, in fact, appear to be a better balanced, and so more attractive, scenario. Indeed, at one point, the writer came to believe in it quite strongly, because of a rather intriguing piece of evidence from the best known of the Gask fortlets, Kaims Castle. For when, yet again, Christison (1901, 18ff) excavated the site he was puzzled to find that he could locate no internal buildings, only a layer of metalling (fig 1.10), whereas one would normally expect to find at least one and often a pair of barrack blocks fronting onto a central roadway. It did not occur to him to look under this surfacing and, at the time, there was perhaps no reason why he should have done. But we now know something he did not which is that a number of the Antonine Wall milefortlets had their interiors cleared of buildings and cobbled over at some point during their operational lives, although occupation of some sort continued (e.g. Wilkes, 1974). The Gask fortlets, if they were Antonine, might well have had a similar history and so their buildings may well underlie a later surface.

There were doubts, however, because although Midgate produced a similar lack of internal structures, its metalling was so poorly preserved that the remains of any underlying buildings should still have been visible over much of its area had they existed. For many years it might have been tempting to dismiss Christison's findings as simply a reflection of the poorer field techniques of the period, especially given the uncertainty over the Midgate tower, but the Gask Project's own work at Glenbank has now produced exactly the same results. The site was surrounded by two much re-cut ditches and had a turf rampart with a massive timber built gate tower at its entrance. But nothing was found in the interior (despite a very intensive search) except for plough damaged metalling, and a single small post hole which need not necessarily be Roman. It would seem, therefore, either that the Gask fortlets simply never had internal buildings or, perhaps more probably, that their buildings are for some reason no longer archaeologically detectable. Perhaps they were of mud brick, cob or turf walled construction or they may have been founded on sleeper beams which rested on, rather than cutting into, the surface. Possibly even tenting was used for seasonal occupation, but whatever the case their remains may have been ploughed away long ago. Whatever the case, only further excavation and a firm date from one of these sites will finally allow us to see where they fit.

This, then was the pre-existing evidence for multiple structural phases on the single ditched sector of the Gask and, although it could be described as suggestive, it was not enough to be conclusive. In July 1998, therefore, the Gask Project excavated the northernmost tower currently known on the system, at West Mains of Huntingtower on the outskirts of Perth, with this specific question in mind. The evidence here was less clear cut than further south, as the post holes had been damaged by modern land drains. Nevertheless, the site was still able to provide relatively clear evidence for a secondary phase and may again even show signs of a third (Woolliscroft forthcoming (a)). For example, fig 1.5, section E-F, shows the site's south-eastern post hole and layer 23, which may represent part of a primary post pit, has certainly been cut by the post hole represented by layer 24, which could, thus, be secondary. Layer 22 seems likely to be a demolition feature connected with the removal of that secondary post, but this seems, in turn, to have been cut by layer 20, which was itself cut by layers 7, 19 and 21. Sadly, such was the damage to the site that it was impossible to make a more three dimensional study of layer 20 and, as sectioned, it seems far too shallow to be a post. But it is perfectly possible that it has been sectioned well away from its centre line

and it may well have gone deeper further to the west in an area now destroyed by a drain. If so, this could be a third post phase, with layers 7, 19 and 21 representing a final demolition. Whatever the case, there do at least seem to be two phases on the site, which means that we do now appear to have tower rebuilds on the northern Gask sector. This in turn means that we should now have a unified history for the entire frontier line, and thus probably a significantly longer one than had previously been thought.

The End of the System.

Whatever its exact life span, the Gask system was eventually abandoned and there has long been evidence to suggest that this was a matter of deliberate Roman policy rather than the result of, at least direct, native coercion. For there is no evidence for the sort of destruction we might expect from hostile action. Instead, we find a picture of careful demolition and the removal, destruction or burial of any material likely to be of use to an enemy. The Gask Project's own work has added further support to this picture, for Glenbank had its gate tower posts dug out. Midgate had its ramparts partly shovelled into its ditch to slight them, and at both Greenloaning and Shielhill South the tower posts had been dug out and burned, along with possible wattle and daub panelling, at the end of the second period. But we can introduce one subtle extra nuance, for although the end when it came may well have been orderly, it might also have been rather sudden and unexpected by the men on the ground. Because Midgate seems to have been abandoned part way through a ditch re-cut, not, one would have thought, a particularly long job on a site of this size, and something that would surely not even have been started had the garrison known that they were about to leave.

The reasons why the Gask was abandoned, and with it all of northern Scotland, when so much effort had gone into their consolidation, remain debatable (Breeze 1988 and Woolliscroft 2000). It is tempting to imagine that the terrain and the indigenous population were simply too tough for the Romans and ultimately made conquest impossible. This seems unlikely, however, for the Romans had overrun far more difficult country, such as the Alps and Pyrenees, along with larger and just as warlike peoples. In fact, the principle trigger for the withdrawal has long been recognised to lie wholly outside the province, in a number of serious Roman defeats on the Danube in the 80's AD. These led to troop withdrawals from various parts of the Empire, including Legio II Adiutrix (probably accompanied by auxiliaries) from Britain (E Birley 1953, 21f). Ultimately, Britannia was a peripheral province and its needs took a lower priority than those of the Danube lands, where military setbacks could open threats to the very heart of the Empire. The loss of 25% of its legionary strength would obviously, though, have forced a major reassessment of the army's local commitments in Britain and, with the newly conquered Pennines and much of Wales also still requiring supervision, it may have been felt that the Scottish territories could simply no longer be held with safety. That said, this may not be quite the whole story and local effects might after all have played some role. For Britain still held the single largest garrison of any Roman province: with three legions, a fleet and a disproportionately large auxiliary force (Holder 1982, 104ff and Jarrett 1994). Moreover, many areas elsewhere had survived the running down of their garrisons surprisingly soon after conquest, but there may have been at least one factor at work to make Scotland an exception. In particular, an interesting idea, first put forward by W. Groenman van Waateringe (1980) with relation to the Rhineland, and since mentioned in a British context by both Breeze (1988, 13ff) and Millett (1990, 54f and 99f), may have some bearing here. The Romans generally sought to avoid leaving large numbers of administrators in conquered provinces, at least for any length of time, and the military presence was also kept to a minimum, especially in areas away from the frontiers. Rome tended instead to take the local administrative, legal and law enforcement systems largely as she found them and simply turned them to her own ends, under the overall direction of provincial Governors and their surprisingly minimal staffs. This meant that, even after quite bloody wars of conquest, at least local elites were often left with their power and wealth intact and simply acquired responsibilities to the Roman state in taxation and judicial concerns which, in any case, they might already have been discharging under their pre-conquest government. In other words, Rome ruled most of her captive states not by the direct supervision or coercion of their populations, but merely by bending their governing classes to the imperial will and, even here, so long as all went well, the Empire frequently seems to have had a fairly light touch. The deal was also reciprocal, often to the point of symbiosis. The local magnates not only survived; their position necessarily acquired imperial backing. They continued to run their communities, albeit on Rome's behalf, and they could profit from doing so well, not only by preserving their local status and power but, with time, the more able and ambitious might also now hope for still more profitable careers on the Empire wide stage and, through Rome's almost unprecedented generosity with her own citizenship, they could aspire to become legally one of the conquering people, rather than one of the conquered. They thus acquired a vested interest in preserving the imperial power, rather than, as might otherwise have been expected, becoming natural focuses for resistance to it.

It was a brilliant system and, on the whole, it worked superbly well. It made efficient use of (and eventually expanded) the meagre pool of scarce Roman manpower.

It was cheap to operate. It made local peoples feel less under the imperial thumb and the provincial elites, being small and readily identifiable, were more easily encouraged, suborned, communicated with and, if needs be, intimidated than entire populations. In short, it was a system that allowed Rome to govern an empire by, at least tacit, consent that she would have found it difficult to rule by force alone. The only problem was that it had grown up on the assumption of finding the sort of centralised, Mediterranean city state or kingdom style societies which possessed the necessary political infrastructure to make them capable of being left to run themselves in this way. Unfortunately, although, as Millet (1990, Ch 2-4) points out, at least the beginnings of such centralisation had already formed in southern Britain at the time of the Roman conquest, they had probably not done so in the north, and especially in northern Scotland.

Scotland certainly shows little sign of the outward trappings of such development. For example, with the exception of a number of poorly dated hill forts, most of which seem to have gone out of use by the time of the Roman incursion, the settlement pattern is largely one of dispersed individual farms and small, possibly extended family, communities, with little in the way of the sort of settlement hierarchy which might reflect a developed social and political hierarchy (Hingley 1992, 7-53). There also seem to have been rather fewer "high status" goods in circulation than in the south and we see no signs of the development of centralised institutions such as coinage, taxation and formalised monarchies. In other words, although communal activity and so, presumably, communal feeling did exist, there is little to suggest the existence of all but the most embryonic central authorities within the individual tribes. The suggestion could be made, therefore, that the Romans may simply have found the socio/political state of Scotland to be too incompatible with their established system of provincial governance to be either practicable or, at least, cost effective, given a situation in which major force reductions were already taking place.

The Construction of the Gask System

Another field in which the Gask Project has been interested is the building and construction sequence of the system. Unlike those working on many later Roman frontiers, however, we do not have the luxury of being able to determine relative dates by means of stratigraphic relationships between individual sites and a running barrier of some sort, such as a wall or palisade. For no such structure has ever been traced on the Gask and, as even ephemeral structures such as palisade trenches should still be detectable from the air, there almost certainly never was such a barrier. Instead the only constant element is the road. Moreover the point is worth making that there is, as yet, no guarantee that even this is Flavian, at least in its current well engineered and surfaced form. For it has yet to provide any dating evidence, and certainly no other part of the Flavian north of Scotland had such a high quality road. In any case no stratigraphic link has ever been shown between the road and any of the frontier installations and it has thus proved impossible, so far, to determine the exact building order of the different elements of the system.

There are, though, a number of clues that might be relevant to the system's construction. We have already seen that the southernmost four towers have double ditches and have raised and then dismissed the possibility that they might not be fully contemporary with the rest of the line; but these towers also share another difference. There have been a number of attempts over the years (none of them convincing) to identify a regular spacing system on the Gask, based on the Roman mile (e.g. Rivet 1964). It does have to be said that this is something of a British obsession. We have grown used to the idea that systems like Hadrian's Wall have their installations set to a fairly rigid spacing and the same pattern may now be emerging with the milefortlets of the Antonine Wall (Woolliscroft 1996). Elsewhere in the Empire, however, we find frontier sites positioned far more flexibly and so archaeologists there tend to have fewer preconceptions and so make far fewer attempts to force the issue. In short, there is no need to expect the Gask installations to show regular spacings. But it is worth taking another look at the data (Appendix 2) to see what, if any, patterns emerge.

Fig 1.11a shows a graph of every known inter-site spacing on the Gask (with a Roman mile mark) and they hardly appear very regular. But, of course, the really large values almost certainly represent sectors where we still have sites to discover and are thus not getting the true picture. For example it would be difficult to doubt that we have at least one and probably two towers missing between Westerton and the fort of Strageath (fig 1.11a, WES-STR). In an attempt to filter out these anomalies, therefore, fig 1.11b shows only those spacings under 2km in length, but the effect still appears to be more or less random. There are four values relatively close to a Roman mile, a few that are a little way over, but most are considerably shorter. There is, though, one small group, at the top of the graph, which do at least appear to be relatively consistent between themselves and these are the southern double ditched towers. Their spacings are all around 900m, which is too long to equate to Hadrian's Wall's 1/3 of a Roman mile turret interval, but it does fit a nominal spacing of 888m, or 3/5 of a Roman mile (1 R.mile = 1479m (1618 yds)). Better still, the graph only starts at Ardoch as there is a long c.2 2/3km spacing between the fort and the final tower to the south, at Greenloaning (fig 1.11a), but this gap happens to be almost exactly three of these 888m spacings, which might be a hint that we still have two more towers to find here.

This is all very promising, but this 3/5 Roman mile spacing breaks down elsewhere on the system. Nor does the longer, northern, single ditched sector, appear to follow any other regular interval. The simple fact is that the southern part of the Gask appears to show regular spacings whilst the northern section does not. Again, then, we appear to have a clear distinction between that southern double ditched sector and the rest of the line. So do we again have face two construction periods? That would certainly be one possibility, but there is an obvious alternative explanation. For on other Roman frontiers, such as Hadrian's Wall, differences in design can often represent not different building periods, but simply the work of different construction teams and the same may well be true on the Gask. If so, can we find evidence for any other such building sectors?

Unlike Hadrian's Wall, the Gask does not provide the huge luxury of building inscriptions to tell us who built what and when, but we can try looking at structural differences and there are a number of possible criteria. Take, for example the shape of the towers. Some are recorded as being square whilst others are markedly rectangular. Might there be a pattern? The answer would appear to be no, because, as is shown by fig 1.11c, the differences are randomly distributed. Moreover, all but one of the towers that have been claimed as square were dug by Christison just over a century ago and published without proper plans. It is thus hard not to question the excavation reports, especially as one of these sites is Raith where, as we have seen, we might even be dealing with a fortlet.

Equally inconclusive are the tower dimensions. Fig 1.11d shows their relative sizes in square metres, but one can use any other measure and still get the same result: a more or less random distribution. Moreover, this is nowhere more apparent than on the southern group from Greenloaning to Shielhill North, which we have otherwise marked as a distinct entity. For, although it is true that all of the southern towers are rather larger then average, which certainly might be considered diagnostic, there is an almost a 100% size difference between Greenloaning, which is one of the largest Roman timber towers known anywhere, and the smallest of the group: Shielhill South.

The sites' ditches (Appendix 2 and fig 1.12) tell a rather different story, however, and have characteristics which may point to there being no fewer than four building sectors on the system. Firstly, again, we have the southern group of four which, with their double ditches, are not surprisingly the largest sites in overall diameter at 24 - 26m. Then we have a group of six towers from Kirkhill to Midgate towards the eastern end of the Gask Ridge proper which, although single ditched, are only 2-3m smaller in diameter than the southern group's outer ditches, at c. 22m. Next, there is an intermediate group,

Gask Ridge Tower Spacings.

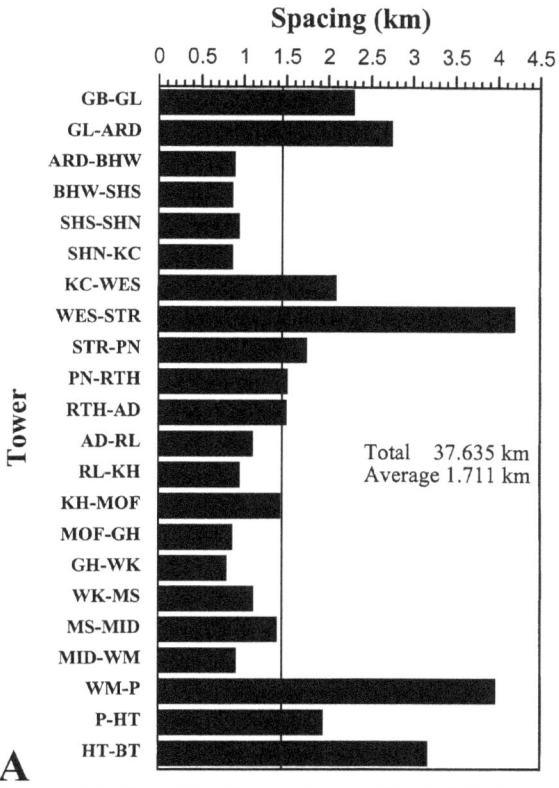

Gask Tower Spacings, Under 2km.

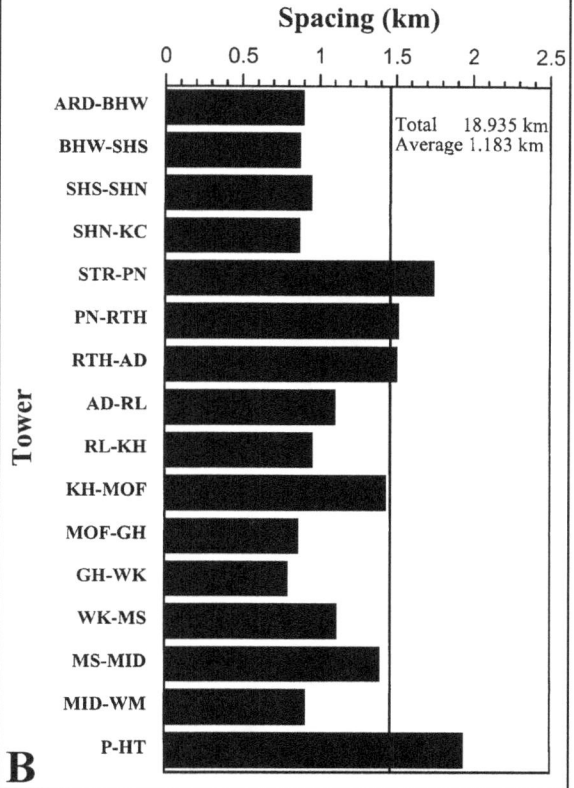

Gask Tower Shapes.

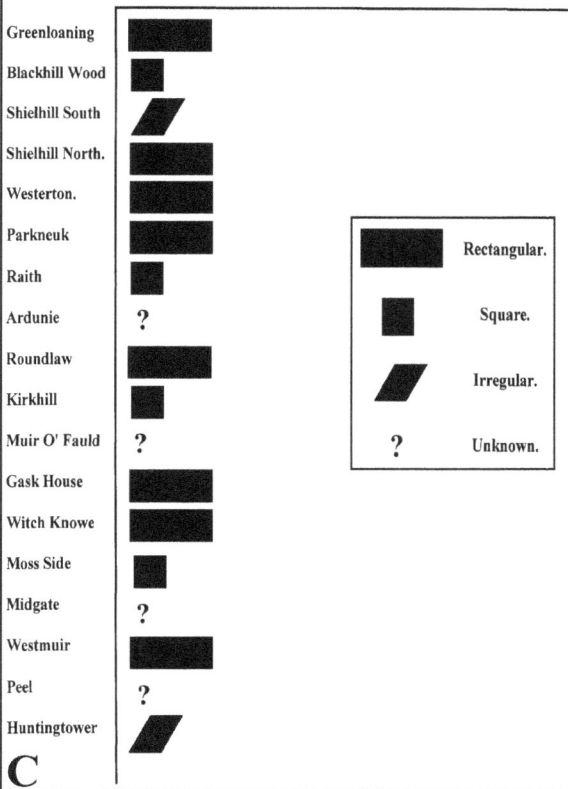

Gask Tower Areas.

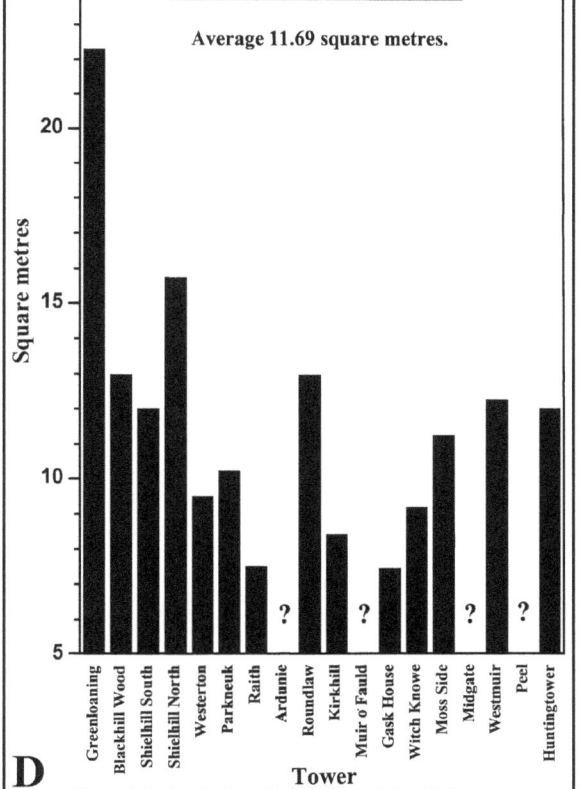

Fig 1.11.

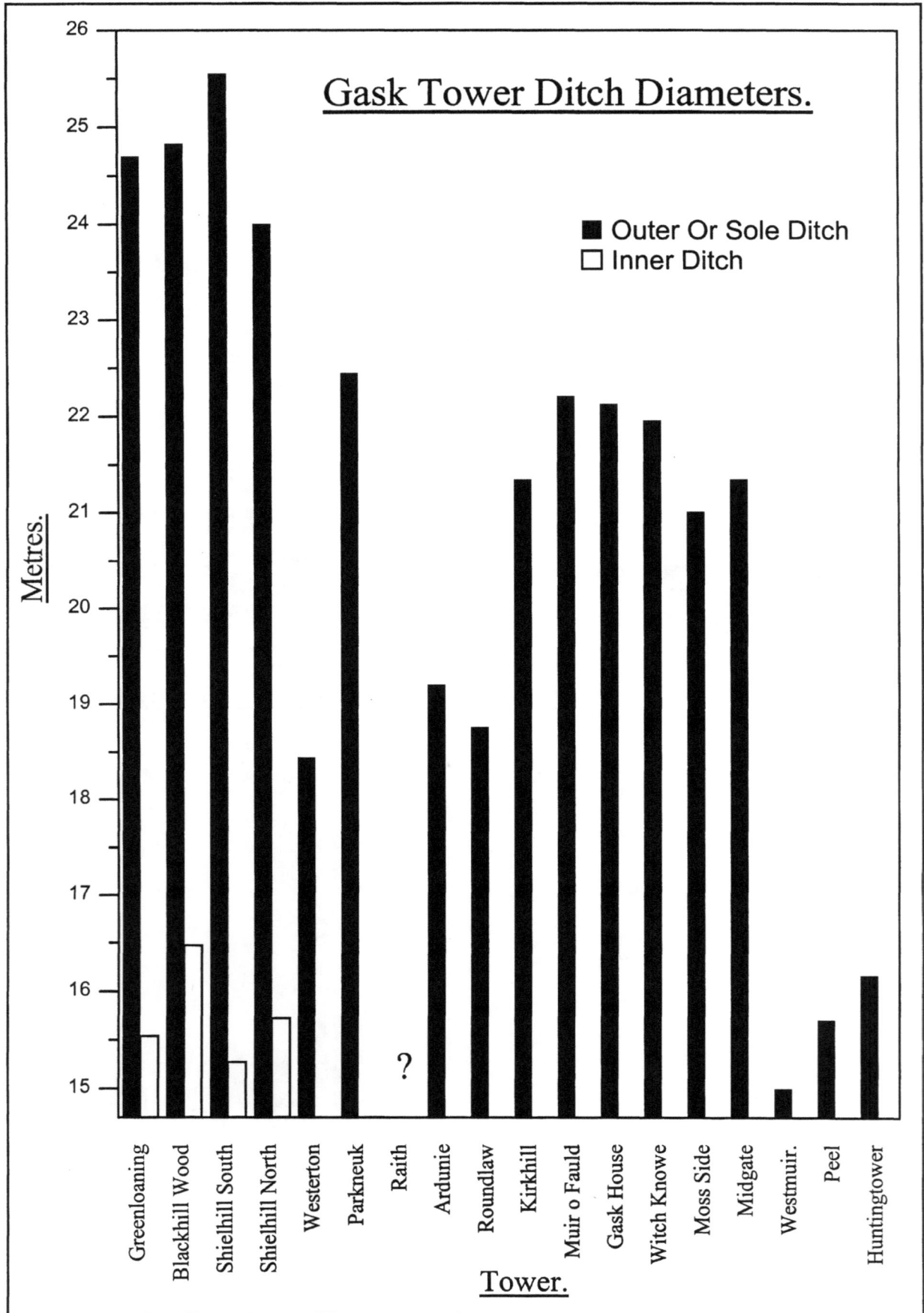

Gask Tower Ditch Diameters.

■ Outer Or Sole Ditch
□ Inner Ditch

Metres.

Tower.

Fig 1.12.

Cubic Metres per metre of ditch.

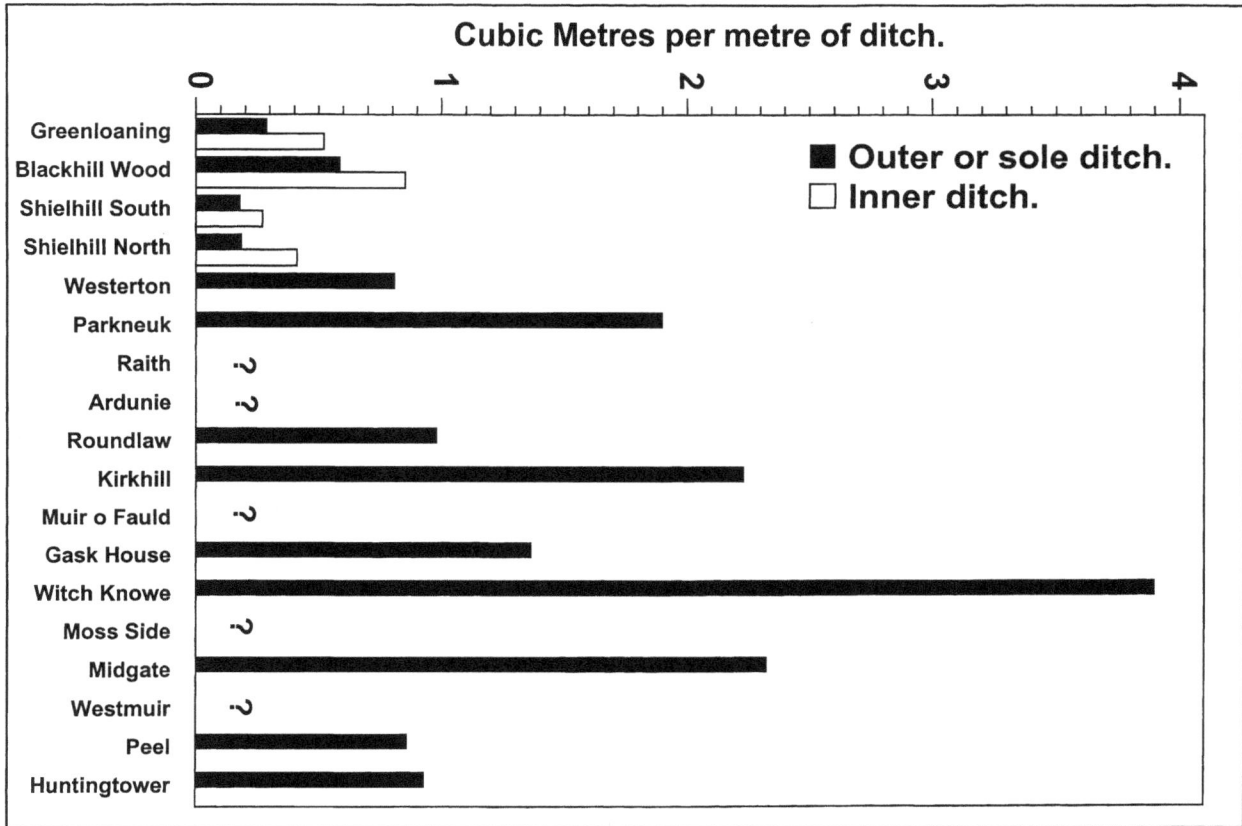

Fig 1.13. Gask Tower Ditch Volumes.

from Westerton to Roundlaw, which are significantly smaller at 18 - 19m and, finally, an eastern group, from Westmuir to Huntingtower, whose ditch are smaller still, at only 15 - 16m in external diameter, which is smaller than some of the southern group's inner ditches.

The ditch volumes, where known, also follow these divisions (fig 1.13). Those of the southern group are abnormally slight, sometimes laughably so. They are often less than 0.5m deep; they can be as little as 0.25m deep and are sometimes barely more than a metre wide. Indeed Blackhill Wood was found to have an oven set into one of its ditches (Glendinning and Dunwell 2000, 277f) and although this may relate to a somewhat later temporary camp, it does at least make the point that these features can have had little if any defensive value. The eastern Ridge towers, on the other hand, have substantial ditches of up to 1.8m deep and 4m wide, and it is interesting in this context that the supposed Midgate tower fits well with the rest of this group in both volume and diameter. Meanwhile both the intermediate and eastern groups have ditches of around 2m wide and just under 1m deep.

Furthermore, just as the southern sites have double ditches and larger than average towers, most of the other groups also have additional distinguishing features. The intermediate group, unlike the eastern Ridge group (but like the double ditched sites), has its rectangular towers set with their long axes facing, rather than at right angles to their ditch entrances. They also have ditches of the asymmetrical *fossa punica* type, with a near vertical outer face, rather than the far more standard, V shaped profiles known everywhere else on the line. Moreover, at least one site, Westerton, had a pair of projecting slots running out from the tower towards its ditch entrance, which might be the foundation for a flight of external steps (Hanson and Friell 1995, 502ff). Meanwhile, the tower shape at Huntingtower, on the eastern group, was distinctly irregular, rather than either square or rectangular, and its rear posts proved to be so far back in the enclosure as to be set into the internal rampart. This may or may not prove to be diagnostic, although faint air photographic traces of Westmuir's tower posts do make them appear to be both more central and more regularly laid out. More importantly, however, there is also evidence that the Eastern group may again be set at a regular spacing interval, this time of 2/3 of a Roman mile (Chap 6), rather than the 3/5 Roman mile spacing seen further south. It might even be relevant that there are also variations in the design of the fortlets, although we have already seen that these might not be fully contemporary with the towers. For Glenbank, on the southern sector, has its entrance set in its short axis, whilst Kaims Castle and Midgate, on the intermediate and eastern Ridge sectors, have theirs in their long axes.

21

This all seems quite clear cut and logical, for the groups are not too dissimilar in length and coincide reasonably well with what one might expect to be the spheres of influence of the forts. Moreover, if we do have four groups, one can hardly resist noticing the fact that there were also four legions in Britain at the time, which are the usual builder units and, as none of these designs repeat on further sectors, we may even have a sign that the entire frontier was built in a single season. There is, however, just one anomaly. For Parkneuk, at the westernmost end of the Gask Ridge and which ought to belong to the intermediate group, has the widest ditch diameter of any of the Ridge top towers (22.5m) and a V shaped ditch whose volume lies in the eastern group range (although its exact depth remains somewhat uncertain). Its excavator (Robertson 1974, 21ff) thought that its tower was oriented in the intermediate group fashion, with its long axis facing the entrance, but not even that much is completely certain as only three of the four post holes were located. This means that, however attractive these potential building sectors may seem, they need to be treated with at least a degree of caution until more towers can be found and studied in this area. As we have already seen, there are gaps in the spacing pattern which suggest that there are still quite a number of towers to be discovered on the Gask (perhaps as many as 12), especially in the intermediate group sector, and hopefully at least some of these will eventually come to light. Once they do, we should be able to form a better idea of whether Parkneuk is really an isolated aberration, and thus of whether the model presented above is more than a figment of the current, incomplete data.

Current and Future Research

In addition to the detailed work on individual installations, the Gask Project has been engaged in wider ranging research in a number of areas and this will continue into the future.

Firstly, the full length of the system still needs to be established. As we have already seen, the line is only known, at present, to run from Glenbank to Bertha, but as little as forty years ago the tower line had only been traced from Parkneuk to Midgate. The known length of the system has thus more than tripled in that time (from 10.7 to 35km), largely through the use of aerial photography. It is tempting to wonder, therefore, whether it might continue still further, especially to the south towards Stirling and/or Doune (where a Roman fort is now known), or even to Camelon near the later line of the Antonine Wall, where the road itself appears to begin (fig 1.1). For although in the north, the system now ends at a reasonably logical point, at a large auxiliary fort on the bank of a major river, the fortlet of Glenbank in the south does not appear strong enough, or in an obvious position to be a terminus. That said, it is noticeable that all of the four possible building sectors mentioned above begin and/or end at a fortlet, but Roman frontiers almost always end at forts and on major geographical features such as rivers, and so a terminus on the Forth or Teith would appear far more likely. Nevertheless, over half a century of air photography, mostly by Cambridge University and the RCAHMS, but more recently also by ourselves, has yet to locate further minor installations and the situation is made more

Fig 1.14. The supposed Roman tower at Fendoch, from the air.

difficult by the fact that even the course of the road is uncertain between a point about a mile to the south of Glenbank and the southern outskirts of Stirling. It is thus possible that we do now have the full extent of the frontier. This does still seem somewhat unlikely, however, and the situation has almost certainly been influenced by the fact that the modern agricultural regime to the south of Glenbank is far more pastoral in nature than that further north. This makes the formation of cropmarks and other air photographic phenomena far less frequent and we can only await the results of future flying, especially in severe drought conditions.

The same is true of the situation north of the Tay where, as yet, there is no really conclusive evidence that even the Roman road continued, despite antiquarian reports of it and despite the presence of additional forts and a legionary fortress. We have already seen that it could be argued that Cargill and Cardean continue the Gask fort line. But, for the moment, the only tower known north of Bertha is Black Hill, on the opposite side of the Isla from the fort of Cargill and, although the possibility of further discoveries cannot be ruled out, it would certainly come as far less of a surprise to find that the system did not continue to the north.

There are, however, at least two more sites outside the frontier which have been claimed as Roman minor installations over the years. The first is the long supposed tower at Fendoch (fig 1.14). This is a circular ditched feature with what appears to be an internal rampart, which sits on a bluff on the opposite side of the Sma' Glen mouth from Fendoch fort, and about 1 km to its north-west. Unfortunately, the site has never been excavated, but although it remains possible that it might be a tower, its view down the glen, even from full height, would not (contrary to popular opinion) have been particularly impressive and a far better site would actually have been on the northern mouth of the glen, which is also closer to the fort. Its ditch, albeit as a surface feature, seems unusually shallow and broad to be Roman and there is no sign on an entrance break, especially in the internal bank, which also leaves no room for a berm between itself and the ditch. It is to be hoped that the site will be more closely investigated at some point in the future, but it may well prove to be a barrow of some sort, with the apparent rampart actually the remains of a robbed out tumulus.

More recently, the Gask Project has excavated a site at Dornoch (fig 1.2), on the bank of the Earn, just to the north-west of Strageath, which had appeared from the air as a possible fortlet. It proved to date to the Victorian period, however, and as it showed heavy signs of metal working it may well have been linked to the construction of the Crieff to Glen Eagles railway bridge over the Earn, whose steel piers can still be seen in the river a few hundred metres upstream.

Next, there is a need to locate additional sites on the known parts of the Gask. This time, there can be little doubt that these are there to be found since, as we have seen, the spacing pattern for the existing installations shows some very obvious gaps. The Gask Project has already excavated one circular air photographic target, at Upper Quoigs, between Glenbank and Greenloaning (fig 1.2), which appeared to be a damaged ring ditch and had been suspected of being the missing Gask tower which should lie somewhere in the vicinity. But, when excavated, it proved to be a late Medieval sand working dug into a knoll. Further progress should only be a matter of time, however, and in the meantime, study of air photographs is, allowing us greatly to refine our knowledge of the course of the Roman road, parts of which have been badly mismapped in the past. The military installations are, almost without exception (appendix 2), built very close to this line, which means that, if nothing else, we should now have a better idea of where to search for new sites in the future.

Thirdly, air photography since WWII has revealed an ever growing number of Roman temporary camps. Over 70 are now known north of the Antonine Wall (Appendix 1), extending up to 57 ha (140 acres) in area. This is one of the richest assemblages anywhere in the Roman world, yet their dating remains largely uncertain and a detailed re-evaluation of the entire corpus is probably long overdue. This is especially true now that recent work has forced us to question the exact role of these sites (Breeze 2000, 49ff), for a number do not seem to fit the traditional picture of a simple, albeit fortified, overnight stop by a body of men on the march. For example, the 46.6 ha (115 acre) site of Dunning has shown signs of two occupation periods (Dunwell and Keppie 1995), as has the camp beside the glenblocker fort of Dalginross (Rogers 1993, 277-286) and we may have to face the possibility of prolonged and/or repeated use of the same camps. To date, the Gask Project's contribution to this issue has been to investigate a series of small possible camps in the immediate vicinity of the Gask. Six have been subjected to trenching and geophysical survey, of which two (both under 0.5 ha (1.2 acres)) still appear to be Roman (Chap 2). A further four are currently awaiting attention, including a particularly promising site at Aldonie Cottage (fig 1.2) near Kaims Castle, and more may be found in the future.

Fourthly, archaeologists have long complained that not enough has been done to study the impact of the Roman incursions on the indigenous population of Scotland. This has been to no small degree the result of the way in which Roman and Iron Age archaeology have been studied in the past, with Romanists and Pre-historians forming very separate groupings, who have traditionally shown remarkably little interest in each other's work. Worse still, much of the attention of the Iron Age specialists in recent decades has been directed towards the so called "Atlantic" cultures of the islands and western seaboard and, although this now appears to be changing to some degree, the more easterly regions, such as the Gask area, have been somewhat neglected as a consequence.

Partly as a result of these shortcomings, the popular view of Roman/native interaction in northern Scotland has been purely one of warfare and oppression. To say the least, it can hardly be denied that all invasions have their negative side but, even so, the situation in reality must have been rather more complex and this is especially true now that the Gask Project's own work has suggested that the first century occupation may have been more prolonged than had previously been thought, so that more sophisticated relationships would have had time to develop. Nor should the effects of 15 - 20 years of Antonine occupation be forgotten, albeit troop levels in the immediate Gask area were then rather lower. There has anyway been speculation in the past that a number of Caledonian tribes may have maintained a strongly pro-Roman policy and might even have actively welcomed Roman intervention as a protection against more traditional, local enemies (Breeze 1982, 56ff). The evidence for these attitudes has always been somewhat tenuous, but amongst the areas for which pro-Roman sentiment has been claimed is Fife, in the immediate hinterland of the Gask (Hanson 1987, 157). Indeed, we have seen that there have been suggestions in the past that the Gask frontier may have been designed largely, or even exclusively, as a protective cordon around some form of Roman protectorate in Fife (Frere 1980, 96). The very idea of invasion may thus be inappropriate for the Gask region, since the native population might not have resisted and might merely have seen itself as admitting an ally. Even if the area was taken by force, however, the negative aspects of occupation may have been somewhat counter balanced by economic and other opportunities.

The Roman forces in first century northern Scotland amounted to garrisons for at least the 13 currently known auxiliary forts and a legionary fortress. Assuming that all of the forts were occupied at the same time, this gives a total of from 12,000 to 18,000 reasonably well paid men, depending on the size of the individual auxiliary garrisons. Both the personal spending power and the corporate logistical needs of these troops should have introduced a significant economic stimulus, especially as there are, as yet, few signs of the usual Roman civilian towns (vici) developing around the forts (Chap 8). An army of this size would have been difficult to supply with nothing but imported materials, especially as the road network seems to have remained unfinished when the area was abandoned and many of the forts lie away from navigable waterways. Local supplies would, thus, have been vital and, although Roman logistical needs may have been met from taxation or even, initially at least,

Fig 1.15. The newly excavated souterrain at Shanzie, from the air.

from simple expropriation, even this is likely to have had effects (especially of an agricultural nature) which may be archaeologically detectable. Trade should also have grown up, with Roman imports being made more available, and personal contacts (both positive and damaging) between individual Roman soldiers and local inhabitants can be expected. These interactions, along with wider political effects, might also have archaeological consequences and the Gask Project has now started to devote more attention to the subject.

For the moment, the principle tool employed has been environmental (particularly pollen) analysis, although this has been hampered by the free draining and acidic nature of many of the local soils, which tend to destroy almost all organic materials, including bone. The picture to date is thus far from complete, but the evidence that has been accumulated points to a virtually treeless landscape, far from the dense primordial forest of popular imagination, given over almost exclusively to grazing with, as yet, little sign of cereal cultivation. This pattern contrasts with a more arable regime seen in the area in still earlier times (e.g. Romans & Robertson 1983) but, as the same picture can be seen in both immediately pre-Roman contexts and in Roman ditch silts, the Roman incursion may have done relatively little to harm local agriculture. Indeed, environmental results from the Gask tower of Peel (Chap 6) would suggest that agriculture actually intensified during the Roman occupation and, again, this may be due to the economic stimulus produced by Roman logistical needs. This would fit well with a recent theory by Armit (1999) that the enigmatic underground structures, known as souterrains (fig 1.15), which are so common in Perthshire and Angus, might have been built to store large quantities of local farm produce intended for the Roman army.

As for the natives themselves and their interactions with the invading power, we have as yet only tantalising glimpses. Three of the Gask minor installations, including Huntingtower and Glenbank, at opposite ends of the line, overlay native groove houses (the third being Cuiltburn), and Peel also seems to supersede native activity of some sort (Chap 6). Circular features, which appear to be of native origin, were detected underlying the forts of Strageath and (on a much larger scale) Cardean by our own geophysical surveys (Chap 8) and similar structures are visible in air photographs taken by the Project and others of Cargill (fort and fortlet) and the glenblocker forts of Dalginross and Inverquharity. Even temporary camps, such as Keithock, Stracathro and Battledykes, were built over native settlements and many more Roman sites, notably the Gask fort of Bertha, have native activity immediately outside their defences. This makes it all too tempting to conjure up a picture of local people being thrown out of their homes to make way for the army, but it has to be stressed that, in the absence of precise enough dating evidence, it

remains equally possible that these features may have been abandoned long before the Romans arrived. Whatever the case, there is a certain amount of, albeit tenuous, evidence that, however they may have treated settlement sites, the Romans may have been more willing to respect native burial and religious monuments and this would fit well with their known attitudes to the gods of their enemies.

Like many pre-industrial peoples, the Romans saw the gods as being far more closely involved in day to day life than even most believers would today. At the same time they saw their relationship with the divine as largely contractual in nature. The good will of the gods could thus be bought by the provision of suitable rites and sacrifices, whilst their anger could be earned, not so much by sin, but by what amounts to breach of contract, by neglecting those same rites and sacrifices. As a result, the Romans assumed that an enemy's gods would be open to better offers. In other words they would seek, not to defeat the enemy's gods, but to bribe them into changing sides, and desecrating their sacred sites was not the obvious way to go about this. The dead might also have spiritual power and so they too might well have been seen as worth appeasing, which may provide some clue as to why a number of Roman military sites (e.g. the temporary camps at Ardoch and Easter Powside) come very close to, but avoid impinging on Bronze Age barrow fields. Indeed, it would not come as any great surprise to find the Romans actually using native cemetery sites, for although there is as yet no evidence for this from the Gask area itself, recent air photographic work on Hadrian's Wall has revealed what appear to be high status Roman tombs set on the fringes of a large native cemetery, c. 600m to the south of the fort of Great Chesters (Jones & Woolliscroft, 2001, 109 & fig 62).

Air photographs of the Gask area have revealed numerous examples of a variety of Iron Age site types but, as always, it is difficult to date such features with any precision from the air to select Roman period targets for excavation and further study. As the Gask Project has neither the resources nor the remit to conduct a more general survey of the local Iron Age, a compromise was needed and a search has been made for multi-phased sites. These should be an indication of prolonged occupation which should, at least, provide a statistically higher chance of continuity into the Roman occupation, and work has now commenced on the first such site, at East Coldoch near the Roman fort of Doune. The site, which shows at least five separate phases, was subjected to reconnaissance work in 1996 (Chap 4) and has since seen the first of two planned seasons of larger scale work. The standard of preservation proved to be excellent, especially for a crop mark site, with one round house surviving complete with its burned down roof and carbonised nut shells on the floor. As yet, there is still no guarantee that it was occupied into Roman times, but

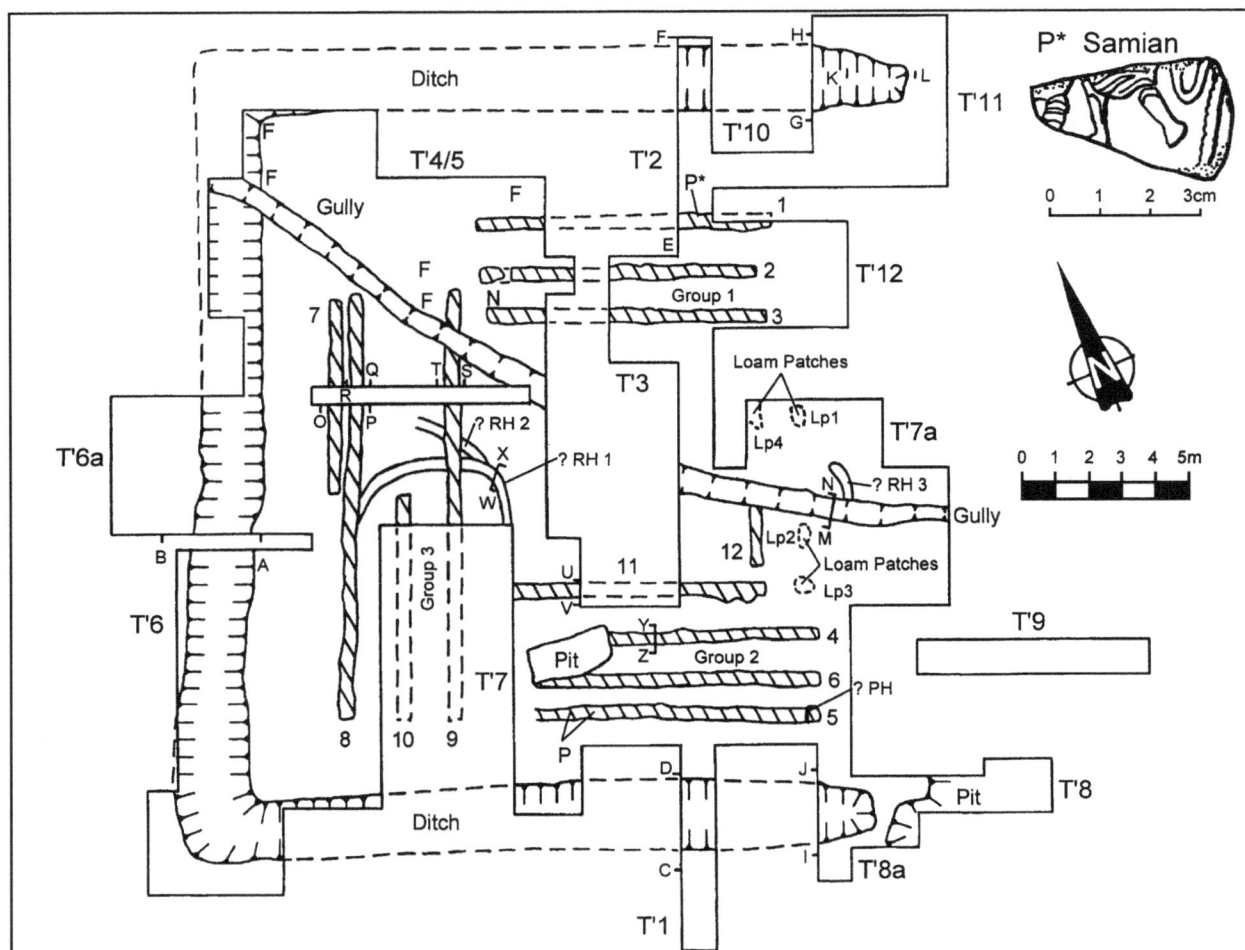

Fig 1.16. Cuiltburn site plan.
Find spots: F = Flints, N = Nails, P + Roman pottery, Lp = ? post stance, RH = ? Roundhouse.

datable carbon was recovered from all its critical contexts which means that, once the scientific post-excavation work has been completed, it should be possible track environmental changes through real time. The site has, though already produced one surprise in that it suggests that the Iron Age population might have traded in bulk goods. For, although a great deal of barley grain was found in the occupation levels, there was no trace of barley pollen in contemporary ditch silts. Quite the reverse, there was clear evidence for the same purely pastoral economy that we have found elsewhere in the area. The grain was thus not grown in the vicinity and must thus have been brought in from elsewhere.

Further such work on other sites is planned for the future and, in time, the Project's work should help towards building a better picture of what the area was like before the Romans arrived and of the impact they had. This, in turn, might give us a better idea of what the frontier was deigned to protect and from whom.

Attention is also being given to the possibility of Roman civilian activity. A large geophysical survey has already been conducted outside the fort of Strageath, in the hope of locating a vicus (Chap 8), and it is also worth mentioning an apparently unique site at Cuiltburn (Woolliscroft forthcoming (b)), a few hundred meters further south, which may have a civilian origin (fig's 1.2 and 1.15). The feature was tentatively identified from the air as a fortlet but excavations by the Project suggest otherwise. The site did produce Roman pottery along with three Roman looking, rectangular, beam founded buildings, grouped around an internal courtyard and fronted by some sort of timber facade, but the defences are not those of a fortlet. The ditch goes around only three of the four sides and, although the site sits right beside and parallel to the Roman road, the open side, unlike the entrances of all of the proven Gask installations (Appendix 2), faces away from the road not towards it. The ditch itself has a steep sided, flat bottomed profile, quite unlike the usual Roman military "V" shape, and there were no signs of an internal rampart or palisade defence. Nevertheless the site is quite probably Roman and, although it has not yet been possible to find a single excavated parallel, a civilian or non-military official function seems possible.

26

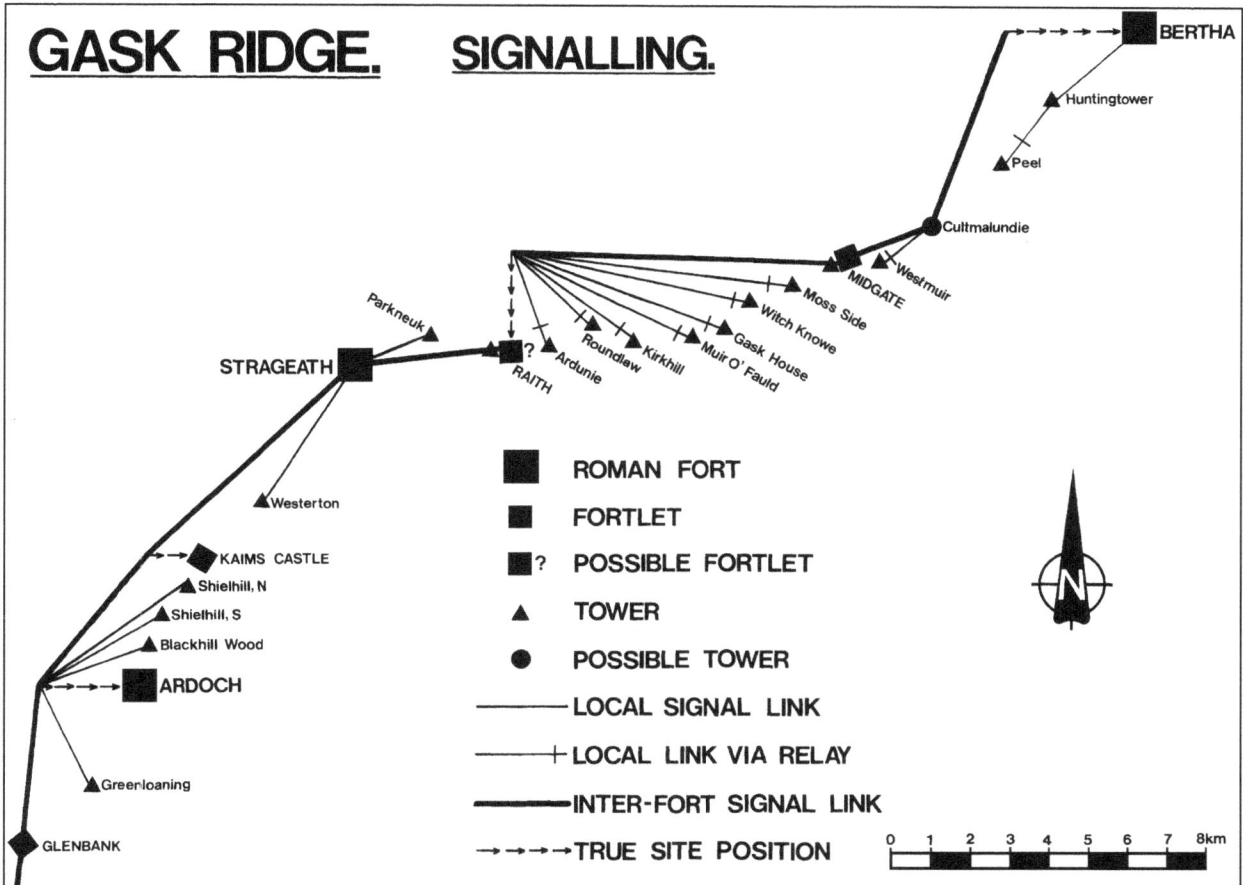

Fig 1.17.

Communications

Like all Roman frontiers, the Gask cannot be seen as just a linear collection of individual sites. It was an integrated defence system, and to behave as such it had to be able to act (on a reliable basis) as a single unified whole. It thus required co-ordination which, in turn, means that it needed efficient communications. Under normal circumstances the Roman road would have facilitated the movements of messengers and dispatch riders, but under emergency conditions more rapid communications by signal would have been necessary. A study has thus been made of the Gask frontier's likely signalling arrangements (fig 1.17). In addition to its own intrinsic interest, this has allowed another useful comparison with later Roman systems elsewhere. For, if the Gask really was the prototype Roman frontier, knowledge of its state of development might help us to judge the level of innovation thereafter, and a technical area like signalling might well be a good indication.

Most Roman frontiers consist essentially of a chain of forts strung out along the frontier line, interspersed with whatever smaller installations, such as towers and fortlets, acted as an observation screen. Various elaborations, such as running barriers, outposts and coastal defences are often found, but this still remains the essential core. It would seem reasonable to expect that the bulk of any signals traffic on a Roman frontier would have been alert warnings sent from these observation posts to the forts and it is easy to assume that signalling would have operated in a linear manner, in other words that signals from individual minor sites would have been relayed from tower to tower along the line until they reached a fort. But on most of the later Roman frontiers of Europe (Woolliscroft 1989, 1994, 1996 & 2001, Woolliscroft and Hoffmann 1991 & 1997 and Gudea 1997) the Romans actually seem to have run things far more efficiently. For these often vast systems, which frequently run through very difficult terrain, have usually been so skilfully laid out so that almost all of the minor installations can see a fort, and thus signal to it directly, using the visual techniques of the day (Woolliscroft 2001, Chap 1). The forts themselves can also usually be linked together to form a long distance strategic chain, either by again being directly intervisible or, much more often, by means of intermediate relay stations.

In real world terrain, this ideal was not always fully achieved, and there are almost always some small sites whose signals would have needed relaying before they could reach a fort. But these are almost always a small minority and even they are usually positioned so as to need the minimum possible number of relay sites. And despite its early date, this is exactly the pattern we find on the Gask. (Woolliscroft 1993). Almost all of the lower lying sites have a direct view to a fort (fig 1.17), whilst the fortlet of Kaims Castle has been skilfully positioned on the only position able to see both Ardoch and Strageath simultaneously (from the full height of a Roman tower) and thus act as a relay between them. The topography of the Gask Ridge itself restricted the east-west views of some of its towers, but even so, there is only one installation on the entire system that would have needed more than one relay to transmit its signals to a fort. Moreover this site, Westmuir, almost certainly has an undiscovered neighbour c.2/3 of a Roman mile to its east in or around the modern Cultmalundie Wood, a position with an excellent view to the north-east and which would have been able to link it to Bertha. It is also noteworthy that the two key positions for signalling on the Gask are Kaims Castle, which has already been mentioned, and Raith. The latter stands on a quite superb observation position with a magnificent 360° field of view which was obviously regarded as important by the system's builders since, to gain it, Raith has been built far further from the road than any other Gask installation (170m as against an average of 27m). The site is able to link every tower between itself and Midgate to the fort of Strageath and it is also in visual contact with both Kaims Castle and Midgate fortlets, which means that it could play a major role in inter-fort communications. Such vital relay sites would almost certainly be hardened, to use modern military parlance. In other words we might expect attention to have been paid to their protection, perhaps by providing more heavily manned and fortified installations. In this context, therefore, it can hardly be irrelevant that Kaims Castle is a fortlet rather than just a tower, and the possibility of a fortlet at Raith can then be seen in a rather more logical (and urgent) light.

It could in fact be suggested that the Gask was nothing more than an arterial signalling system to link the three forts. Indeed the towers are often referred to, rather casually, simply as "signal towers", with all that that implies for their function (e.g. Robertson 1974). Such an argument is untenable, however. There are far more towers far closer together than would have been needed for such a role and so the minor installations were almost certainly meant primarily to provide observation cover. But there is obviously little point in having observers unless they can tell someone what they see. Moreover that someone would need the information quickly enough to act on it and the forces necessary to do so, which once again means, in practice, that the operation of the system depended on efficient communications with the principle garrison forts. The towers were thus watch towers that needed to be able to signal, rather than signal towers per se but the Gask does seem to have had an efficient signalling system right from the start, which ran on exactly the same principle as those of Rome's later frontiers. This means that, apart from the lack of a running barrier, we already have on the Gask all of the basic elements of a classic Roman Limes system. The Gask would have been a more open line than barrier systems such as Hadrian's Wall and may reflect a slightly different approach, but it still held the working core of Roman frontiers to come. These may now appear more complex and they were certainly often more grandiose, but in reality the differences are largely matters of (sometimes cosmetic) detail. The Gask frontier has often been seen as little more than a footnote even in the history of Roman Britain, so much so that people who live within sight of it can be totally unaware of its existence. But this little prototype frontier was the start of a trend which was to sweep over thousands of miles around the entire Roman world. Its basic design was built into systems which effected centuries of history over a vast area, and it is time that it was recognised as a monument of major importance.

2. Excavation and survey on six suspected small Roman temporary camps.

D J Woolliscroft, A J Hughes and N J Lockett. With contribution by S Ramsay.

The last fifty years have seen a spectacular growth in our knowledge of Roman temporary camps in northern Scotland thanks mainly to the use of air photography. The final word has yet to be written, but the vastly increased number of sites now known, coupled to more detailed analyses of their size and morphology, have permitted at least reasonably plausible attempts at reconstructing Roman campaigning routes and even the approximate strengths of different invading forces (e.g. Hanson 1987, chap 6 and Maxwell 1989, chap 3). These advances have, however, mostly concerned the larger camps, whose size can range up to 58ha (144 acres). Yet in other Roman military areas (e.g. Hadrian's Wall), far smaller camps are also found. These have been variously interpreted as construction camps and as practice camps built during training exercises, but some may simply reflect small detachments on the move. It should thus come as no surprise that there are a number of enclosures amongst the wealth of air photographic images of the Gask region which could be similar small camps. Indeed, one such site has long been known from surface traces at Gask House, immediately to the south of Gask House tower (Christison, 1901, 35). This site measures just 1.82 ha (4.5 acres) over the ditches, but still has all of the features of a full sized camp, including four entrances with titulus gate defenses. Three of the latter have been known since the end of the 19th century at the North, West and East gates and the fourth came to light at the South gate during one of the Roman Gask Project's air photographic flights (neg: 00CN4#31). In an attempt to confirm the existence of more such diminutive sites, the writers have investigated six more camp like air photographic targets, some of which were smaller even than Gask House. The work was conducted in 1998 and 1999 as part of a wider study of the camps on and around the Roman Gask frontier and, although four of the features no longer seem likely to be Roman, two, interestingly the two smallest, do seem to be genuine Roman camps.

Easter Powside.

This enclosure is known from a number of air photographs (e.g. RCAHMS Neg: A29091 and Gask Project neg GPAP01 CN1.31) and takes the form of a slightly irregular parallelogram with rounded corners (fig 2.1A). The site is located at NO 056245, 1.5 km to the west of the Gask system tower of West Mains of Huntingtower and, despite its name, it lies on the farm of Marlefield. It sits on a low bluff overlooking the tiny River East Pow from the 35m contour and has excellent views in all directions. Its form is at best a distinctly distorted version of the classic Roman military "playing card" shape, but less than regular site plans are far from unusual in temporary works. The design is certainly well suited to the ground on which it stands, since the bluff line projects to the north at the site's northwest corner and the enclosure ditch simply follows it to take advantage of the most defensible line. Air photographic indications have shown that the site lies just to the north of a significant native barrow field, but it does not appear to impinge on any of the burials.

The entire ditch circuit has never been visible from the air and the writers have not as yet had time to trace the missing sections, by either trenching or geophysical means. Nevertheless, a reasonable approximation can be interpolated. The enclosure can be shown to have measured c.76 m (n-s) along its western ditch, by c. 69 m (e-w) along the southern side, over the ditches. The eastern ditch does not show in full from the air and the northeast corner has been destroyed by a, now disused, railway which bisects the site from east to west, but it was probably in the region of 10 m shorter than the western side. The northwest to southeast diagonal is c. 102 m. In all, the site probably measured c. 0.45 ha (1.12 acres), which would make it one of the smallest Roman camps currently known in Scotland. The only visible entrance break lies in the center of the north ditch, closest to the river, and there is a short length of ditch just outside it which might represent a titulus defense. This is, though, offset by some 12 m to the west of the entrance center line and so the identification must remain doubtful until further study can be organized.

The excavation consisted of a single ditch section at the enclosure's southeastern corner and revealed a standard Roman, military style, V shaped ditch 1.9 m wide and 0.85 m deep, with signs of an "ankle breaker" sump (fig 2.1B). The ditch had lain open for long enough to silt naturally to almost half its original depth, whereupon the silts (L'6) had reached a reasonably stable angle of rest. This may represent a considerable period of time, but the ditch had then been back filled from the direction of the enclosure interior (NW) with a mixture of turf and loams (L's 3, 4, 8 and 9) which may have derived, at least partially, from an internal rampart. The trench only extended for about 1 m into the interior and so may not have reached the position of any surviving rampart base remains, but no traces of any other internal defense, such as a palisade, were encountered in that area. No small finds were recovered, but the ditch shape, the site's overall morphology, and the possible indications of a turf and earth rampart do seem highly suggestive of a Roman date. The site does thus seem quite likely to be a small

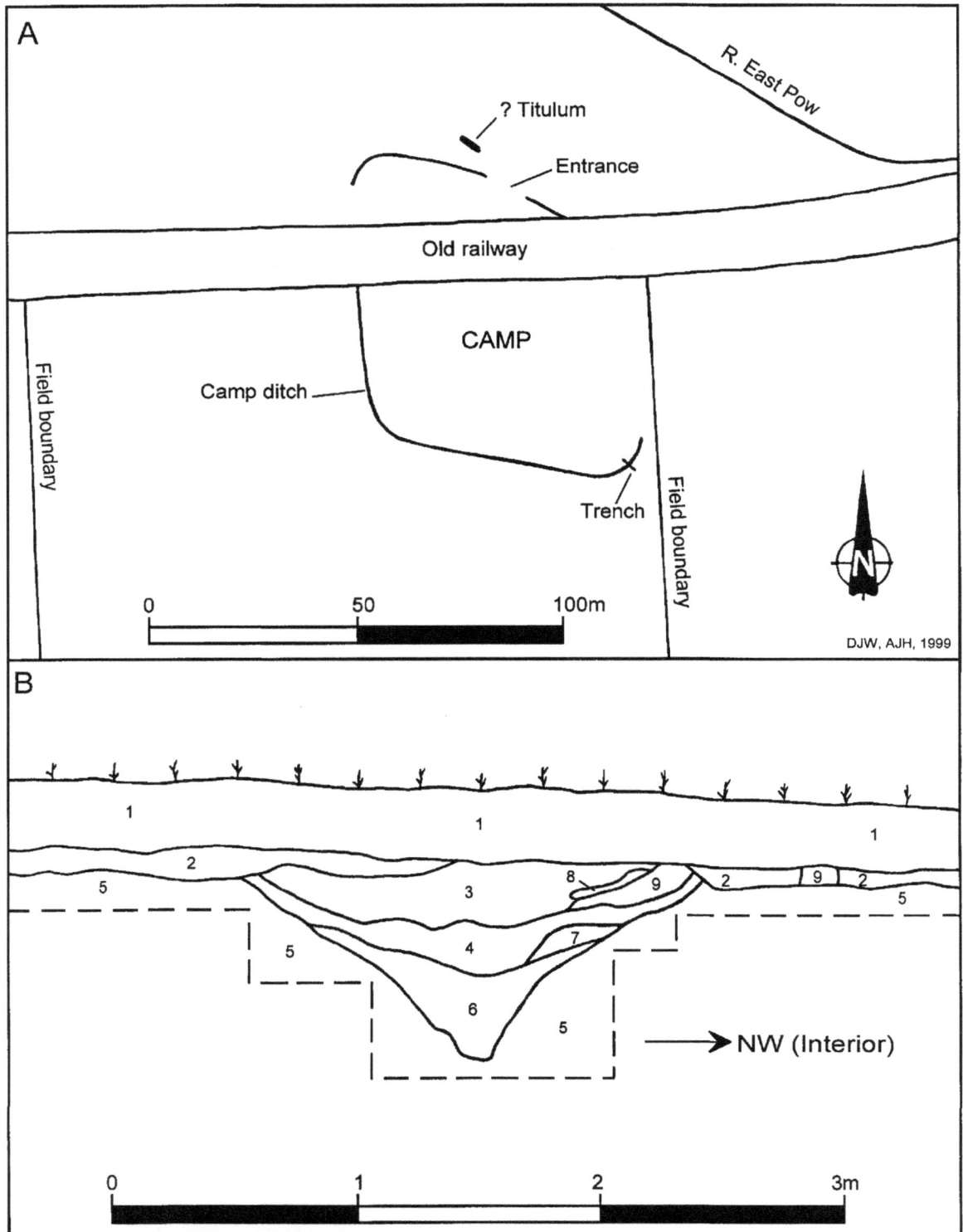

A

? Titulum

Entrance

R. East Pow

Old railway

CAMP

Camp ditch

Trench

Field boundary

Field boundary

0   50   100m

DJW, AJH, 1999

B

1

1

1

2

5

3

8

9

2

9

2

5

5

4

7

6

5

NW (Interior)

0   1   2   3m

1. Turf and topsoil. 2. Red/brown loam. 3. Mixed turf and loam. 4. Dark brown loam. 5. Natural orange
sand and gravel. 6. Brown silty sand and gravel. 7. Dark brown loam with gravel. 8. Carbonised vegetation.
9. Brown loam with turf flecks.

Fig 2.1. Easter Powside: plan and ditch section.

temporary camp (albeit this may not yet be regarded as proven), perhaps connected with the building of the Roman road from the Gask Ridge to Bertha, which lies only c. 200 m to the south.

Ardunie.

A single air photograph (RCAHMS Neg B5176) taken in 1988 showed what appear to be two overlapping rectangular enclosure ditches, with rounded corners, towards the western end of the Gask Ridge at NN 943186. The sites lie immediately south of the Roman Gask road on the farm of Ardunie, c. 450 m to the west of the watch tower of the same name (fig 2.2). They have reasonable views of their surroundings including a view along the Gask Frontier from Raith to Roundlaw and have long range views over Strathearn to the south. Neither feature showed a full ditch circuit on the air photograph, assuming that they did indeed have such circuits, but the two enclose approximately 2.33 ha (5.76 acres) and at least 1.96 ha (4.86 acres) respectively. Both appear to be at least potentially more perfectly rectangular than Easter Powside, and this again led to the suggestion that they might be small Roman camps, albeit only Enclosure 2 showed recognizable signs of an entrance break in the visible portions of its ditch. If so,

these sites could have been of particular importance since Enclosure 1's ditch (at least) seemed certain to intersect, and so perhaps precede, the Roman road, whose own date still remains uncertain.

As at Easter Powside, a single trench was laid out, this time at the one intersection between the two enclosure ditches, with a view to examining both the ditch morphology and the chronological sequence between the two features. The excavation would appear to dispel any possibility of the features being Roman camps. The two ditches were found in the positions expected and, although both were badly damaged by plough scarring, a modern pipe land drain and two older, gravel filled trench, land drains, it was clear that the Enclosure 2 ditch had cut that of Enclosure 1 and was thus later. Both ditches, however, proved to be very shallow saucer shaped features. Enclosure 1's ditch was 1.7m wide and, although land drain damage made it impossible to obtain a full section within the excavated area, its maximum depth is probably around 90mm (fig 2.2, plan and section A-B, L'3). Enclosure 2's ditch was a maximum of 1.6m wide, within the trench and only 78mm deep (fig 2.2, plan and section C-D, L'4). Both were thus quite unlike any normal Roman military ditches and, although the possibility cannot be ruled out that these were marking out features for camps which

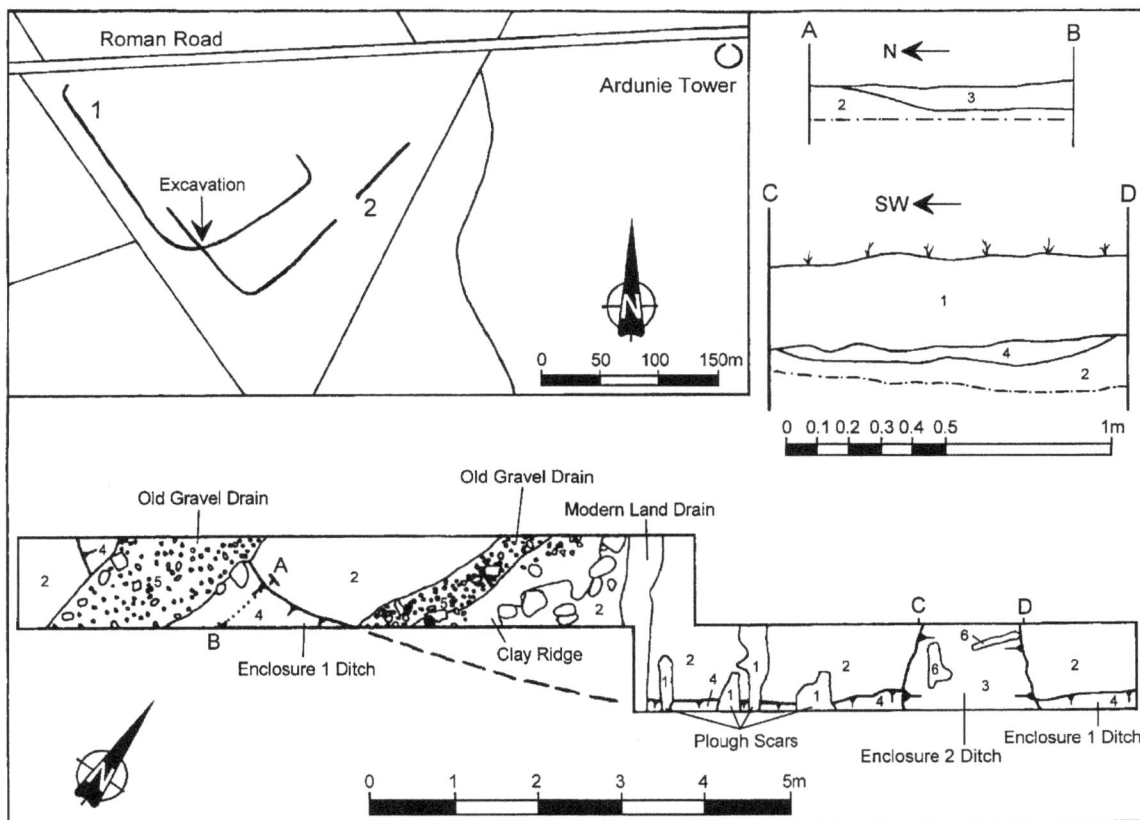

1. Topsoil.   2. Natural orange/red clay.   3. Smooth clayey grey/brown loam.   4. Silty grey loamwith clay.
5. Packed gravel in brown loam matrix.   6. Mixed orange red clay with brown loam.

Fig 2.2. Ardunie enclosures: location map with excavated plan and sections.

were laid out but never completed, perhaps as a training exercise, the enclosures seem more likely to have been more modern agricultural features. They may perhaps represent old field or plantation boundaries, although as no root holes were found in their bottoms, they are unlikely to be old hedgerows, and their relationship with the topography makes it unlikely that they were connected with drainage. No artifacts or datable carbon were recovered, so no absolute dates can be assigned to the enclosures, but as the Enclosure 1 ditch was also cut by the plough scarring and all three land drains, it is clearly the oldest feature within the trench. The Enclosure 2 ditch was not cut by any other feature within the excavated area and so its relationships with the land drains and ploughing remain unresolved.

Upper Cairnie.

In the 1950's and early 1960's R.W. Feachem and then J.K. St.Joseph (1958, 90 and 1965, 82) recognised the ditches of two adjoining enclosures at NO 038192, on air photographs taken by the R.A.F. The sites lie on the land of Bankhead Farm, although they are usually named after the nearest farmstead: Upper Cairnie. Both are rectangular enclosures with rounded corners (fig 2.3a) and they have since shown repeatedly as, often well defined, crop marks.

The sites occupy a commanding position on a gentle south facing slope, just below the summit of the Gask Ridge, 1.6 km to the SSE of the Roman tower at Westerton (fig 1.2). To their south the ground slopes away much more steeply and they enjoy superb views, especially to the south and east, where they overlook Strathearn from a height of 135m. Neither ditch circuit has ever shown in its entirety and nothing is visible at the surface, but the larger, western site is the most complete and measures approximately 3.3ha (8.16 acres) over its ditches. Almost the whole of the southern end of the eastern enclosure is missing, but the faint suggestion of a turn at the southern end of its eastern ditch, as if to form a southeast corner, does at least imply that there was originally a southern ditch and suggests that the enclosure would not have been much larger than 1.63ha (4 acres). Both sites are slightly irregular in shape, but the western enclosure is c.182m (e-w) by 190m (n-s), whilst the eastern site is c.125m (e-

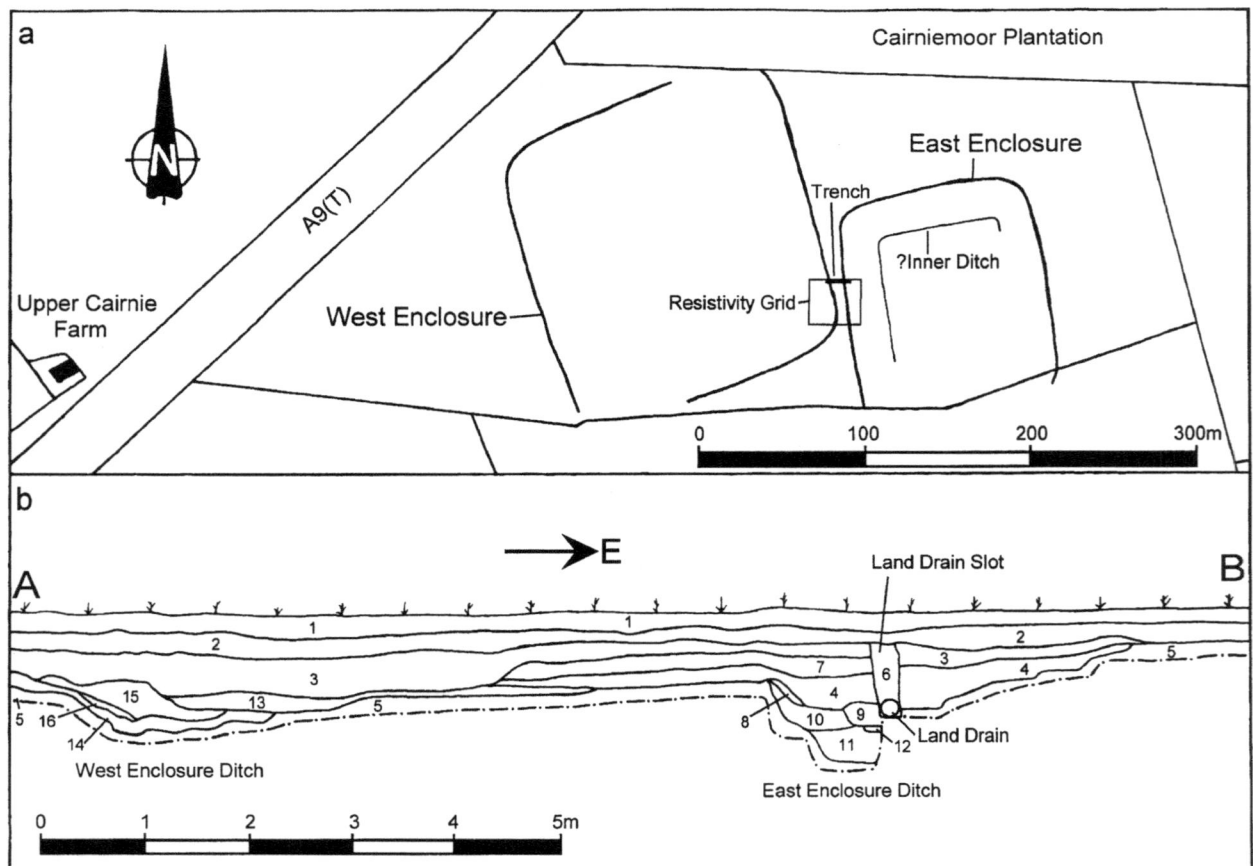

1. Turf and topsoil. 2. Grey/brown loam. 3. Pink/brown loam with charcoal. 4. Clean pink/brown sandy loam. 5. Natural boulder clay. 6. Brown clayey loam. 7. Rusty loam with iron slag. 8. Brown loam with sandstone. 9. pink.beige clay. 10. pink/brown clayey loam with sandstone. 11. Grey silt. 12. Red/brown clay. 13. Brown loamy sand. 14. Pink/grey silt. 15. Dirty brown/grey siltyclay. 16. Clean brown/grey silt.

Fig 2.3. Upper Cairnie: section and location plan.

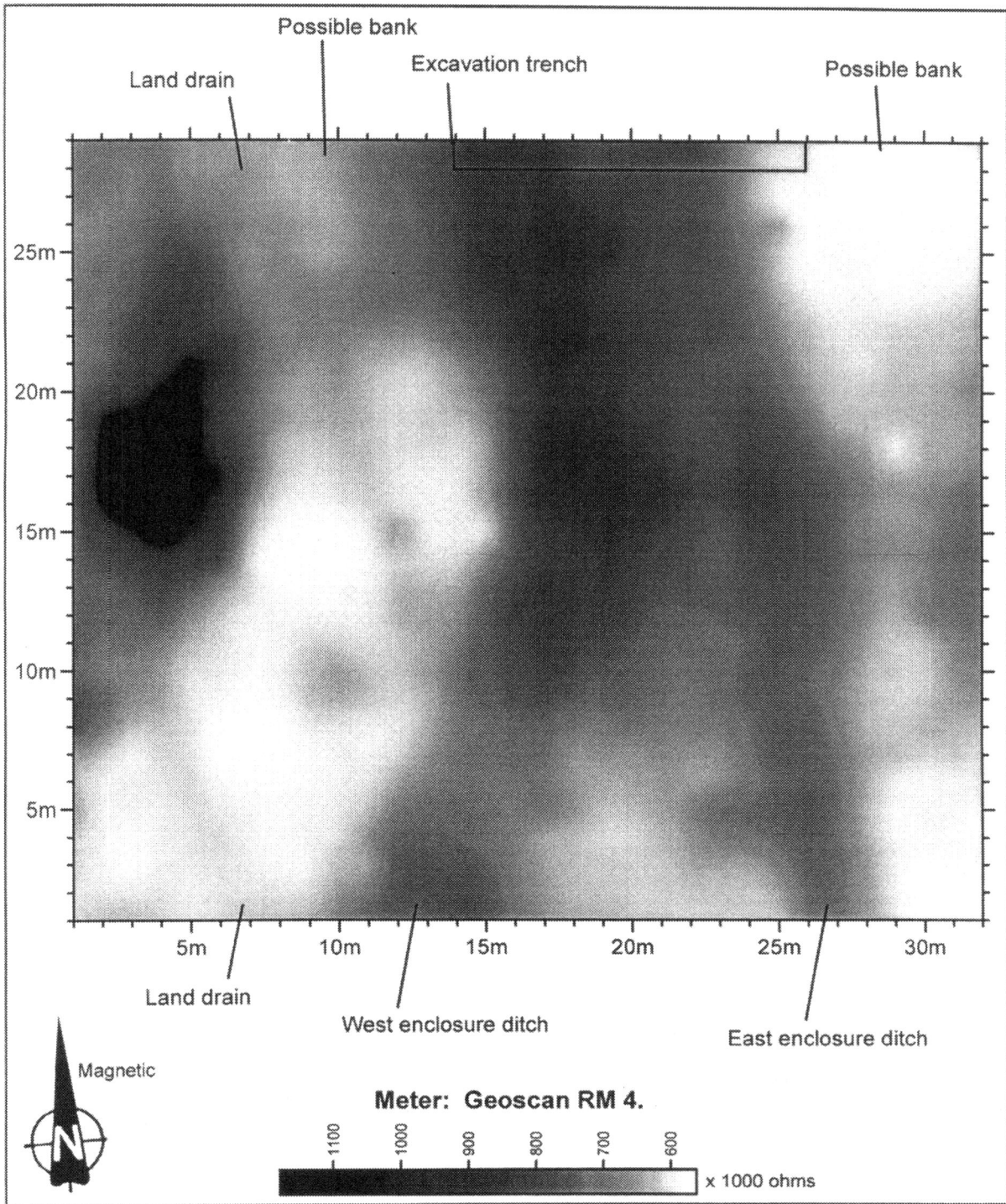

Fig. 2.4. Upper Cairnie: Resistivity.

w) by at least 140m (n-s). Some air photographs show much fainter indications of an inner ditch inside the eastern enclosure, which appears to run almost exactly parallel to at least parts of the bolder outer ditch and roughly 23m inside it. The feature is so narrow that it may represent a fence slot or an insubstantial drainage feature, although its morphology makes it appear certain that it does relate to the enclosure rather than to the pattern of modern land drains in the same field.

St.Joseph (1958, 90) initially interpreted the Eastern enclosure as a Roman fort, but the slightly later discovery of the western site in such close proximity seems to have been enough to cause him to dismiss both sites as Medieval. The possibility remained, however, that both may have been small temporary camps. There was, though, one objection to such an interpretation being made from the aerial evidence alone for, although both enclosures had the correct general shape, neither showed signs of entrance breaks in their ditches. In April 1999, therefore, the Roman Gask Project attempted to settle the question by conducting a resistivity survey and trial section on the site.

The resistivity survey (fig 2.4) covered a 31m (e-w) by 28m (n-s) grid around the two enclosure ditches' point of closest approach (fig 2.3) and was undertaken primarily to ensure that the two ditches could be sectioned by a single trench of the shortest possible length. Nevertheless, it did produce useful additional data. The two ditches were found on exactly their expected lines but, unusually, both were detected as bands of high rather than low resistance. This pattern appears to be relatively normal in this particular area, however, with similar results known from the Gask towers of Peel (Chap 6) and Huntingtower (Woolliscroft forthcoming a). It seems to result from the ditch fills being freer draining than the heavy boulder clay subsoil and it is noteworthy that the modern land drain tracks also appear as lines of high resistance. The ditch anomalies ranged from 2 to 4m in width, with that of the western enclosure being noticeably wider than its counterpart. More interestingly, however, both ditches appear to be backed by parallel bands of low resistance and it is possible that these may represent the ploughed down remains of internal earth banks or ramparts. Finally, one area of extremely high resistance was detected behind the possible bank, right in the southeast corner of the western enclosure, although no interpretation can be offered here with any confidence and the feature may represent nothing more than a rock outcrop or a large boulder.

A single trench was cut across both ditches at the northern end of the resistivity grid (fig 2.4), to determine their nature and stratigraphic relationship (fig 2.3b). The top of the natural subsoil was noticeably lower in the center of the trench (by c. 0.25m), and also sloped down slightly towards the west. This would suggest that this part of the field was once a slight hollow, whereas the modern ground surface is level from east to west. Both ditches proved to be relatively slight and to have been buried to a considerable depth so that it is perhaps surprising that they are still so readily detectable both by the resistivity meter (with a half meter probe spacing) and from the air. This did, however, mean that the intervening stratigraphy survived well, despite many years of ploughing.

The East enclosure ditch was the more substantial of the two and appeared to have a flat bottomed, U shaped, profile (fig 2.3b), although the intrusion of a modern land drain (L'6) made it impossible to excavate it fully. The ditch was 0.75m deep from the subsoil top and a

maximum of 1.25m wide. It seemed to have filled naturally for some time, firstly with a fine grey silt (L'11) and later with a weathering product of the natural pink boulder clay (L'10). This ditch may then have been re-cut (although this was less than certain) to a rather shallower depth and with a more saucer shaped profile, after which it again started to fill with erosion products from the natural clay (L'9). It was then finally filled with loams (L's 4 and 8), which may have been deposited by plough action, rather than deliberate backfilling. The modern land drain prevented the excavation of the primary ditch's eastern (inner) face, but the fact that nothing but the subsoil was visible immediately to the east of the drain suggests that it may have been markedly steeper than its western counterpart. This profile differs markedly from the usual Roman military V shape, albeit camp ditches tend to be more variable than those of more permanent installations. The writers have been trying to locate the records of two sections cut by R.W. Feachem on the northern side of the same enclosure, which were mentioned in print by St.Joseph (1965, 82), but otherwise never published. These should provide a useful comparison with our own results, but to date they have not come to light.

The uppermost fill of the eastern enclosure ditch was a layer (L'7) containing substantial quantities of iron slag: in all 3.24 kg in a layer whose total volume (within the trench) amounted to only c. $0.52m^3$. Two small crucible fragments were also recovered and the rusty colour of the loam matrix of the layer itself also suggests a high iron content. No remains of hearths, furnaces or other metal working infrastructure were found within the trench, but this layer does suggest a period of smithing or iron smelting somewhere close by.

The western ditch is both less substantial and more complex, with a total of three cuts visible which, combined, give the impression of a broad linear scoop, rather than anything that could be recognised as having defensive value. The primary cut is represented by siltation layers 14, 15 and 16 (fig 2.3b) and seems to have been a shallow flat bottomed ditch a little over 2m wide and 0.5m deep. Its center line lay roughly 6.5m west of that of the eastern ditch. Like the eastern ditch, it was cut directly into the natural boulder clay, but there is no surviving stratigraphy to determine whether or not the two were contemporary or, if not, which came first. The second cut is represented by silt layer 13 and may have taken the form of a slight step cut into what had, as stated, been slightly rising ground in the west, rather than a true ditch. The feature as it survives takes the form of a shallow saucer shaped depression 1.9m wide, but only 0.2m deep, with its center line c.1m to the east of that of the primary cut. The siltation deposit has, though, spread over an area c. 2.1m to the east of the feature as actually cut. Again, there is no stratigraphic connection to give a relative chronology between this feature and the primary cut of the eastern ditch, but the

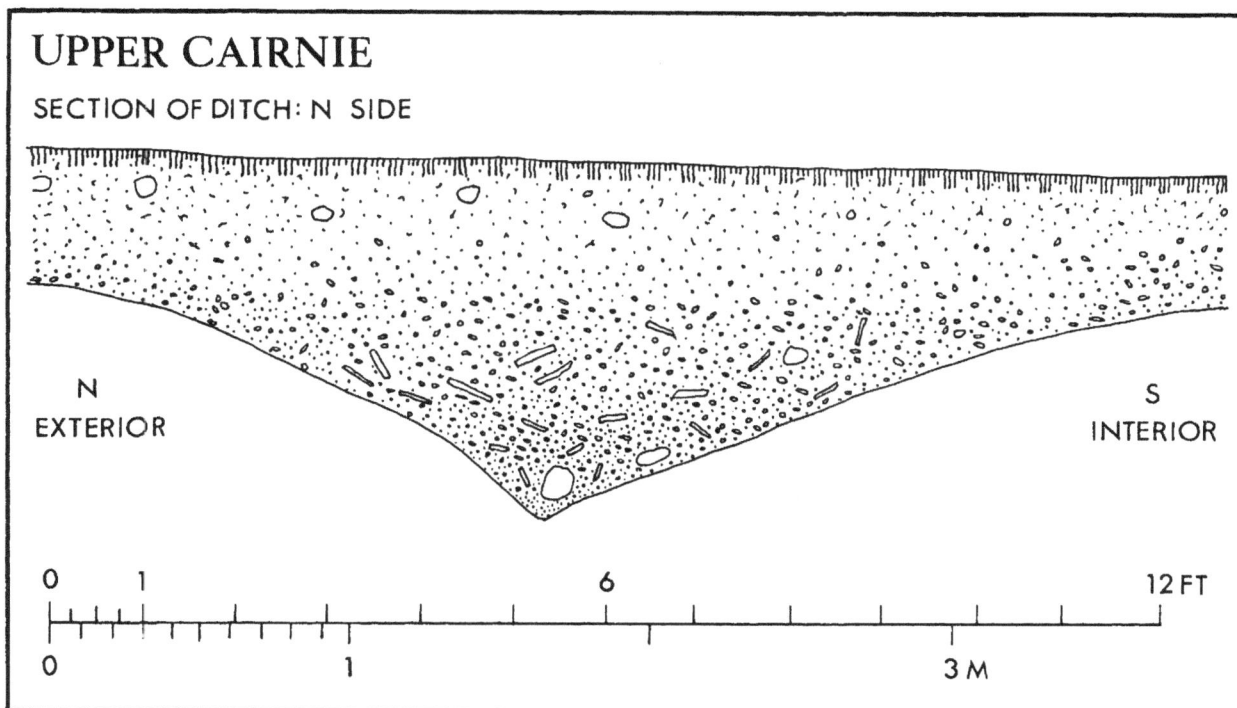

Fig 2.5. Upper Cairnie, Western Enclosure, North Ditch: St.Joseph's Section.
Crown Copyright: Royal Commission on the Ancient and Historical Monuments of Scotland (Professor St.Joseph Collection).

silt does underlie layer 4, one of the upper fill layers of the eastern ditch's secondary cut and so certainly predates the fill of this ditch, albeit not necessarily its cutting. The final cut of the western ditch was a broad (3.25m), shallow (0.2m) saucer shaped depression represented by layer 3. This cuts both upper fill layers of the eastern ditch (L's 4 and 7) and is thus the latest ditch cut on the site.

Since the excavation, a drawn section has come to light of a trench cut through the northern part of the western enclosure ditch by the late Prof J.K. St.Joseph, in September 1963 (records held by the RCAHMS). The drawing shows this part of the ditch to have a much more Roman appearance, but was never referred to at all in print by St.Joseph himself. It is thus presented here (as fig 2.5) for the first time. It shows a markedly wider profile than our own section, but of similar depth, at 3.56m wide and 0.72m deep. No layer descriptions or other field records have been found to accompany the drawing, except that the fill is said to be of "Tough clayey silt with marl fragments", but the ditch does show a clear, albeit shallow, V shaped profile and does not appear to have any evidence of re-cutting.

No datable artifacts, or charcoal flecks large enough to enable C14 dating, were recovered from these excavations and so it is currently impossible to provide absolute dates for any of the activity on the site. Layer 3 (fig 2.4b) had, however, spread some way to the east to overlie the eastern ditch, in which location it has been cut by a modern land drain slot. The drain is thus later than any of the ditch phases, which means that it is at least possible to say that the entire sequence of both ditches took place before the modern era. Nevertheless, there now seems even less reason to disagree with St.Joseph's (1965, 82) opinion that neither enclosure is likely to be Roman. The shallow ditch profiles of both enclosures are quite unlike those of normal Roman camps and, although the St.Joseph section shows the western enclosure ditch to be V shaped and slightly more substantial in the north, the absence of entrance breaks would still seem to all but rule out a Roman military origin. The features may have been agricultural in nature, but the tenuous geophysical evidence for earth banks on the interior sides of both ditches might suggest that they are actually old plantation boundaries. Similar demarcation features can still be seen around many of the older plantations in the area, with a shallow ditch backed by a low bank built from the ditch upcast and, if this interpretation is correct, it would be easy to see how small scale iron working might have been attracted to a ready source of wood and/or charcoal fuel.

35

East Mid Lamberkin.

East Mid Lamberkin (sometimes spelt Lamberkine) was discovered from the air (as a crop mark) in the 1950's by the late Prof J.K. St.Joseph (1955, 87). Nothing is visible on the surface. The site takes the form of a rectangular enclosure, 0.41 ha (1.02 acres) in area, over the ditches (fig 2.6), with sides of c. 68m (n-s) by c. 62m (e-w). The site lies at NO 074 225, c.4km west of the center of Perth and sits on the 100m contour with excellent views, especially to its north and east. When first found the enclosure had already been damaged by a modern road, the A9, which bisected its southern half, running on a heading of WSW to ENE. Since that time, however, massive additional damage has been done by the conversion of the Stirling to Perth section of this road into the A9(T), a duel carriageway, which here runs in a broad cutting which has irredeemably destroyed the entire southern part of the site, apparently without prior archaeological investigation. Fortunately, a number of superb air photographs survive in the Cambridge Air Photography collection (notably negs CKO57 and AAG40) which show the site before this mutilation took place and so it remains possible to reconstruct plans of virtually the entire ditch circuit.

The site was initially identified as a possible small Roman temporary camp (St.Joseph 1955, 87), but St.Joseph himself then appeared to become disillusioned with the feature and never mentioned it in print again. There is, however, a reference in the site's data sheet in the National Monuments Record (Scotland) to a letter from St.Joseph to the Ordnance Survey of 7th December 1976 in which he said that further work had shown that the site was not Roman. What this work actually was is not recorded, however, and the writers have been unable to trace either the letter itself or any reference to field work on the site in either St.Joseph's own surviving papers or those of the Ordnance Survey Archaeological Section (both held by the RCAHMS). This is a great pity, for any additional insight from the site's discoverer would have been valuable. Certainly the enclosure's overall morphology is perfectly compatible with a Roman military site. It has rounded corners and a general playing card shape. Three entrance breaks are visible, one each in the north, south and western ditches, and a fourth, in the eastern ditch may already have been destroyed by the A9 when the site was first seen. Moreover, although all three gates are different in design, each is of a recognizably Roman type. The west gate is a very narrow postern style gap in the ditch, whilst the south gate is a much broader gap of a type more common in temporary camps, and (although it was not strong enough to be marked on fig 2.6) one of St.Joseph's air photographs (CUCAP neg AAG40) shows what might be the faint trace of this type's usual

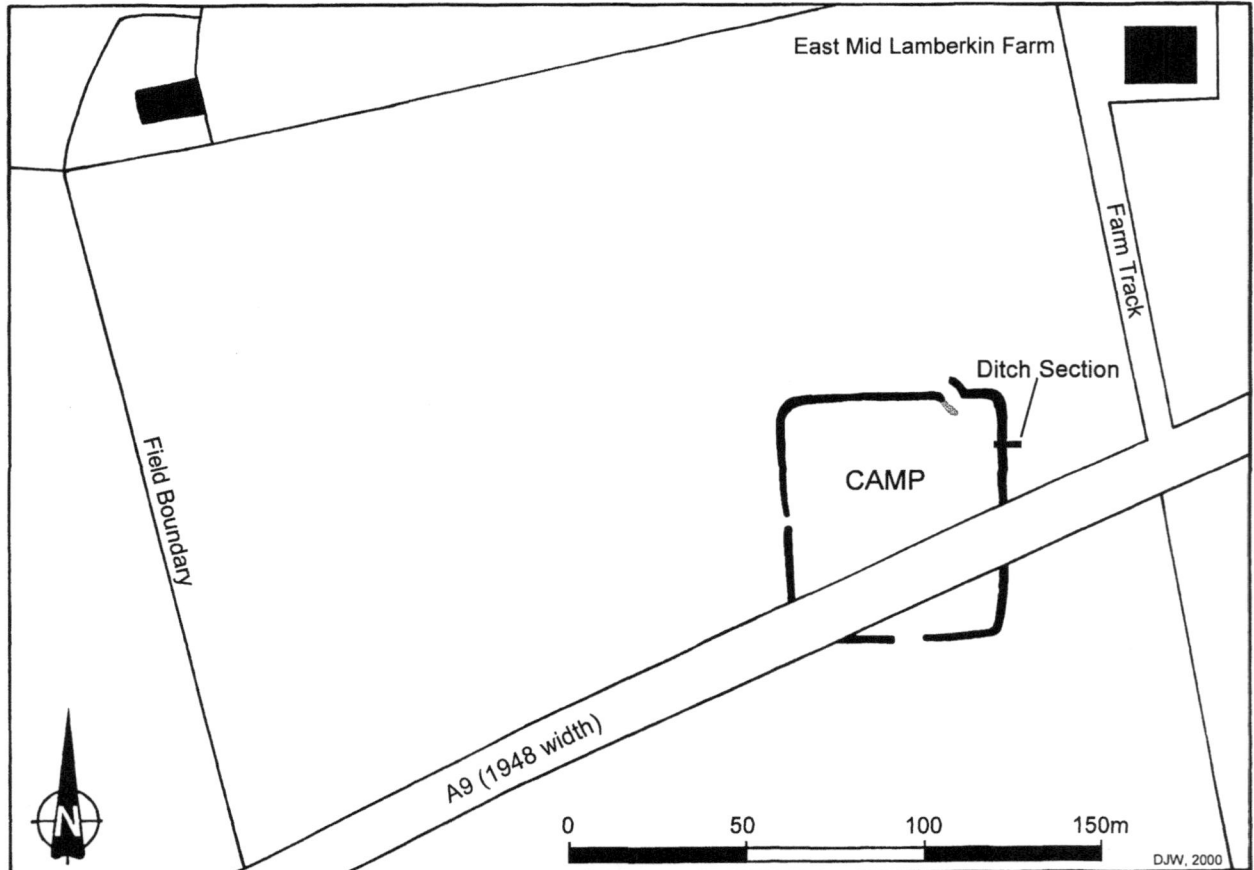

Fig 2.6. East Mid Lamberkin temporary camp.

36

covering titulum. Finally, the north gate shows an outward curving clavicula on its eastern side, of a type best known in Scotland from the famous "Stracathro" series of camps (e.g. Maxwell 1989, 50 and plate 12b). This is not itself a Stracathro style gate, however, since it lacks the usual straight out turn on its western side. Instead, a single air photograph (now in Perth Museum) taken by local flying instructor, Mr W. Fuller, shows signs of what may be an answering inward curving clavicula on the gate's western side (dotted on fig 2.6), which would produce a more symmetrical gate type previously known from sites such as Cawthorn camps B and C in Yorkshire (Welfare and Swan 1995, 12).

Given this positive morphological evidence, but remembering the doubts eventually expressed by St.Joseph, the Roman Gask Project undertook a resistivity survey and trial ditch section on the site in September 1999. The geophysical results proved to be relatively unhelpful, with the ditch showing only patchily, probably because the survey had to be undertaken after a period of heavy rain. Nevertheless, they did provide tenuous additional confirmation of the inward curving clavicula suggested by the Fuller air photograph at the north gate. The section, however, gave more clear cut results (fig 2.7). It revealed a ditch 3.64m wide and 1.12m deep, when measured from the subsoil top (1.41m deep from the modern ground surface). This proved to have a near perfect V shaped profile of standard Roman military type, despite being

cut into an extremely hard clay and rock subsoil, albeit it lacked an "ankle breaker", bottom sump.

Despite this further, and apparently persuasive morphological evidence for a Roman date, the history of this ditch still remains somewhat ambiguous. Once dug, it had silted naturally for some time, with a mixture of loamy silt washed in from the surface, and erosion products from the boulder clay, to form a layer (L'8) up to 0.38m thick. Immediately above this, was a thin layer of carbonised vegetable matter (L'10), only 56mm thick and extending only over the western half of the ditch. Two samples were taken from this deposit, one of which was sent to Dr S.Ramsay (University of Glasgow) for environmental analysis (report below), whilst the other was C14 dated and, somewhat unexpectedly, provided a two Sigma calibrated date of AD 585 to 700 (Cal BP 1365 to 1250). This would put the formation of the layer well beyond the date of any likely Roman military occupation and into the Pictish period. The remaining fill layers with the possible exception of layer 2, then seem to have entered the ditch from the interior and L's 4, 5, 6 and especially the turfy layers, 7 and 9, seem compatible with former rampart material being dumped into the ditch, either deliberately or, less probably, through plough action, although L's 7 and 9 could also represent colonization of an open ditch by plant life.

The carbon date is, however, only a terminus ante quem. The layer itself is clearly not primary, being some way

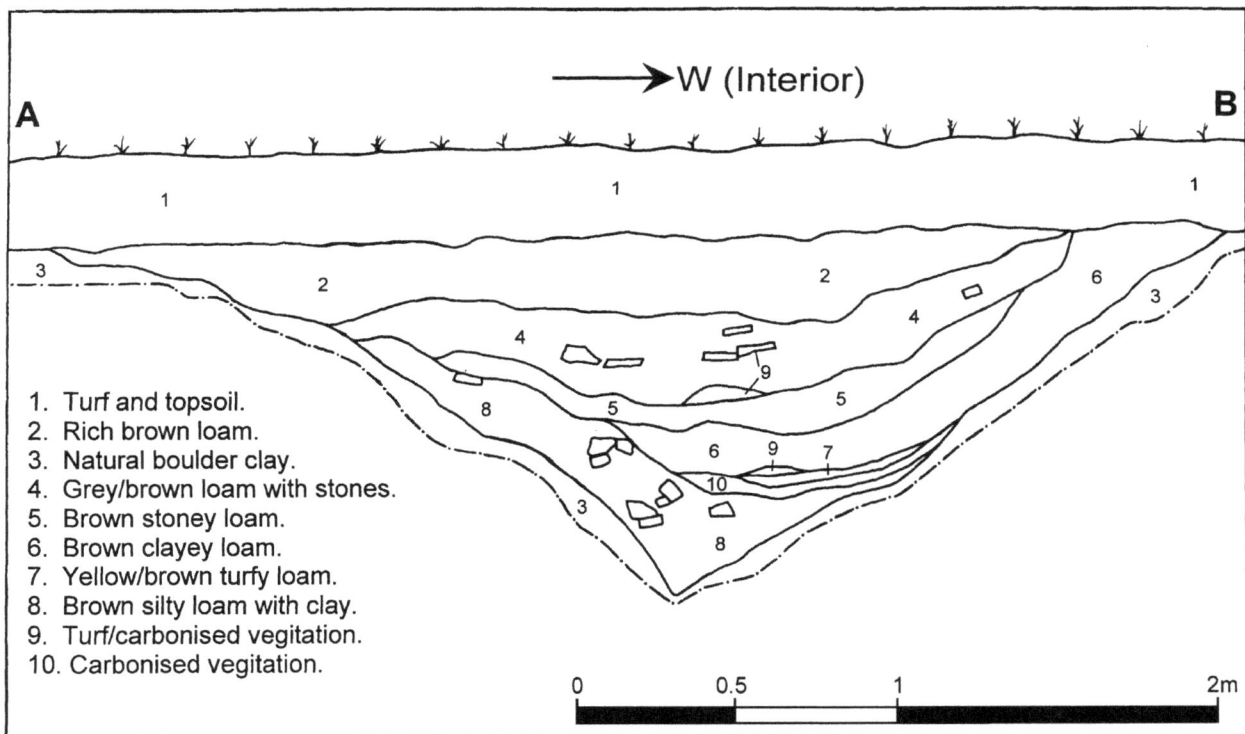

1. Turf and topsoil.
2. Rich brown loam.
3. Natural boulder clay.
4. Grey/brown loam with stones.
5. Brown stoney loam.
6. Brown clayey loam.
7. Yellow/brown turfy loam.
8. Brown silty loam with clay.
9. Turf/carbonised vegitation.
10. Carbonised vegitation.

Fig 2.7. East Mid Lamberkin: ditch section.

above the original ditch bottom, which means that the ditch as a feature must be rather older. Even so, other things being equal, such a relatively narrow band of primary silt need not have taken more than a few years to form and so the ditch construction date might still have fallen well within the C14 date error range, in which case the ditch (and thus the entire enclosure) may well be Pictish. If so, however, its morphology would be without precedent and, in fact, all things may not be equal, for there are difficulties in explaining the mechanisms by which the layers observed in the ditch section could have formed if only a single continuous process of deposition is envisaged. In particular, the primary silt layer is unusually asymmetrical. On the eastern (external) face it forms a thick layer which reaches much of the way up to the lip, but on the western (interior) side only a thin deposit was found, and even this stretches considerably less far up the ditch face. The carbonised vegetation layer (10) is then left in physical contact with the ditch side at a depth where on the opposite face it would be separated from it by 0.36m of silt. Indeed layer 10 and, above it, a thin turfy layer (L'7) appear to have formed in a somewhat suspicious looking hollow in the top of the primary silt and it seems more than likely that the entire bowl shaped cavity now filled by layers 4, 5, 6, 7, 9 and 10 is a re-cut. If so than the C14 date for layer 10 may have little if any relevance for the date of the original ditch and instead of a Pictish site resembling, or even possibly imitating a Roman military feature, we may have the perhaps more plausible scenario of pictish reuse of an existing small Roman camp. It should be stressed that this cannot yet be regarded as proven and it would certainly be useful to undertake further work here, especially around the north gate and in the interior, but for the moment the site does still appear to be best explained as, at least in origin, a Roman camp, in which case it is currently the smallest known north of the Antonine Wall. Furthermore, if this interpretation is correct, this site is also the most tempting to explain as a Roman practice camp, rather than as a work camp or as an overnight bivouac for some small detachment on the move. For the ditch seems unusually substantial for the tiny area enclosed, especially given the extremely hard nature of the subsoil. Moreover, so far as the writers have been able to ascertain, the presence here of three different gate types in one Roman camp is unique, although sites, such as Cawthorn camp A (Welfare and Swan 1995, 12, No 72) are known with two gate types, and although it cannot be proven (and may never be) it is tempting to wonder if a group of Roman recruits might have received training here in constructing a range of different gate types.

Environmental Sample from East Mid Lamberkin

Susan Ramsay

This sample (Organic sample 2) comes from the ditch fill of a Roman temporary camp at East Mid Lamberkin but derives from a layer (L'10) which lies significantly above those of Roman date. The sample itself has been radio carbon dated to Cal AD 585-700. The organic sample was sieved through a 300μm mesh and the residue left to dry before examination. The residue was sorted under low magnification (x 8 - x 40) and carbonised plant remains were removed, and identified where possible. The results are shown in the table below. Vascular plant nomenclature follows Stace (1997).

The significant quantities of carbonised c.f. heather stems along with abundant remains of what appeared to be carbonised grass or sedge rhizomes and seeds of spike rush would suggest that this area had once been heath land and was probably deliberately burned perhaps to provide agricultural land. The few carbonised cereal remains of both barley and oats may have come from grain left after stubble burning of subsequent crops which was ploughed back into the soil or trickled down through spaces in the soil. A larger sample would be required to determine any further information relating to the agricultural practices on the site.

Acknowledgments.

The work was directed by the first writer and conducted by volunteers and students of the Universities of Nottingham and Edinburgh, with the kind permission of the farmers, Mr J Christie (Easter Powside), Mr A Scougall (Ardunie), Mr W Fotheringham (Upper Cairnie) and Mr W Rob (Lamberkin). Thanks are also due to the Dupplin Estate and their factor Mr R. Smith for permission to work at Upper Cairnie and Lamberkin.

Table 1: Organic material from East Mid Lamberkin.

Taxon	Common Name	Part	Organic sample 2
Avena sp.	oats	caryopsis	1
Betula	birch	charcoal	<0.05g (2 fragments)
Calluna vugaris	heather	seed capsule	2
Eleocharis sp.	spike rush	seed	4
c.f. Calluna vulgaris	c.f. heather	stems	3.7g (abundant fragments)
Hordeum vulgare sl	barley	caryopsis	2
Persicaria lapathifolia	pale persicaria	seed	1
Poaceae / Cyperaceae	grass / sedge	rhizomes	1.5g (abundant fragments)
Bone	bone	fragment	1

3. Fieldwalking finds from the Roman forts of Bertha, Dalginross and Strageath

By D J Woolliscroft

with finds reports by
F C Wild, A T Croom, K F Hartley and A C Finnegan

Introduction

In the mid 1970's the Cumbernauld Historical Society undertook a program of field walking at four Roman forts in northern Scotland: Carpow, the two Gask series forts of Bertha and Strageath, and the glenblocker fort of Dalginross (DES 1976, 73). At the time, all four sites were poorly dated and the Society's considerable haul of surface finds, almost all of pottery, should have allowed them to make a significant contribution to our understanding of the history of Roman Scotland. Sadly, however, no funding was available at the time to support specialist analysis of the material and, although most of the corpus has been conserved in storage, the Carpow finds now appear to have vanished.

Since the 1970's large scale work at Strageath (Frere and Wilkes 1989) has largely solved that site's chronological questions, but the passage of almost thirty years has left Bertha and Dalginross almost as mysterious as ever, despite the publication of excavations from both sites (Adamson 1979, Adamson and Gallagher 1986 and Robertson 1964). The Cumbernauld Society's remaining finds were thus still potentially a very precious resource and in 1998 the Society was kind enough to lend them to the Roman Gask Project[1] for analysis, prior to donating them to Perth Museum. The pottery finds were analysed by Mrs F C Wild (Manchester), Dr A T Croom (Tyne and Wear Museums) and Dr K F Hartley, to all of whom the Gask Project is most grateful. The Bertha material also contained a number of lithic finds and these were very kindly examined by Mrs A C Finnegan.

Results

Strageath

This fort provided much the smallest corpus of finds from the Cumbernauld Society's field walking program: a total of only eight sherds, with no fine wares, were recovered. Nevertheless, the three mortarium fragments present have added some small confirmation to the picture of both Flavian and

Antonine occupation already established by the much larger finds body from the Frere and Wilkes (1989, 117-138) excavations.

Bertha

As one of the three Gask system forts, it has usually been assumed that Bertha would have followed the same sequence as its sister forts at Ardoch and Strageath, both of which show Flavian and Antonine occupation. Excavation has now confirmed Flavian activity (Adamson and Gallagher 1986), but the only evidence for later occupation has remained an inscription to Discipulinae Augusti (Keppie 1983, 402) recovered from the Tay beside the fort, a type which tends to be 2nd century or later in date and thus seemed more likely to be Antonine, or even Severan, than Flavian. Antonine occupation now seems to have been firmly substantiated by the Cumbernauld Society's finds, since all of the fine ware and mortaria fragments have been designated below as either "Antonine" or "probably Antonine". The material has thus provided welcome confirmation for an aspect of our existing model of the history of Roman Scotland. The fort also yielded five fragments of Medieval pottery, suggesting later occupation on or near the site, and a number of flints.

Dalginross

This site is a member of the line of so called "Glen blocking" forts which run along the southern highland fringe from Drumquhassle to Stracathro and which include the legionary fortress of Inchtuthil. This line has always been regarded as a purely Flavian, and probably fairly short lived system for, when excavated, its installations have rarely shown more than a single structural phase. Moreover, with the exception of a single coin of Trajan (Scots Magazine 1771, 501 and Macdonald 1918, 245) found on or close to the fort of Drumquhassle and a coin of Severus Alexander which may have been found near to (but not in) Dalginross (Macdonald 1924, 326), no finds of any other period have ever been recovered from these forts. Dalginross has long been one of the worst dated of the line but, even here, the position seemed assured for, although no finds whatever were recovered from the only excavation to have been conducted on the site (Robertson 1964, 198), two stray coin finds (Macdonald 1924,326), an aureus of Titus and an As of Domitian (dated to 86 A.D.), appeared to confirm the Flavian date. Here, however, the Cumbernauld finds are able to offer their biggest surprise and, arguably their greatest contribution to our understanding of the Roman occupations of Scotland. For the site was found to have yielded both Flavian and Antonine material. Indeed, only one of the five Samian sherds recovered can be assigned to the Flavian period (see below) and all three of the mortarium fragments appear to be Antonine.

---

[1] Our thanks to Mr J J Walker for arranging access to this material.

Fig 3.1   Dalginross fort from the air showing double enclosure, with temporary camp in foreground.

The Samian from Dalginross had not been marked with field reference numbers, and so unexpected were the Antonine identifications that on receiving the fine ware report (the first to be completed), the writer contacted the Cumbernauld Society to ask if there was any possibility that the material could have been mixed up since its discovery. The answer was that the fine ware finds had once been taken to show a school class and that although careful precautions had been taken, it was just possible that material from one fort could have been replaced in the wrong finds bags. This appeared to put some doubt on the Samian analysis, but the coarse ware fragments had been marked in the field and these were certainly all found to be in the correct bags. This means, at the very least, that the coarse ware reports can be completely relied upon and, as the material was all bagged together in one bag per fort, it might also suggest that none of the material had been mixed, which would allow us to regain rather more confidence in the Samian datings.   Whatever the case, however, the mortaria datings alone are sufficient to provide a firm indicator of Antonine occupation at the site, which means that we are forced to re-evaluate our picture of Antonine activity in northern Scotland. As has already been said, the Gask forts of Ardoch and Strageath were already known to have been reoccupied in the Antonine period, presumably as outposts to the Antonine Wall, and the Cumbernauld material has now confirmed the long held assumption that Bertha would also have fitted this pattern (the position at Doune remains unclear). It

would now seem that we must also add Dalginross to the list and this may have wider repercussions.

Firstly, with the (possible) exceptions of Inchtuthil and Fendoch, the entire glenblocking line has been almost uniformly under studied, especially by excavations using modern techniques. Indeed some sites, such as Malling, remain virtually untouched.   For many years archaeologists simply seem to have felt that the dating issues were secure and that there was, thus, little point in devoting additional effort to a series of sites which were not (Drumquhassle to some extent excepted) under threat. It would now seem that this confidence may have been misplaced,, and the possibility arises that other glenblocking forts might also have seen Antonine activity. This might appear at least somewhat unlikely, because air photographs of Dalginross have long revealed what might now be seen as an important feature which is, so far, unique on the line: two concentric fort shaped enclosures (fig 3.1).   It has usually been suggested that the inner of these represented the fort (with a small annex) and the outer, a larger annex or construction camp (e.g. Robertson 1964, 198, although c.f. St Joseph 1951, 64) but it is possible that they are simply the successive defences of the Flavian and Antonine forts (although the exact Cumbernauld find spots were not recorded, making it impossible to determine which is which). Nevertheless, Drumquhassle is also completely encircled by an, albeit less regular and much larger, enclosure, which has also been generally regarded as an annex (Maxwell 1983, 168-172 and fig 2), and it might now seem desirable to conduct further work on the glenblockers, either excavation or, at the very least, additional, more precisely controlled field walking, to gain a clearer picture of events.

Secondly, Dalginross is accompanied by a c. 22 acre (c. 9 ha) temporary camp with Stracathro type gateways (St Joseph 1951, 64). Such camps have usually been assumed to be Flavian in the past (e.g. Maxwell 1981), mainly by association with nearby sites which are themselves often assigned to the Flavian Period by less than conclusive evidence. This dating may well prove to be correct, but given the evidence from Dalginross it might be safest if we were not to take it for granted until more positive dating evidence can be obtained from the camps themselves.

Finally, the fort also yielded ten fragments of Medieval pottery suggesting later occupation on or near to the site.

The Fine Wares from Bertha and Dalginross

By F C Wild

The Samian sherds from both sites were in a poor state of preservation, but included pieces identifiable as of Central Gaulish origin. Although of Antonine date, the possibility should not be overlooked that they could be survivals into the Severan period, though this seems less likely in the case of the Hadrianic-Antonine form 18/31.

BERTHA

Six Samian sherds were present, of which two were from the same vessel. Field reference numbers were given for only three of the pieces.

1.   (X221), Form 37, Central Gaulish. Small sherd from a bowl decorated with panels with beaded borders. The panel shows a double medallion containing part of an uncertain type, just possibly a vine scroll (c.f. Rogers 1974, M14) used by Acaunissa. In the absence of an ovolo, panel junctions, or even a complete type, there is nothing that is diagnostic of a particular potter, but a date in the Antonine period seems certain.

2.   (X220). Probably form 18/31R or 31R , Central Gaulish. Antonine.

3.   (no field ref) Two joining fragments, probably of form 18/31. Central Gaulish. Hadrianic or early Antonine.

4.   (no field ref) Bowl fragment, possibly form 37. Central Gaulish, probably Antonine.

5.   (no field ref) Bowl fragment. Central Gaulish, probably Antonine.

DALGINROSS

Five Samian sherds were present, none decorated, with none obviously from the same vessel. One sherd was certainly of Flavian origin, the others are all more likely to be Antonine. No field reference numbers were given.

1.   Base fragment from form 15/17 or 18, Southern Gaulish, Flavian.

2.   Form 18 or 18/31. Probably Central Gaulish and Hadrianic or early Antonine.

3.   Bowl fragment, Central Gaulish. Presumably Antonine.

4.   Footstand scrap, Central Gaulish. Presumably Antonine.

5.   Scrap of uncertain form, Central Gaulish. Presumably Antonine.

The Coarse Wares

By A T Croom (identification of mortaria by K F Hartley)

Catalogue

The pottery was quantified by sherd count, estimated rim equivalent (ERE) and weight (kg). Individual reference numbers, where known, are given in brackets.

Pottery

STRAGEATH

	no	ERE	wt
Amphora: (P&W Class 25)			
1) bshh, 1 burnt	3		0.926
Mortarium: Colchester			
1) incomplete rim with spout, 150-200 (X213)	1		0.071
Mortarium: Mancetter-Hartshill			
1) incomplete rim, Antonine (X212)	1		0.070
Mortarium: N France			
1) Gillam (1970) type 238, 65-100 (6517)	1	7	0.050
Coarse ware			
1) bsh sandy grey fabric, cp or store jar	1		
2) base sh bowl/dish, sandy micaceous grey fabric, pale core	1		0.072

BERTHA

	no	ERE	wt
Amphora: (P&W class 25)			
1) rim	1		
2) rim, battered	1		
3) handles (7310, 7311, 7311 [sic])	3		
4) ?handle	1		
5) bshh, 3 slightly burnt (7300, 7323, 7325, 7345)	24		3.196
Amphora: Cadiz fabric			
1) b sh	1		0.038
Mortarium: Colchester			
1) complete rim, part of left facing spout, 140-170			
2) bsh and b/bsh, 2 vessels, 140-170 (7331)	2		0.180
Mortarium: ?Corbridge			
1) bsh cream fabric, 2nd century	1		0.018
Mortarium: Scotland			
1) b/bs, burnt, second century	1		0.029
Fine ware			
2) very worn bshh, most of cc lost	2		0.016
Coarse ware			
1) BB2 cp two joining rim fragments, Antonine (X222)	1	9	

	no	ERE	wt
2) bshh, battered (7322, 7324, 7334, 7344)	7		
3) rims, poor condition, possibly medieval	2		0.064

Medieval
1) bshh (1957, 3674, 4200, 7340)   5

Clay object
Worn conical object (?plumb bob), date unknown (7332)

DALGINROSS

	no	ERE	wt
Amphora: (P&W class 25)			
1) rim (6767)	1		
2) handle (6700)	1		
3) handle stub			
4) bshh (6619, 6620, 6621, 6622, 6623, 6627)	31		2.528
Mortarium: Colchester			
1) b/bs 140-170	1		0.043
Mortarium: Scotland/N. England			
1) rim, Antonine (2805), c. AD 120-160	1	8	
2) flange fragment, second century (2805)	1	13	0.127
Fine ware			
1) bsh, lost most of cc	1		0.002
Coarse ware			
1) flange from bowl	1		
2) bshh (6626, 6628)	4		0.051
Med pot			
1) bshh (1948, 3785)	10		

Tile

BERTHA

Box tile
1) corner sh
2) corner sh with knife-cut vent edge, & incised lattice keying (7388)
3) ?box tile, coarse fabric with incised right-angle keying (7329)

Bessalis or other brick
1) cream fabric with pink core

Abbreviations

b/bs	=	base/body sherd	cc	=	colour coat
bsh	=	body sherd	cp	=	cooking pot
bshh	=	body sherds			

headings
no = sherd count
ERE (%)
wt (kg)

Report.

The coarse and fine wares, mainly body sherds, are generally in a very poor condition and little can be said about them. The majority of pottery recovered from the sites are body sherds of Peacock and Williams 1991 (P&W) Class 25 amphorae, of little use for dating; the best dating evidence must thus come from the Samian (see above) and the mortaria.

Strageath

There were only eight sherds from this site, three of P&W Class 25 amphora, two reduced ware unidentified coarse wares, a rim of Gillam 1970 type 238 mortarium dated 65-100, and an incomplete Colchester mortarium rim, dated 150-200.

Bertha

There was a single sherd of Cadiz fabric amphora, used in particular for P&W Classes 17-18, dated late first to early second century. The mortaria, however, are all likely to be Antonine, including a Colchester rim dated 140-170, and there is a single BB2 rim, probably Antonine in date.

Dalginross

The pottery from this site was mainly P&W Class 25.

There was a single fine ware body sherd, in very poor condition, and a flange from a bowl in an oxidised fabric. There were two sherds from mortaria made locally in Scotland or possibly Northern England (probably both Antonine in date) and a base/body sherd of a Colchester mortarium dated 140-170.

Lithic Report

By Abigail C Finnegan

Bertha

262 - Pyramidal single platform flint core. Crushing of the base of the core suggests direct percussion by a striking hammer to detach flakes as the preferred knapping technique.

263 - Primary flint flake. Weathered. There is some evidence for retouch on the dorsal and ventral surfaces which could suggest use as a scraper.

261 - Flint platform core.

7348 - Secondary irregular flint flake. Retouched to create a scraper edge.

unnumbered - Flint chunk. No evidence for anthropogenic modification.

4 Excavations and Survey at the Ring Ditch of East Coldoch, Blairdrummond.

By D J Woolliscroft and N J Lockett

The Site

East Coldoch was discovered from the air by the RCAHMS as a ring ditch of approximately 30m in external diameter and damaged by the insertion of a modern water tank. It is located in plough land and nothing is now visible on the surface, but air photographs show a slightly ovoid form, somewhat narrower east-west than north-south and with a single entrance break oriented towards the Northeast. The site lies at NS 703986 (fig 4.1) on the summit of a low hill which, although only 41m high, offers a superb vantage point, with long range views in all directions, especially to the south, over the Forth valley and the hills beyond. Stirling Castle, for example, is in full view at a distance of 10 km to the ESE, as is Leckie Broch to the south.

The writers originally became interested in the site during a search for possible Roman watch towers south of the known Gask series, and especially between Stirling and the fort of Doune, where they might also help to trace the route of the lost Roman road through the area. The available air photographs showed the site to be sitting amongst a palimpsest of at least three separate lighter ditched structures which are usually classified as Iron Age or late Bronze Age in date. Fig 4.2 is a composite plan derived from a number of rectified air photographs and shows the current state of knowledge. There is one small ring ditch immediately to the south of the main site, which represents a probable barrow, whilst a faint, but larger diameter, ditch apparently intersecting the main site's own ditch appears to be a palisaded enclosure. A second segment of a similar light ditch intersects both this feature and the barrow ditch and may be a second palisaded enclosure.

Another large (apparently multi phased) palisaded enclosure is visible to the north of this group, on a second low mound on the opposite side of the modern road, as are a number of pits, which may be interpreted as posthole structures, and a series of small sub-rectangular enclosures which may be Iron Age fields or even square barrows. The site itself was interpreted as a ploughed out barrow or ring ditch house on the NMRS record sheet (NS79NW 34), but its ditch stood out in marked contrast with its neighbours, being markedly heavier which, coupled to its vantage point,

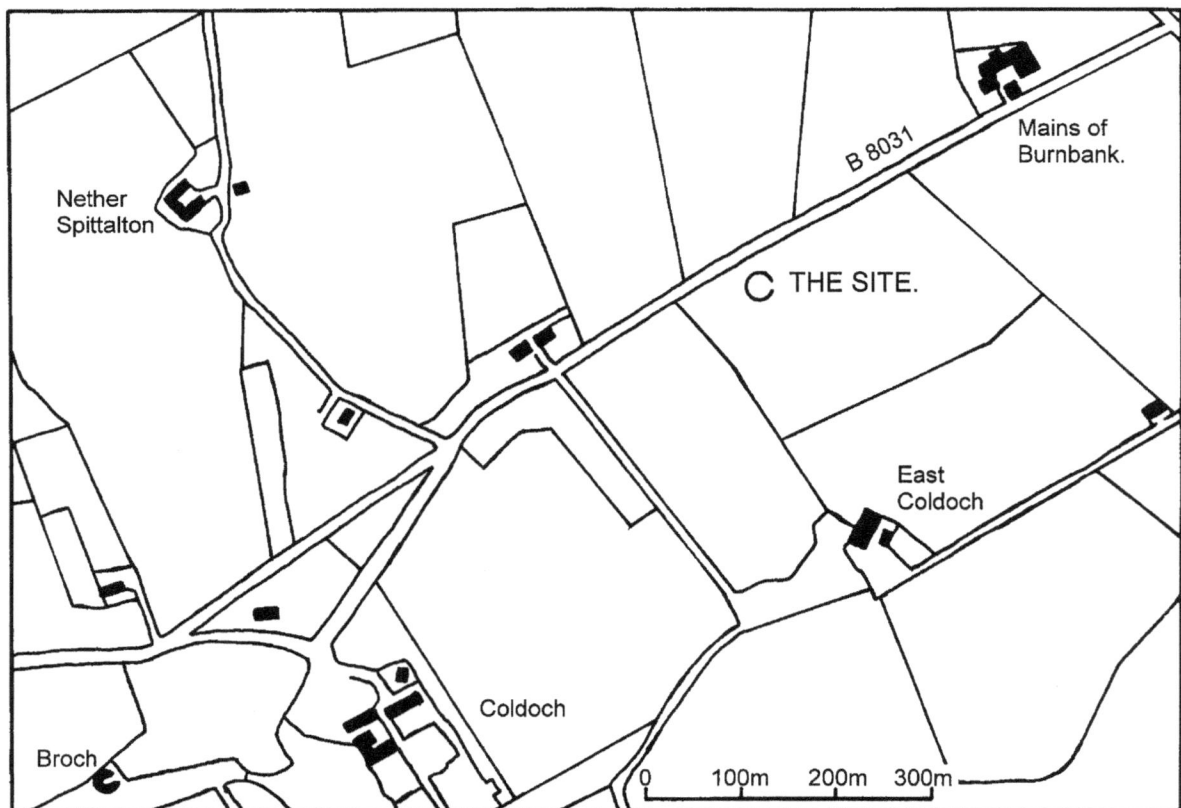

Fig 4.1. East Coldoch: location plan.

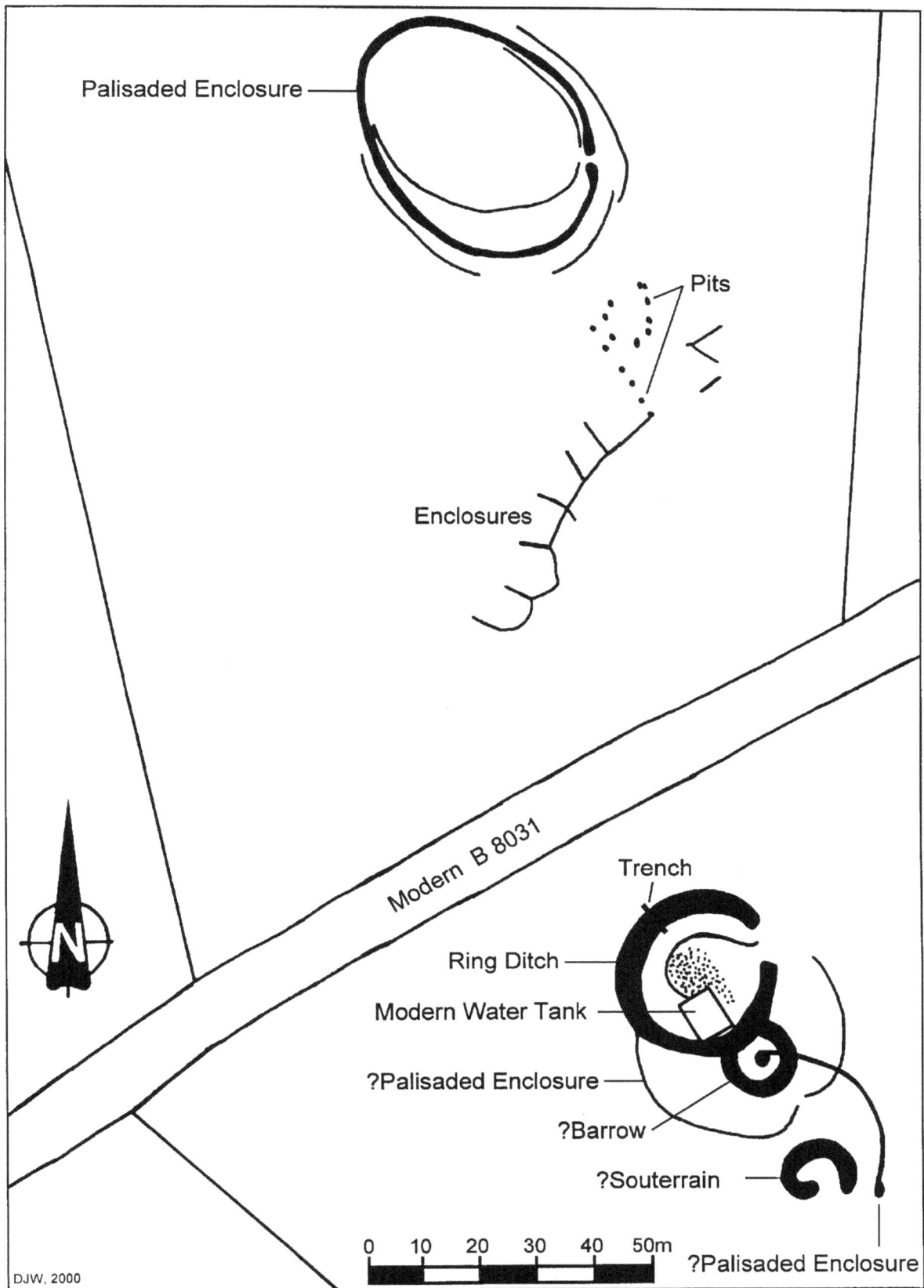

Palisaded Enclosure

Pits

Enclosures

Modern B 8031

Trench

Ring Ditch

Modern Water Tank

?Palisaded Enclosure

?Barrow

?Souterrain

0 10 20 30 40 50m

?Palisaded Enclosure

DJW, 2000

Fig 4.2. East Coldoch: air photograph rectification.

47

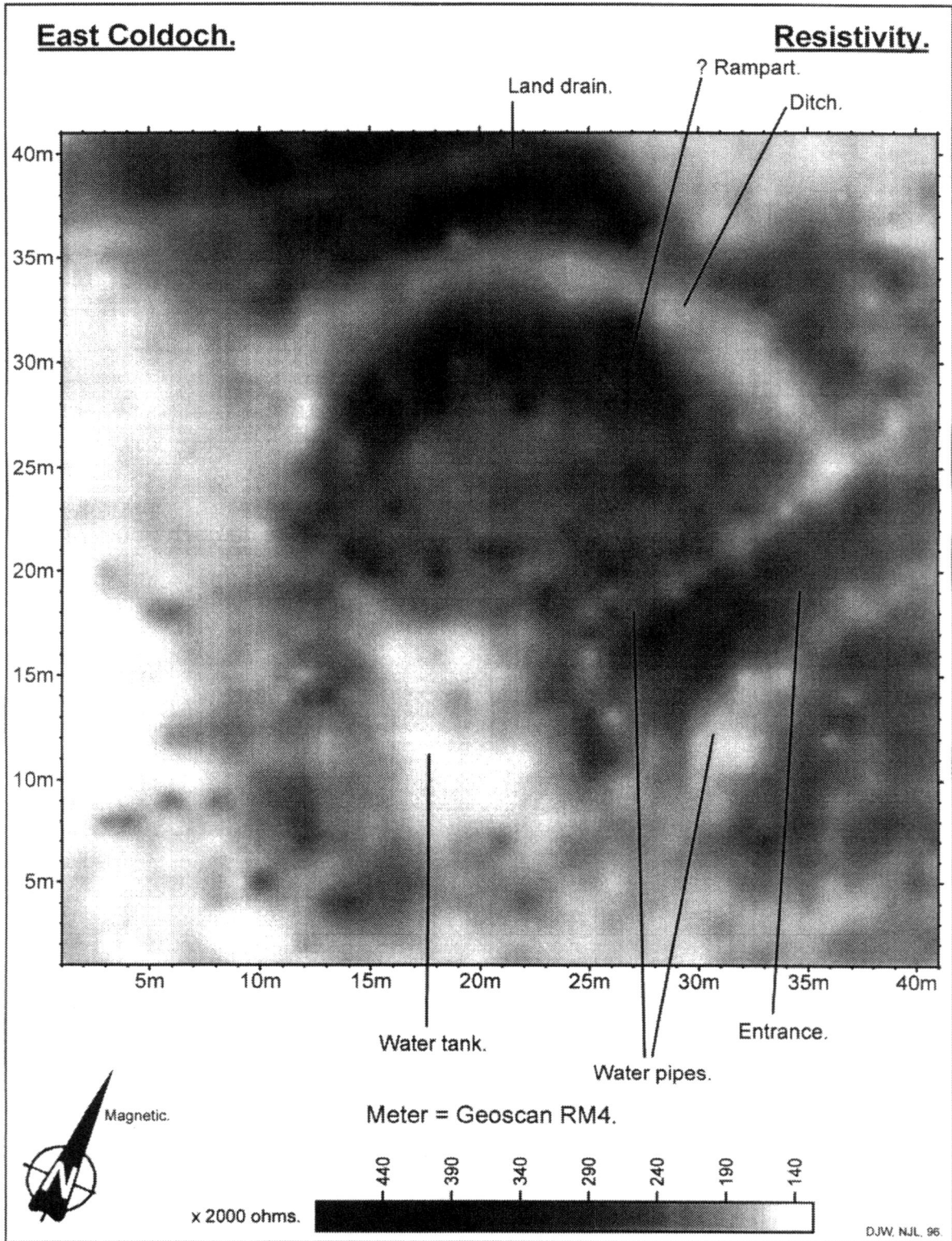

Fig 4.3. East Coldoch: ring ditch resistivity survey.

raised the possibility of a Roman military installation superimposed, like so many of the Gask area, on a group of native features.

The Geophysical Survey

With the kind permission of the farmer, Mr D Graham, a resistivity survey of the main ring ditch was conducted in 1996, which confirmed the slightly ovoid form and the estimated dimensions derived from the air photographs (fig 4.3). The site is 29m in external diameter east-west and approximately 32m north-south, although interference from the modern water tank and disturbance, which may have been caused by the still more recent burial of its concrete cap, made the results in the southernmost part of the ditch circuit less than clear. The entrance break is roughly 10m wide and shows a slightly tucked in appearance caused by the southern ditch butt end being positioned noticeably to the west of its northern counterpart. The ditch appeared to be about 4m in width, which would leave an internal area of around 21m x 24m. Air photographs had shown

a dark area in the centre of the interior, which might represent a filled in hollow of some sort, and the resistivity plot shows a corresponding area of low readings. It also, however, shows a band of readings, just inside the ditch, which are higher than the normal background for the field and which might represent the remains of an internal rampart. Finally both the survey and the air photographs show a number of modern pipes, including two running c. 5.5m apart, which cross the site on a near parallel path from the Southwest to the Northeast and which pass through the ditch entrance break. These approach the modern water tank and had been interpreted as water pipes from the air photographs, but the resistivity survey was able to trace them running straight past it, and it now seems possible that they might be field drains.

The Excavation

Once the resistivity survey had been plotted, a single test trench was excavated to section the ditch at the northernmost end of the ite (fig 4.4). This revealed a

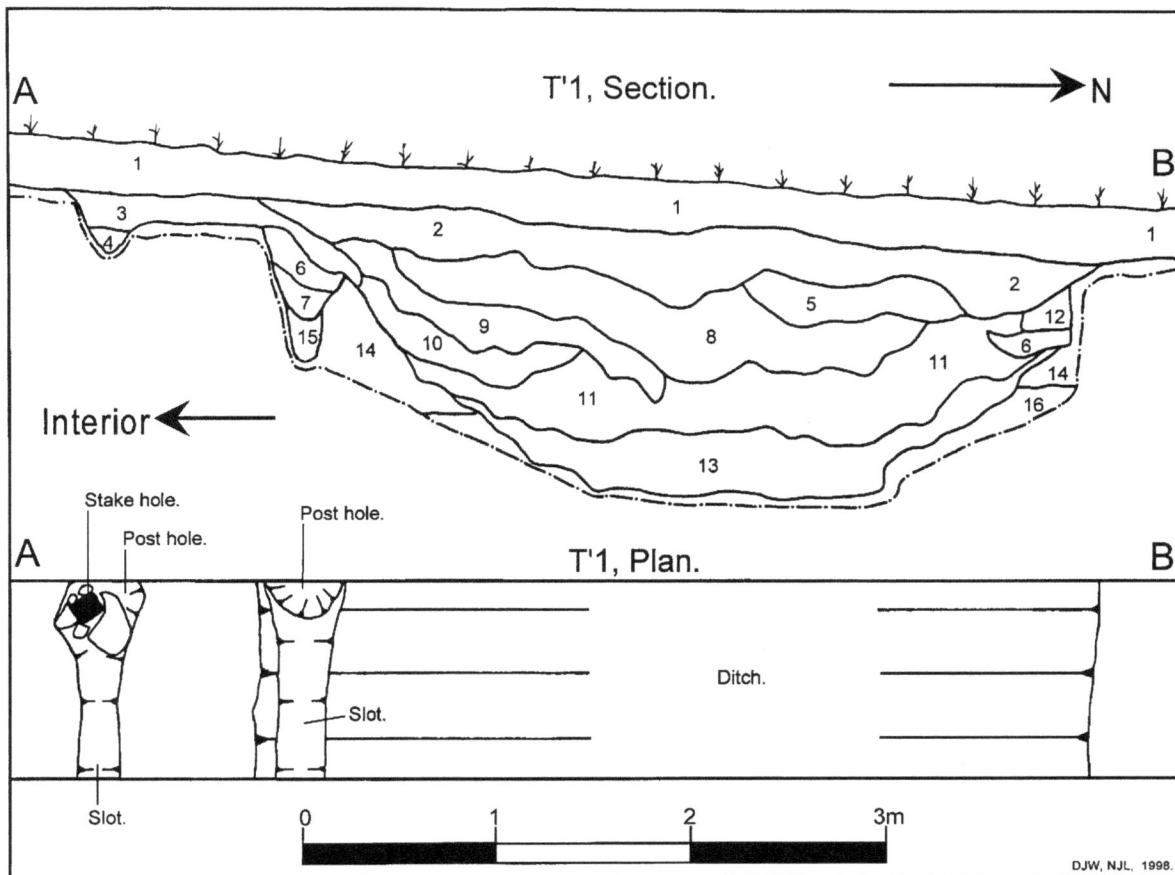

1. Turf and topsoil. 2. Brown loam. 3. Dark grey/brown loam with charcoal. 4. Brown sand. 5. Grey/brown loam. 6. Gravel. 7. Silty brown loam. 8. Grey loam. 9. Mixed turf and charcoal. 10. Brown loam with gravel. 11. Grey loam with gravel. 12. Yellow Sand with gravel. 13. Grey silt. 14. Natural sand/gravel aggregate. 15. Black loam. 16. Natural plum clay.

Fig 4.4. East Coldoch: ditch section.

substantial, flat bottomed, "U" shaped ditch, 4.3m wide and 1.6m deep. Immediately inside and parallel, to both this feature and to each other, two slots were located, each of which produced a single post hole within the 1m width of the excavation trench. The outer (northernmost) of the two was the broader by a small margin at 0.25m (as against 0.21m) and the features lay 1.04m apart at their centre lines. The two slots appeared to be broadly contemporary, both with each other and with the ditch, since both were cut into the same natural layer (fig 4.4, L 14) and both were overlain by the same loam and charcoal deposit (L'3), whilst the outer slot had been cut into the inner ditch lip, apparently when the latter was still open. If this interpretation is correct, they may represent either a double internal fence of some sort (such widely spaced uprights can hardly be called a palisade), or possibly some form of box rampart. It remained possible, however, that they were simply successive fences.

The only post hole within the slots whose original form could be ascertained was that shown in plan in the inner feature (fig. 4.4). The timber here had been stone chocked and had rotted in situ. It was rectangular in section, measuring 0.15m x 0.12m. It was sunk just 0.36m into the subsoil (it appears shallower in the drawn section which was measured against the trench side, slightly off the post pit's centre line) and set at an angle of almost 45° to the lines of both the ditch and its own slot. None of this would suggest a timber designed to support a box rampart of any weight, but then the two slots are too close together to provide for more than a fairly lightweight fill content. Even so, if we are dealing with a box rampart, its southern side, at least, must have been fairly low to have been adequately supported by such a post. On the other hand, the single post hole found in the outer slot was rather more substantial. Here the post itself was missing, so no exact dimensions can be given, but the post hole was considerably deeper, at 0.67m, and at least slightly wider at 0.16m which suggests a rather stronger arrangement which should have been able to support a greater depth of rampart.

The only real evidence for a rampart, however, apart from the resistivity data, lies within the ditch fills. The ditch had initially begun to silt naturally, probably over a considerable period, with a thick (up to 0.35m) layer of grey, waterlogged, primary silt (fig 4.4, L'13) overlain by an equally thick, fairly even, layer (L'11) of gravely grey loam. These deposits, however, had then been partly buried by two layers which had clearly slumped into the ditch from the site's interior. Layer 9 was a band of mixed turf, which still preserved a complex jumble of carbonisation lines whilst, below this, layer 10 was a loose deposit of clean brown loam which appeared to have collapsed or been dumped into the ditch in one event rather than being washed in over time. Layer 3, a plough truncated deposit of grey/brown loam with charcoal flecks, which sealed the two post

slots, might also have been turf derived and all of this would sit well with a rapid demolition or collapse event, perhaps involving a turf and earth bank or the contents of a turf filled box rampart, for which the posts might have formed a revetment. Moreover, the surviving (sloping) shape of the top of the outer slot's post hole might suggest that the post had eventually snapped off at, or just below, ground level and then fallen, or been pushed out into the ditch, whilst the relatively small volume of material involved in these layers would again suggest that only a relatively slight rampart was involved. It seems possible, therefore, that we might be dealing with the remains of a turf bank of some sort, which may have sloped down from the ditch face into the interior, hence the lighter timber revetment at its lower inner face. It might be equally likely, however, that the heavier posts on the outer face were provided simply because the rampart approached so close to the ditch lip and thus required greater stabilisation here to prevent its being undermined, rather than because the physical weight of material was greater. Whatever the case, it is not hard to see why the site's builders should have wanted to both constrain the width of their rampart and to place it so close to the ditch. For, even as things are, the feature would have reduced the size of the internal area to around 19m x 22m and a more conventional self supporting turf rampart would have reduced it still further.

Finally, there was no obvious sign of a buried topsoil, vegetation layer or similar deposit at any point to suggest that the ditch had stood open for any significant period after the rampart collapsed. Layers 6 and 12 against the outer face of the ditch were small lenses of gravely material which appeared to have been dumped, but the rest of the ditch fill, (L's 2, 5 and 8) is made up of loam deposits which may have entered the ditch through plough action It is possible that material may have been dumped into any surviving hollow when the water tank was cut into the site, but the present farmer has only been on the land for a few years, which means that there is no family tradition to record what the site might have looked like before the tank was installed. The writers have, however, been unable to find any reference to the ditch being visible at the surface within near modern times, let alone within living memory and the ditch may well have been obliterated relatively soon after the putative rampart collapsed.

Interpretation

No datable material was found during the excavation and although small flecks of charcoal were recovered from layer 3, there was no material suitable for carbon dating within any context that could be confidently regarded as primary. It is, thus impossible to make more than an intelligent guess at the site's date and identity. Certainly, the ditch diameter is somewhat large for a Roman tower, but it is not abnormally so, for the tower of Garnhall on the Antonine Wall has a not dissimilar external diameter at 28.97m (Woolliscroft in Keppie 1996, 400f and Woolliscroft & Hoffmann forthcoming). The ovoid shape is also not unprecedented for a Roman site in this area since the Gask tower of Midgate (Christison 1901, 34f and Woolliscroft 1993, 302ff) has a similar form, albeit the identity of this site has been challenged in recent years (Hanson and Friell 1995, 514). The size and form of the entrance break would, however, be highly unusual for a Roman tower, where symmetry and an entrance width of only 2-4m is the norm and the ditch would appear to be both too substantial and of completely the wrong shape to represent a Roman military site. If anything it resembles a ditch found some years ago c.20 miles to the northwest, at North Mains of Strathearn henge, in Perthshire (Barclay 1983, 134, fig 10, section E-F).

The site does, however, sit amongst a group of features which appear to be Iron Age/late Bronze Age in date and Coldoch Broch lies only c.850m to the Southwest, all of which means that a site of the traditionally envisaged Iron Age date would still seem likely to be the best interpretation. That said, the ditch does appear unusually heavy for a homestead site and especially for one with such a small internal diameter and so the possibility of a small Medieval defensive site, such as a motte, might also be worth considering. The Gask Project is currently engaged in a much larger scale excavation on the site to study the interior, which although damaged by the water tank still appears to be substantially intact, and it would seem prudent to leave any further interpretation until this work is complete. It is worth mentioning, however, that the possible cropmark indications of a souterrain on the site, marked in fig 4.2, have now been proven to be illusory.

5. Parkneuk Wood Roman Road, Perthshire
Excavations in 1967 and 1997

D J Woolliscroft and M H Davies with contribution by S Ramsay

The Site

Parkneuk Wood stands on the western shoulder of the Gask Ridge, c. 25m above and 1500m to the east of the Roman crossing of the River Earn at Strageath. The wood contains a number of Roman antiquities (fig 5.1), notably the Gask series tower of Parkneuk (the westernmost on the Ridge itself), part of the north rampart and ditch of the 130 acre (52.6ha) temporary camp of Innerpeffray East and, immediately to the north of these two, and the subject of this report, one of the best preserved sections of the Roman Gask road anywhere on the system.

Background

In 1967 the Perthshire Society of Natural Science under Mr J.K. Thomson and the late Mrs D.M. Lye sectioned the Roman road at NN 915185, c. 140m to the west of Parkneuk tower, and followed this in 1969 with a watching brief during the construction of a forestry track through the road, c. 112m (367') further to the east. Sadly, although brief notes did appear in print (DES 1967, 28f and DES 1969, 38, 25f), Mrs Lye, who held the field records, died before a full report could be produced. As part of the Roman Gask Project's program of disseminating previous research on the system, the first writer therefore obtained Mr Thomson's permission to publish this work and was fortunately able to almost totally reconstruct the original records from material held in the possession of Mr Thomson himself, Perth Museum and the RCAHMS.

The results were largely straightforward (fig. 5.2). The road was c.19' (5.79m) wide and consisted of a 6" - 9" (152 - 228mm) cambered layer of gravel metalling (L'2), overlying what was described as an 18' (5.48m) wide and 6" - 8" (152 - 203mm) thick layer of, again cambered, compacted red/brown clayey loam (L'3). In its central 12' (3.66m), a central spine had been formed by embedding fairly closely packed rubble into this layer, which acted both as a foundation and to further build up the camber. There were no stone kerbs and, although the trench was later extended up to 23' 11" (7.29m) to the north of the road edge, to give a total trench length of 47'

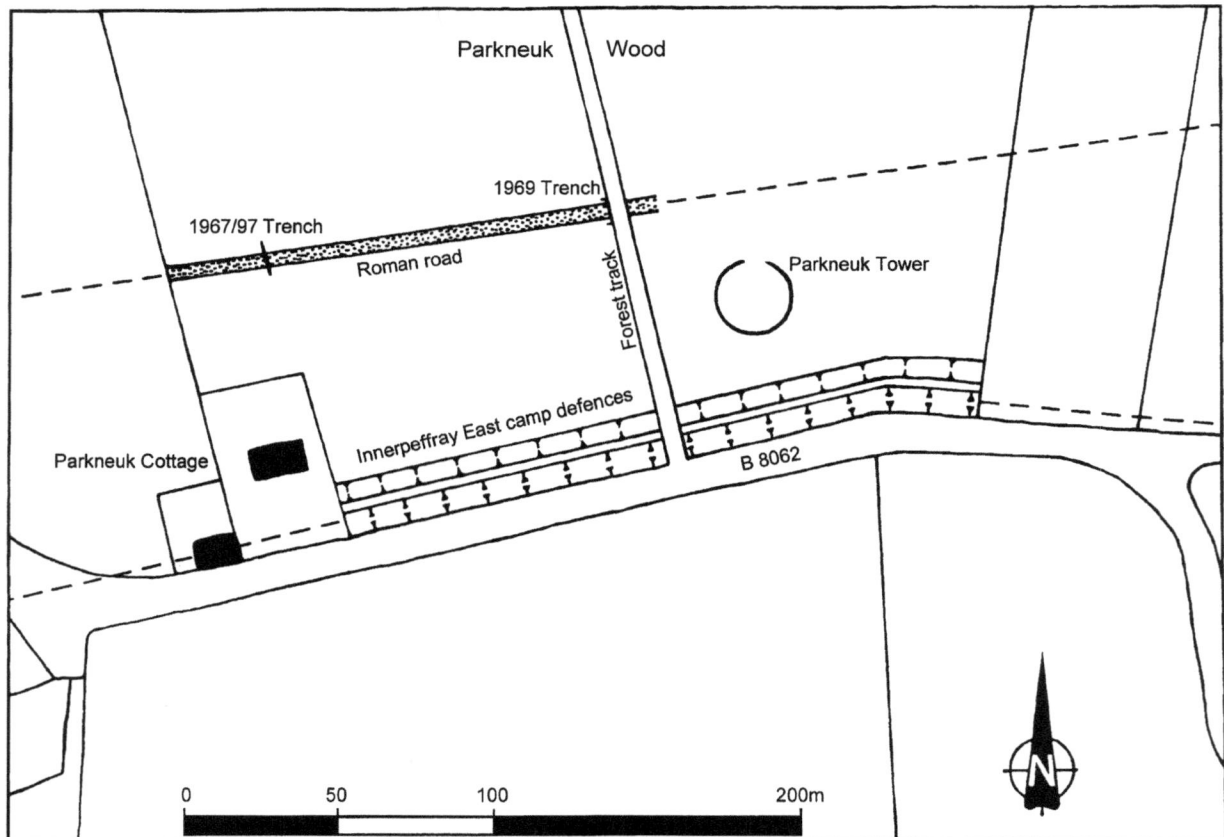

Fig. 5.1. Parkneuk Wood: location plan.

52

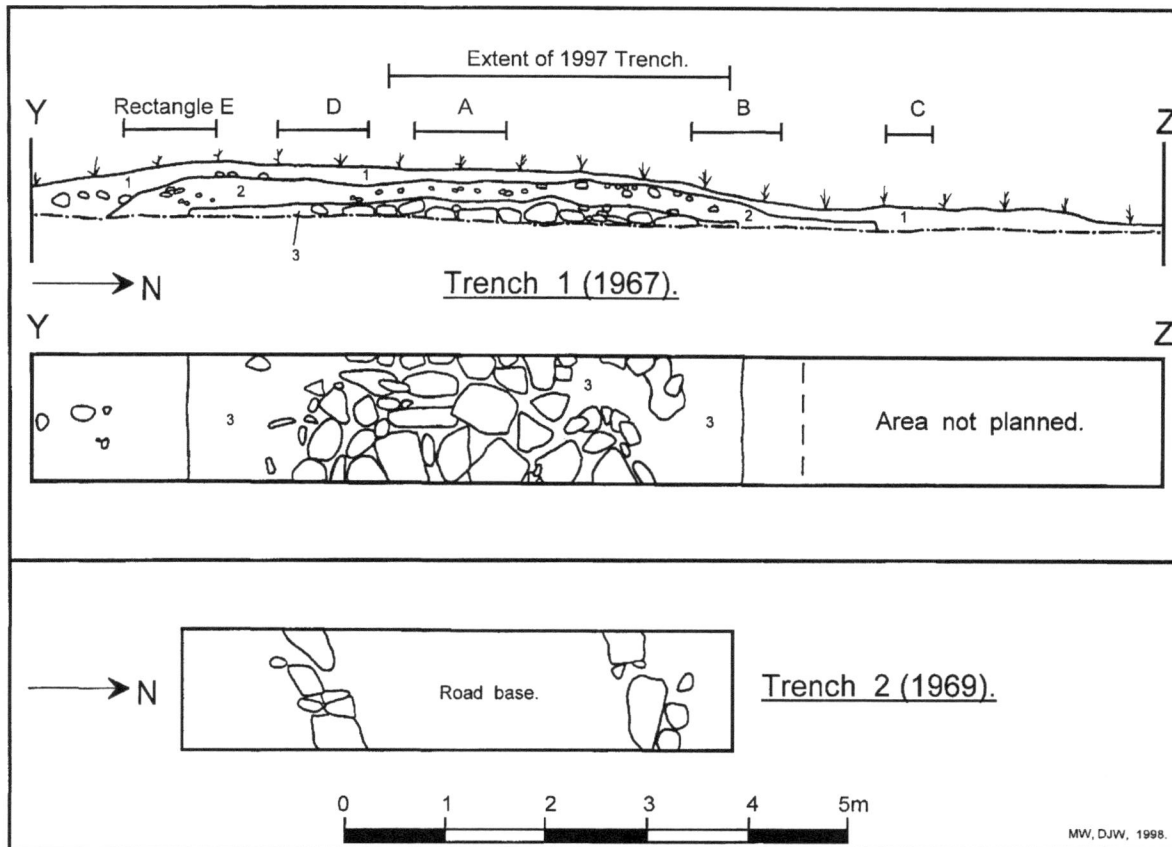

1. Turf & topsoil.   2. Rammed gravel.   3. Rubble in compacted pink clay.

Fig 5.2. Parkneuk Wood: the 1967/69 excavations.

(11.27m), no sign of a side ditch was encountered, despite the fact that the gleyed sub soil uncovered beneath the road provides evidence for prolonged water logging of the site. The results from the 1969 section further to the east were broadly similar, except that here L'3 was missing. No drawn section has survived from this latter work, but a rough plan is provided in Fig 5.2.

Perhaps the most interesting aspect of the road, however, was its substructure for, although this was only studied closely in the 1967 trench, there were signs here that, although much of the road had been built directly onto the original ground surface, the central area had been further built up on a low platform of laid turf, perhaps to improve its camber and/or drainage. Two small areas of the original trench, designated Rectangles "A" and "B", were reopened some months after the main excavation specifically to allow Mr B.M. Shipley of the Macauley Institute for Soil Research, Aberdeen, to study these layers. His opinion was that two rows of laid turves were present (in addition to the natural surface turf), with the lower layer deposited grass side down and the upper layer grass side up. This had produced two black carbonisation streaks through the deposit: a thicker lower stripe, which also extended over the original ground surface further out, and a thinner upper

streak which directly underlay the road foundation. There was, though, speculation that this latter layer may have been discontinuous and may only have represented attempts to fill in hollows so as to produce an even building surface. Samples of this turf were later subjected to a pollen analysis by Dr S.E. Durno.

The 1997 Excavations

Once the 1967 records had been assembled, a number of problems became apparent which made it difficult to produce a thorough and confident report:

1.   The pollen samples taken in 1967 were potentially very important, since they derived from the contemporary ground surface sealed by the Roman road and were thus both reasonably firmly datable (although see the doubts expressed over the date of the Gask road in chapter 7) and representative of the local environment immediately prior to the road's construction. Unfortunately, although a copy of Dr Durno's raw pollen data had survived, his interpretation had not and the data sheets were thus sent to Dr S. Ramsay (University of Glasgow) for re-examination. Her analysis of the species represented suggests that the site

53

lay in reasonably open country, but she also suggested that the original samples may only have been fairly hurriedly examined so that only pollen from a few of the most common species present had been detected, whereas one would also have expected to see many more "trace species" which would have enabled a more detailed evaluation. Dr Durno can hardly be blamed for this situation, since he seems to have made his analysis unpaid as a personal favour, but as the original samples appear to have vanished and so could not be re-examined, it seemed desirable to try to obtain new ones.

2. Although the 1967 plan and section drawings had survived, these did not include the turf substructure layers and Mrs Lye's correspondence makes it clear that they were not drawn. They also appear not to have been photographed. A rough sketch by Mr Shipley has been found, but neither this nor the interpretation he based upon it appear wholly consistent with the excavators' written descriptions of these layers. For example, the carbonisation streaks were drawn as two neat, flat and parallel lines, whilst a letter from Mrs Lye to Mr Thomson describes them as irregular. This is hardly surprising since Shipley drew his sketch to explain his ideas and it was thus presumably meant as a schematic rather than an archaeologically true representation. But, more seriously, the surviving written descriptions also make the entire turf deposit sound rather too thin to fit Shipley's hypothesis (even allowing for almost two thousand years of settlement and the compression caused by traffic that has continued to use the road long after the Roman occupation), for the entire central, three turf layer, sequence is said to have been only half an inch (13mm) thick. Once again, therefore, it seemed desirable that these layers should be re-examined.

3. Aspects of the 1967 plan and section did not appear to match either each other or the excavation photographs, although the latter were generally taken at rather oblique angles and with the sections somewhat under exposed so that they were difficult to evaluate fully.

In an attempt to clarify these difficulties, part of the trench was reopened in September 1997 under the direction of the second writer. Little trace of the 1967 work was visible at the surface, but the trench was relocated without difficulty from the original survey data, which was thus proven accurate. As the original work was conducted in imperial measurements and Scheduled Monuments Consent had been granted on condition that the minimum of further disturbance took place, the re-excavation was obliged to follow suit.

The 1997 trench (fig 5.3) was designed to include the 1967 areas: Rectangle "A" and "B", in which the turf substructure had been most fully examined. It was thus 4' (1.22m) wide (e-w) x 11' 2" (3.4m) long (n-s) and located so that its northern end lay 13' (3.96m) south of

the 1967 base line, and 23' (7m) south of the northern end of the original trench. The backfill was removed and the plan and section redrawn and photographed. The limits of the 1967 excavation, including Rectangles "A" and "B", were clearly evident and, on the whole, the 1997 results matched those of the earlier work. It was, however, discovered that Rectangle "A" had extended 1' (0.3m) to the west of the main 1967 trench and so a 1' (e-w) x 3' (0.914m) (n-s) wing was added (fig 5.3, C-D) 1' from the southern end of the 1997 trench to relocate the original section.

As expected, the modern topsoil (L'1) overlay an 80-200mm thick (slightly shallower than recorded in 1967) layer of gravel metalling, set in an orange/brown loamy matrix (L'2). There were no visible signs of repair or resurfacing, but considerable disturbance by root action may have destroyed the evidence, especially given such a small trench. This layer overlay the road foundation stones which, as expected, ended c.0.6m from the northern edge of the trench. These were set in a compacted pink clay/loam (L'3), as stated in 1967, to form a layer up to 0.24m thick (somewhat deeper than described in 1967).

Only Rectangle "A" was excavated to natural in 1967 and the 1997 dig followed suit. Here at least, however, a complex stratigraphic pattern was uncovered beneath the principle road materials. The natural subsoil (L'10) is a grey, water logged, clayey loam identified by B.M. Shipley as a surface-water gley soil, probably originating as a red boulder clay with loam. The water logged environment had produced reducing conditions so that "The bright coloured ferric iron compounds present are reduced to dull and greyish coloured ferrous iron compounds hence the predominantly grey colour". As expected, a number of turf layers were encountered between this deposit and the road foundations, and these do conform better to Mrs Lye's written description as "irregular" than to the neat layering of Shipley's 1967 sketch, although neither is wholly accurate.

For the most part, two carbonisation layers (L's 5 &, 8) were present, but these were neither flat nor parallel and nor was the lower of the two uniformly thicker than the upper, being thinner than it towards the centre of Rectangle A. The actual sequence seems to be as follows: the subsoil (L'10) is overlain by a turf layer (L'9). This is essentially homogenous, and appears to represent the original turf and topsoil, but it was interrupted by a narrow (c.80mm) slanting gap filled with material identical to L'10. The latter resembles a tool cut, but might be an animal burrow or the result of a small sapling being extracted when the site was cleared. These layers were completely covered by the lower of the two black lines of carbonised grass (L'8), which continues right across the gap in L'9 just mentioned, although it becomes noticeably thinner at this point. As this gap does seem to represent a genuine breach in the

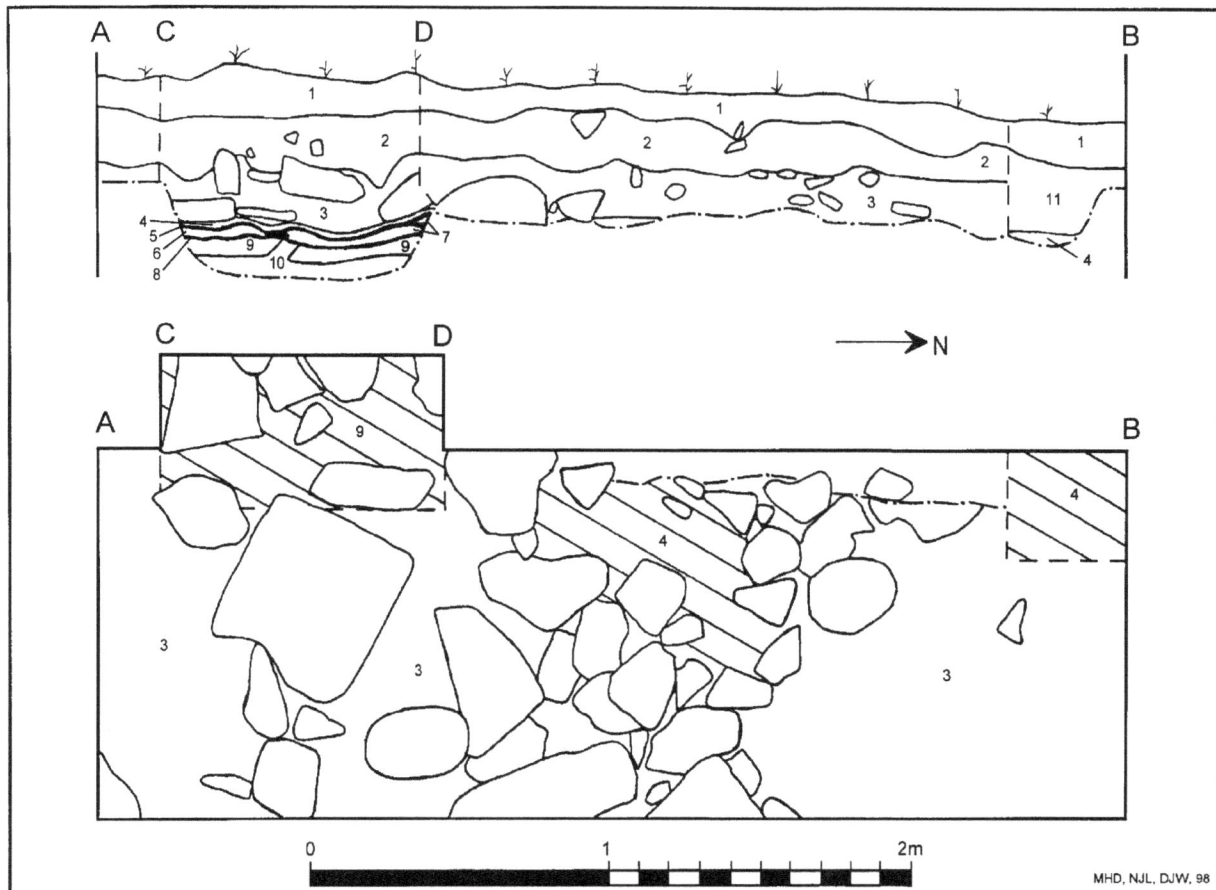

1. Turf and Topsoil. 2. Gravel in Orange/brown loam. 3. Rubble in compacted pink clay. 4. Grey turf. 5. Black organic stripe. 6. Grey turf with yellow patches. 7. Grey clayey turf. 8. Black organic stripe. 9. Pale grey turf. 10. Pale grey gleyed loam. 11. 1967 backfill.

Fig 5.3. Parkneuk Wood Roman road: the 1997 plan and section.

top soil (and thus also its grass layer) present at the time the road was built, this narrowing would appear to support Shipley's theory that the lower line was a double feature made up of both the original surface grass and that from a layer of turves laid grass side down upon it, and this has been confirmed by a thin section examination by Mr J.C.C. Romans (pers com). Above L'8 are two more turfy deposits: L'6 in the southern half of Rectangle "A" and L'7 in the north, separated by a brief, c. 0.18m, area where the upper carbonisation line (L'5) becomes so thick and smudged that the two black streaks become merged. L's 6 and 7 are almost identical, both to each other and to L'9, except that L'6 contained a number of small yellow patches in its upper half which Shipley's interpretation would suggest represent areas where air had penetrated the gleyed soil and allowed localised re-oxidation to take place. The fact that these patches only occur in the upper half of L'6 might support the 1967 conclusion that the overall layer made up by L's 6 and 7 is made up of two layers of laid turves, with the upper layer set grass side up and the lower grass side down.

Contrary to its description in 1967, the upper of the black carbonisation lines (L'5) did not directly underlie the clay/rubble road foundation. Instead a further thin layer of turfy material (L'4) lay between the two, which appeared identical to L's 6, 7 and 9. This might be interpreted as a layer of trample formed over the laid turf platform during the construction of the road itself, but the layer was so clean that it seems more likely to represent a fourth layer of turf, laid grass side down. Certainly, this layer is approximately half as thick as the supposedly two turf thick L's 6 and 7 and there is further corroboration in the fact that at one point, close to the northern end of Rectangle A, L'5 splits in two, briefly dividing L'7 into two roughly equal halves. This might suggest that one turf from the upper half of L'7 was accidentally laid the wrong way up (grass down) and if so, the fact that L'5 splits, rather than simply dipping, would imply that a second grass layer was available, which can only have been provided by L'4. Again contrary to the 1967 description, the total thickness of the turf layers is c. 0.1m when measured from the original pre-road ground surface and c. 0.29m to the subsoil (making the road's total thickness, on average, c.

55

0.7m). This is considerably greater than the half an inch (13mm) quoted in Mrs Lye's correspondence and seems far more compatible with the idea of a low, settled, turf stack, although it remains unknown how consistent this turf deposit might be elsewhere along even this stretch of the road. Samples were taken from all of the archaeological strata and subjected to pollen analysis by Dr S. Ramsay (see below)

Finally, Mr J.C.C. Romans, also formerly of the Macauley Institute for Soil Research, has kindly made available the results of a "Bright ring" and soil thin section analysis conducted on the 1967 turf samples collected by Mr Shipley. In conjunction with samples taken from the 1969 Forestry Commission section these reveal a similar, although much smaller scale, infield/outfield pattern to that discovered by Mr Romans at Strageath fort (Romans Pers Com and Romans and Robertson 1983, 139) using the same technique. Here the 1967 section fell in the outfield area whilst the 1969 section was in the infield, where the presence of some scattered soil pores with oriented clay suggested shallow, possibly hoe, cultivation in the more distant pre-Roman period. This agricultural pattern may have been in force on the site 800 years or more before the construction of the Roman road. The presence of unbroken bright rings in the original surface material, however, and a thin undamaged layer of wind blown diatoms at the original surface, suggested that the site had come to be used for grazing rather than cultivation for quite some time, perhaps 200 years $\pm$ 100, before the road was built, which matches well with the results of Dr Ramsay's pollen analysis (see below).

No datable material was recovered in either the 1967 or 1997 excavations, or during the 1969 watching brief.

Parallels

The width of the road, at 19' (5.79m) is slightly small by the standards of the Gask line as a whole, although not dramatically so. Young (PSAN 1898, 99) reported it as 20' (6.09m) wide a little to the east in 1897, as does the New Statistical Account (p282) for the Parish of Gask. A section excavated by St.Joseph (Glendinning & Dunwell 2000, 262ff) at Blackhill Wood, just to the north of Ardoch (in 1974), found it to be around 24' (7.4m) wide, as did Pennant (reported in Christison 1898, 429) who measured the road as a surface feature at the eastern end of the Gask Ridge, near Dupplin. A 1971 watching brief of a section cut for drainage purposes at Kirkhill, near the centre of the Gask Ridge (DES 1971, 57), found it to be 25' (7.61m) wide and Christison (1898, 432) reported it as 26' (7.92m) wide as it passed Ardoch.

As regards the road's construction, a similar turf substructure may also have been present, in the 1969

Forestry Commission section 367' (112m) to the east of the 1967/97 trench, although this is less than certain as the road foundation is simply said to have been "laid on turf" (DES 1969, 38). But nothing of the kind was reported at any of the other three sections through the Gask road for which information has survived: Blackhill Wood, Kirkhill and a series of rather poorly located sections dug by Young between Raith and Gask House in 1897 (PSAN 1898, 99). A single carbonisation line was, though, found beneath the road at Kirkhill which presumably represented the original ground surface. The turf work may thus have been a purely localised response to waterlogged ground in the immediate vicinity, by lifting the road foundation slightly above its surroundings, and does not appear to have formed a classic Roman road agger. Similar turf work may have existed occasionally beneath Roman roads in analogous conditions elsewhere in Britain, notably on the road between Drumburgh and Kirkbride in Cumbria, which is built up on a low mound of peat sods, where it crosses moss country (Bellhouse 1952, 41ff and pers com), and possibly also on parts of Dere Street in Northumberland, although here absolute proof is lacking (Snape and Speak 1995, 26ff).

The absence of side ditches is far from unusual on the Gask. On the many occasions the road has appeared on air photographs it is usually flanked by roughly parallel lines of quarry pits, but only occasionally by ditches (although see fig 7.1). St.Joseph's section at Blackhill Wood found none, despite extending more than the road's own width to the south, and nor did the 1969 Forestry Commission section in Parkneuk Wood. Indeed, the only excavations so far to have produced ditches are Young's 1897 section at Gask House (PSAN 1898, 206), which found them to be 36' (10.97m) apart, and the watching brief at Kirkhill, where they are reported as being "V" shaped in section and 2' (0.61m) deep. But as both these observations come from the Gask Ridge itself, where much of the road has remained in use to the present day, there is no guarantee that these are original features. As already stated, however, the fact that in Parkneuk Wood the road may have been passing through damp ground might have been expected to have encouraged the provision of drainage and, for exactly this reason, the modern forestry road whose construction produced the 1969 section is flanked by significant ditches. It is possible that the 1967 trench simply wasn't long enough to intercept a ditch running some way from the road, but this does seem unlikely. For the trench extended 23' 11" (7.29m) from the road whereas Young's 1897 ditches ran only 8' (2.44m) from the kerbs, whilst the Kirkhill ditches are simply said to have been "close to the road". One possibility is that the turf stripped areas which must have resulted from the central turf platform might have functioned as a shallow ditch as well, perhaps, as a marking out line for the construction of the road itself. The laying of three courses of turf on the original ground surface would obviously have necessitated the stripping of an area three times the size of that covered, in other words, an area 3 x c.12' = c.36' (c.11m) wide, or a band c.5.5m wide on either side of the road. Such an operation would obviously have only produced a hollow a few centimetres deep, but this may have had some drainage effect and may not have been detected by the 1967 dig. It should be noted, however, that the pollen analysis (below) contains suggestions that the turf used may have come from more than one source and so it is possible that the material may not all have come from the site.

As to the structure of the road proper, a cambered surface of rammed gravel laid on a foundation bed of larger stones is hardly unusual for a Roman road and, although the site's own clay subsoil is remarkably stone free, there was a plentiful supply of both available close by in the bed of the River Earn. Indeed almost all of the stones used in the road's construction appear water worn. Details in construction vary considerably along the line of the Gask, however. For example, the red clay into which the 1967 foundation stones were set, was already absent in the 1969 section only 112m to the east and has not been reported in any other known section. But the stone bottoming itself is a normal feature, although St.Joseph at Blackhill Wood, reports that the road there had "no special bottoming layer" (field notes held by RCAHMS) but consisted entirely of compacted gravel with a few larger cobbles. Elsewhere, however, it is the gravel layer that is missing. The New Statistical Account for Gask parish has the road consist simply of "rough stones, closely laid together". Walker and Maxwell report its absence at Kirkhill, and Young is uncertain, saying: "large stones were found all over the road but I do not think the centre had ever been paved but had been of gravel". This might suggest that in any given spot the Romans simply used whatever materials came to hand, rather than following any set design, but again these reports come from areas where the road has remained in use into modern times and it is perfectly possible that the original Roman surfacing may simply have been worn away. Certainly Christison (1898, 432) at Ardoch revealed a fine gravel surface which he described as being "tightly compacted.....slightly arched, free from ruts and as smooth as a cyclist could wish".

Finally, Thomson and Lye specifically say that the road showed no sign of kerb stones in either of the Parkneuk Wood sections and St.Joseph also found none at Blackhill Wood. Again none are mentioned at Kirkhill and Ardoch, but Young does report his road to have "very large stones" at its edges, so there may have been kerbs in places.

The variations within the Gask road make it possible that different sections were built by different building teams, something which may also be true of the towers

(Chap 1). As yet, however, not enough data is available to prove this conclusively, let alone to suggest where the construction sectors might begin and end.

Pollen Analysis from Parkneuk Wood Roman Road

By Susan Ramsay

Introduction

During the re-excavation of the Roman Road at Parkneuk Wood, the excavators sampled many of the contexts for subsequent pollen analysis, in particular the turf layers and original ground surfaces. The aim was to pollen analyse these contexts to investigate the local environment of this part of Perthshire at the time the road was built. Pollen in the turves used in the construction of the road would have been derived from the vegetation growing in the local environment immediately prior to the Roman presence and the building of the road, as would pollen preserved in the original ground surface under the road.

Method

The samples of soil for pollen analysis were dried then gently ground to produce a fine powder. Approximately 5cm^3 of this powder was subsequently used for each pollen preparation. Standard pollen preparation techniques were used as outlined in Moore, Webb & Collinson (1991), with a hydrofluoric acid treatment used to remove the mineral component. Pollen residues were mounted in silicone oil prior to preparation of slides. Counts of at least 500 pollen grains and spores were made using a Vickers microscope at x400 and x1000 magnification. Pollen identifications were made using the keys and photographs in Moore *et al* (1991) and the pollen reference collection held in the Hopkirk laboratory, University of Glasgow. Vascular plant nomenclature follows Stace (1997). The term Coryloid covers both hazel (*Corylus*) and bog myrtle (*Myrica*) pollen but at this site it is thought that the majority of this pollen will be from hazel. A sum of total identifiable pollen and spores was used to calculate the pollen percentages and unidentifiable pollen was also expressed as a percentage of this pollen sum, although not included within it.

Results

The results of the pollen analyses are shown in Table 1 along with the results obtained from the pollen analysis of a single turf sample from this site by S.E. Durno in 1967.

Discussion

Although problems can occur with soil pollen analyses in terms of movement of pollen through the profile and differential pollen preservation, it is possible to use these results to provide a general idea of the environmental conditions present just prior to the construction of the Roman road.

Context 001 (L' 2, S.002)

This context represents gravel metalling of the road and is set in a loam matrix. This context showed severe disturbance by plant roots and is therefore not secure in terms of its pollen content. This is clear from the pollen spectrum obtained which includes pollen of the exotic conifers fir (*Abies*) and spruce (*Picea*) which have only become a significant part of the vegetation of Scotland in the last hundred years through the planting of large tracts of coniferous forestry. It is therefore likely that this sample contains much "modern" pollen, particularly in view of its extremely high grass (Poaceae) content which reflects the open nature of today's landscape.

Context 002 (L'3, S.003)

This sample was prepared from the clay matrix in which the road foundation stones were set. There is no evidence for exotic conifers in this sample and so it is more likely to be a true reflection of the pollen influx to this site at the time in question. Particularly notable is the extremely high percentage of alder (*Alnus*) in this sample. This suggests that the clay was perhaps collected from the banks of a river or area of fenland where alder woodland predominated. Alder is a moisture loving tree and tends to grow along riverbanks and loch shores where it often is the dominant canopy former in the woodland flora. However there is strong evidence for areas of grassland in the locality, with evidence for pastoral agriculture in the suite of "weedy" herbaceous taxa identified in this pollen spectrum. These include buttercups (Ranunculaceae), a wide range of the daisy family (Lactuceae, *Aster* type and *Anthemis* type), ribwort plantain (*Plantago lanceolata*), greater plantain (*Plantago major*) and several other grassland types. This diversity of herbaceous types perhaps reflects a grassy meadow, used for grazing animals, adjacent to a river, and perhaps enriched by periodic flooding. The proximity of this site to the River Earn would support this hypothesis.

Turf samples:

Context 004 (L' 4, S.004); Context 005/006 (L's 5+6, S.005); Context 007 (L'8, S.006); Context 007/010 (L's 8+9, S.001)

These samples will be considered together as they all represent turf layers either laid down during the construction of the road or on the original ground surface. There are significant differences in the pollen percentages obtained from these turf samples. Whether these are true differences reflecting different local environments from which the turves were cut, or whether they are a product of some differential preservation and mixing within the profile it is difficult to say. However, in broad terms they show a generally open grassland landscape with areas of alder woodland, perhaps restricted to wetter soils along the banks of the river. The only other tree types recorded in the turf pollen spectra are birch (*Betula*) and oak (*Quercus*) but these are only present in very low quantities and are unlikely to have formed a significant component of the local vegetation at this time. Much of the original wildwood of this part of Scotland was cleared in the pre-Roman Iron Age to provide land for cultivation of crops and for grazing animals. This is seen over much of lowland Scotland (Dumayne 1992, 1998; Ramsay 1995; Whittington & Edwards 1993) and suggests a thriving agricultural economy prior to the Roman occupation of central and southern Scotland.

Although canopy forming trees, other than alder, are rare in the pollen spectra, hazel (Coryloid) is well represented. It may be that hazel was selectively kept as areas of shrubby woodland and actively managed to produce a sustainable supply of hazel rods for constructing wattlework panels, to provide wood for fuel and to produce a supply of hazelnuts for food.

Three of the four turf samples show significant values for heather (*Calluna vulgaris*) indicating at least some areas of heathland in the vicinity of Parkneuk. Why one of the turf samples should have very little heather present is difficult to determine unless it came from a source some distance from the rest of the turves.

Although there is evidence for pastoral agriculture being practised in the area there is no evidence from the pollen analyses for arable agriculture. This is not surprising as cereal pollen is very poorly distributed, travelling only short distances from the parent plant. This absence of cereal pollen from the pollen spectra of the turves is not evidence for the absence of cereal growing in the area.

Context 011 (L'10, S.007)

This context represents what was considered to be the original topsoil beneath the turf on which the road was built. This pollen spectrum shows a similar one to that obtained from the turves. Alder is the only significant woodland component and generally the area is open grassland but with areas of hazel scrub. There is little evidence for heath land in this spectrum making it more similar to the turf from context 004.

Conclusions

The pollen spectra obtained from the Roman Road at Parkneuk Wood indicate that the environment prior to the building of the road was one dominated by open grassland which was used for the grazing of animals. The wide diversity of weedy species present within this grassland community is characteristic of a farmed landscape in which there are a variety of niches which can be exploited. Meadowsweet (*Filipendula*) and devil's-bit scabious (*Succisa*) would have grown in wetter areas of grassland, whilst nettles (*Urtica*) are indicative of enriched soils either around a settlement or in areas where livestock have congregated. Although no evidence was found in the pollen record for cereal growing in the area, it cannot be ruled out.

The native wildwood of this part of lowland Scotland had been cleared in the centuries prior to the arrival of the Roman force in the area, resulting in the only significant stands of woodland remaining being dominated by alder and restricted to wetter soils along the river banks. Areas of scrub woodland dominated by hazel were probably preserved to provide wood for fuel and construction, as well as hazelnuts to supplement the diet.

The results obtained from these analyses correlate well with the analysis of a single turf from the Roman road at Parkneuk Wood, undertaken by Dr. S.E. Durno in 1967, at the time of the original excavation. It is also interesting to note that these pollen spectra, dominated by alder, hazel, grass and heather are very similar to those from turves analysed by Boyd (1984) from the Roman forts of Bar Hill and Mollins on the Antonine Wall where a thriving agricultural economy based on pastoralism was indicated prior to the Roman occupation.

The analysis of soil pollen from a site such as Parkneuk Wood is more problematic to interpret than that from more conventionally stratified mire and lake sites. Nevertheless it is possible to produce a broad outline of the local environment around such a site and to add significantly to the information available from purely archaeological sources.

Acknowledgements

The writers are grateful to Mr J.K.Thompson for his advice on the 1967 and 1969 excavations and to Mr M.A.Hall of Perth Museum and Mrs L.Ferguson of the RCAHMS for their considerable efforts in tracing the original field records. We would particularly like to thank Mr J.C.C.Romans for visiting the 1997 excavation to recheck and explain his earlier soil analysis, and the factor of Shearerston farm for allowing access to the land.

Table 1: Parkneuk Wood, Roman Road - pollen percentages

	Context	1	2	4	005/006	7	007/010	11	Durno
	Sample	2	3	4	5	6	1	7	
	Description	gravel	clay	turf	turf	turf	turf	orig. soil	
Taxon	**Common Name**								
Trees									
Alnus	alder	9	42.5	36.2	19.9	32.9	29.3	54.2	34.8
Betula	birch	5.1	7	+	+	1	+	1.1	1.5
Fagus	beech	+							
Quercus	oak	2.1	2.5	1.1		3	+	1.5	+
Tilia	lime	+	+						
Ulmus	elm								+
Abies	fir	+							
Picea	spruce	+							
Pinus	pine	2.1	+						
Shrubs									
Coryloid	hazel / bog myrtle	10.9	14.9	42.6	28.4	12.1	17.5	20	16.2
Salix	willow	+					+		
Heaths									
Calluna	heather	5.3	5.1	1.5	29.2	14.3	26.7	1	23.1
Herbaceous									
Anthemis type	chamomile type	+	+						
Apiaceae	carrot family		+			+			
Artemisia	mugwort						+		
Aster type	daisy type	+	+						
Caryophyllaceae	pink family								+
Chenopodiaceae	goosefoot family	+							
Cyperaceae	sedge	1.2	+	+	+	1.6	1.9	0.6	2
Fabaceae	pea family						+		
Filipendula	meadowsweet	+	+	+	+	+	+	+	
Galium type	bedstraw	+	+						
Lactuceae	dandelion type	2.5	+						
Lotus type	bird's-foot trefoil		+					+	
Plantago	ribwort plantain	+	+	+	+	1		+	
Plantago major	greater plantain		+	+	+	1	+		
Plantago	plantain								+
Poaceae	grass	47.5	20.2	11.4	12.2	26	17.8	12.2	17.7
Potentilla type	cinquefoil	1.2							

	Sample	2	3	4	5	6	1	7	Durno
	Description	gravel	clay	turf	turf	turf	turf	orig. soil	
Taxon	**Common Name**								
Herbaceous									
Ranunculaceae	buttercup	2	1	+	1.4	+	1.2	+	
Rosaceae	rose family	+							
Rumex acetosa type	docks	1.2	+		+				
Silene dioica	red campion							+	
Sinapis type	mustard type			+	+	+	+	+	
Stellaria holostea	greater stitchwort		+	+	+	+	+	+	
Succisa	devil's-bit scabious	+		+	+	+		+	
Urtica	nettle	+		+		+	+	+	
Spores									
Filicales	ferns	1.2	1	+	1.4	2.4	+	3.2	2.7
Polypodium	polypody fern	3.1	+	2.4	4.8	1.8	+	3.2	
Pteridium	bracken	+		+		+		+	
Sphagnum	bog moss	+							+
Total pollen count (TP)		512	511	542	624	504	566	525	402
Unidentified (%) (TP)		3.5	2.7	20.5	6.7	16.5	14.8	12	

(+) denotes less than 1%

6. Resistivity Survey and Trenching at the Presumed Gask Tower at Peel.

D J Woolliscroft

The Site

Peel lies at NO 0604 2323 (figs 1.2 and 6.1), c. 4km to the west of Perth and stands at the southern edge of a field long ploughed for cereal and root crop cultivation. There are no visible surface indications. The site was discovered from the air in 1986 by the RCAHMS (e.g. neg: PT/15159) as a clear, single, penannular ring ditch. Its southern side is slightly truncated by a substantial open field drain and it has a single entrance break on its northern side. It has not yet proved possible re- photographed it in any subsequent season and no surface work had been done following its discovery.

The immediate surroundings contain a significant concentration of prehistoric monuments, notably two henges at North Blackruthven (NO 068246), a barrow field at Marlefield (c. NO 056243) and the large Huntingtower tumulus (NO 069249), but the site itself has since its discovery been tentatively, identified as one of the Roman Gask series watchtowers (Frere 1987, 309). This certainly appeared to be the most plausible interpretation. The feature's morphology matched the other sites in this northern part of the system, where the towers have only a single ditch and, as no central cist or pit was visible on the air photographs, it seemed unlikely to represent a ring barrow. Furthermore, the ditch entrance faces onto what may, on aerial evidence, be the line of the Roman road running down from the Gask Ridge itself towards

the Tay. Nevertheless the site could not safely be assumed to be Roman on the evidence of the ring ditch alone and a degree of follow up work seemed desirable.

The site stands on the 65m contour some way up the southern side of the Pow Water valley but, although only 35m above stream level, it enjoys superb views in all directions and especially across the entire 180° sweep to the north. Even to the south, however, where it faces gently rising ground, the view still stretches for several kilometres in places and would have been greater still from the full likely height of a Roman tower. More specifically, the site is intervisible with the Roman towers of Westmuir and West Mains of Huntingtower, along with the temporary camps of Easter Powside and East Mid Lamberkin. The fort of Bertha to the north-east, however, probably lay just out of sight, although it is intervisible with Huntingtower (Woolliscroft 1993, illus 2).

The Resistivity Survey

As a non destructive means of obtaining additional data, the Roman Gask Project conducted a resistivity survey of the site in October 1999 (fig 6.2). The ring ditch with its entrance gap showed clearly on the resulting plot, although there was a marked weakening of its trace towards the southern side, where the line of the ditch is masked by the field headland and possibly by upcast from the modern field drain.

The site had appeared rather small from the air, perhaps no larger than 16m across (although the RCAHMS oblique photographs contained too few registration points to be accurately rectified) and this was confirmed by the survey. The ditch proved to

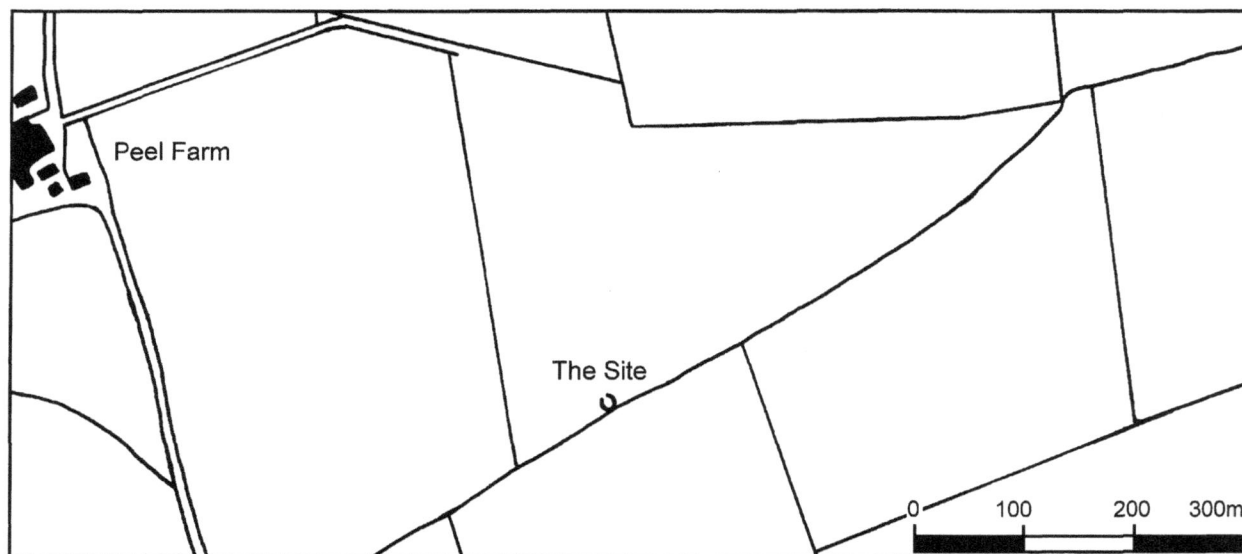

Fig 6.1. Peel: location map.

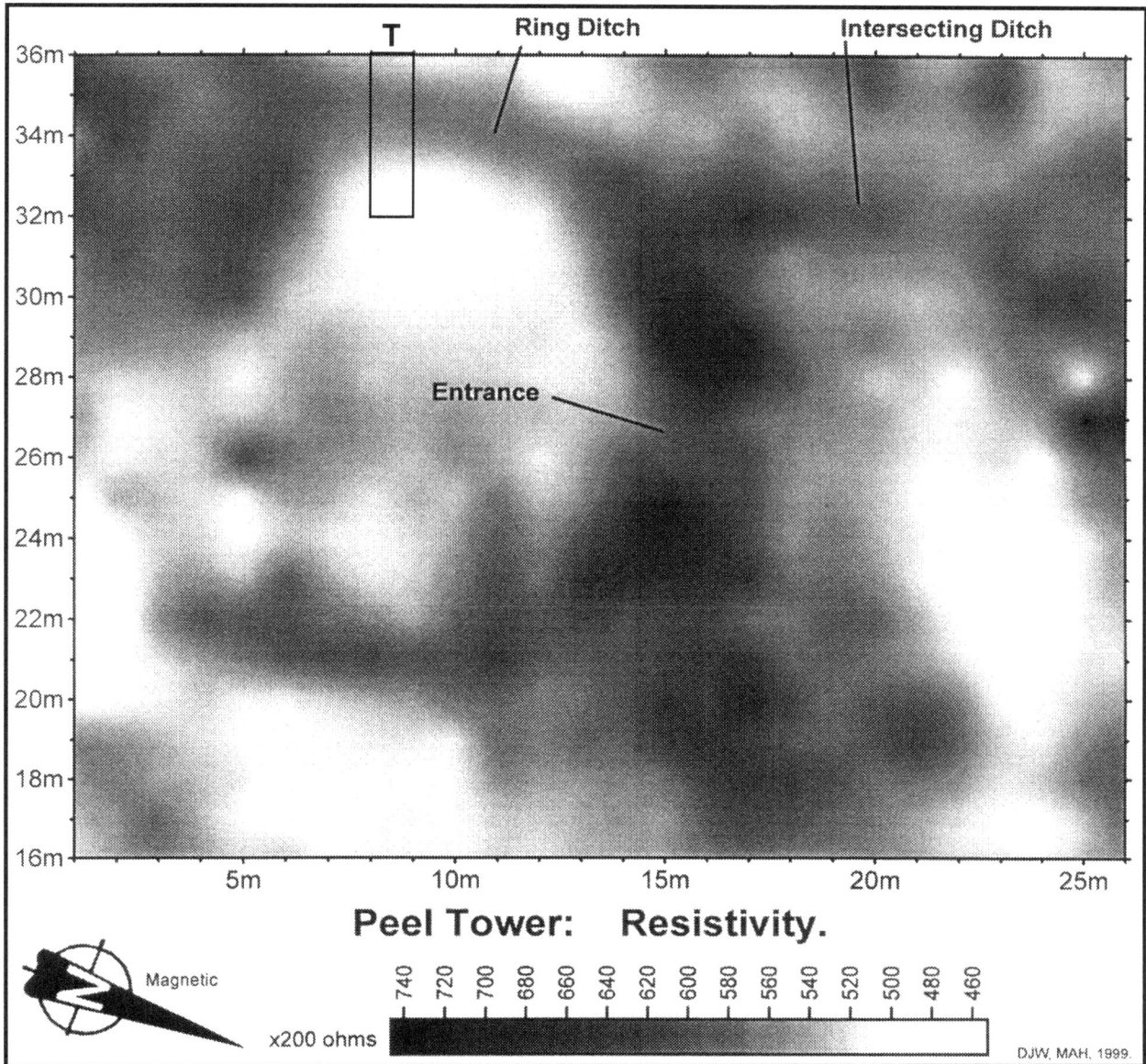

Fig 6.2. Peel: resistivity survey.

average c.15.7 m in external diameter, although it appeared to be slightly elongated along the entrance axis. The opposite effect was noted in the Gask Project's excavations at nearby Huntingtower, where the entrance axis was slightly flattened (Woolliscroft forthcoming a).

Where the ditch shows most clearly, it is probably in the region of 2m wide, with an entrance break of around 3m. Unusually, despite the fact that the site showed from the air as a positive crop mark, the ditch appeared as a series of high resistance readings, rather than as low readings as is more normal. This phenomenon is far from unknown, however, especially on sites where the ditch backfill is more free draining than the natural subsoil (or where it contains a significant quantity of stone) and it appears to be quite common in this

immediate area. The Roman tower of Huntingtower showed an identical pattern (Woolliscroft, forthcoming a), as did the supposed temporary camp at Upper Cairnie (Chap 2). There was no geophysical trace of an upcast mound outside the ditch, although this may have been completely ploughed away, and again there was no sign of a central cist. There was, however, a band of high readings running north-west from a point on the ditch c.5m west of the entrance break, whilst a second heads roughly north-east from a point c. 5m east of the entrance. It is possible that these could represent additional intersecting ditches which might form part of an outwork of some kind. For, although the air photographs show two modern land drains heading for exactly these points, neither feature could be tracked by resistivity running across the ring ditch interior. This could be a defence or a drainage feature for an external

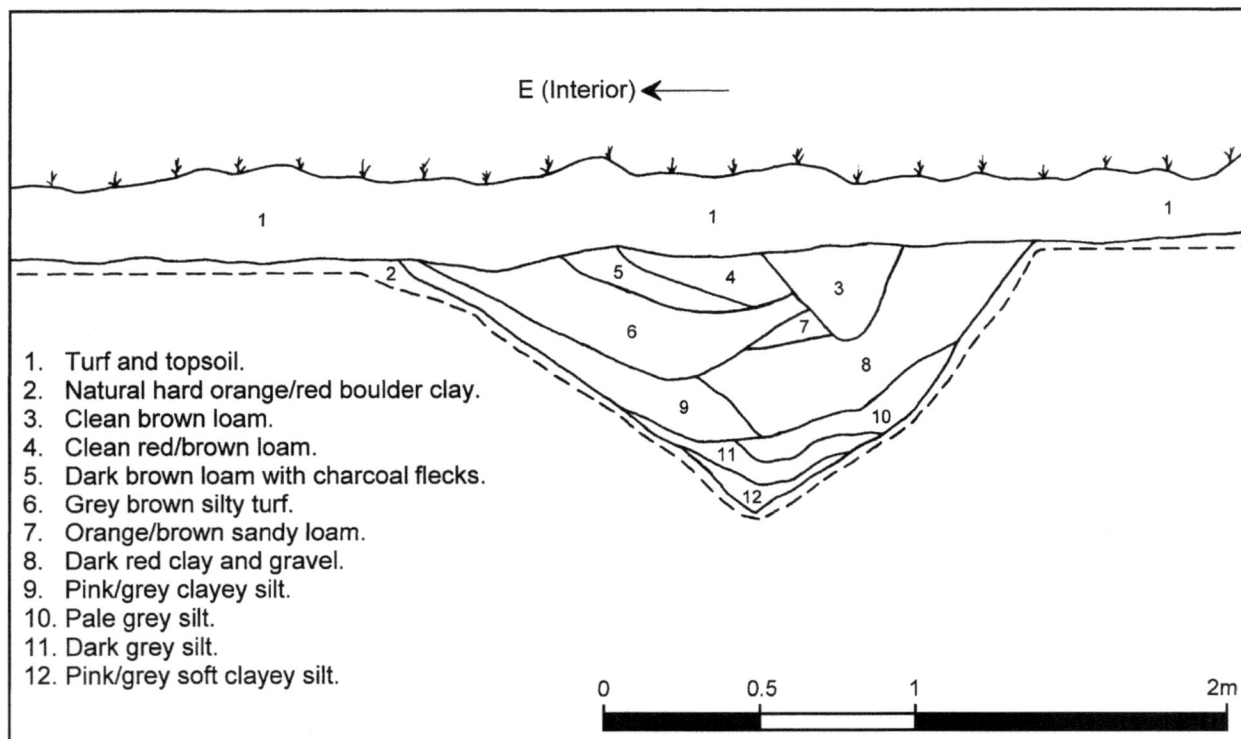

1. Turf and topsoil.
2. Natural hard orange/red boulder clay.
3. Clean brown loam.
4. Clean red/brown loam.
5. Dark brown loam with charcoal flecks.
6. Grey brown silty turf.
7. Orange/brown sandy loam.
8. Dark red clay and gravel.
9. Pink/grey clayey silt.
10. Pale grey silt.
11. Dark grey silt.
12. Pink/grey soft clayey silt.

Fig 6.3. Peel: ditch section.

structure of some sort, such as the rectangular building found outside the Roman tower at Garnhall on the Antonine Wall (Woolliscroft and Hoffmann, forthcoming). It seems more likely, however, that the features might represent the remains of a native enclosure of some sort.

The Excavation

Following the results of the resistivity survey a small excavation was planned to study the intersection between the main ring ditch and the features detected to the north of its entrance. The work took place in October 2000 in the short gap between harvest and ploughing, which unfortunately coincided with one of the wettest autumns on record. As a result, the relevant part of the field was found to be partially flooded and so the principal objective of the excavation had to be abandoned until a future season. It did, though, prove possible to cut a section (rectangle marked "T" in fig 6.2) across a more southerly point on the ring ditch itself, albeit in exceptionally muddy conditions, in the hope of further testing the site's Roman identity.

The trench revealed a V shaped ditch (fig 6.3) of the usual Roman military type except that, as is common on the Gask, it lacked the so called "ankle breaker" bottom sump. The ditch was 2.05m wide (which confirms the geophysical indications), by 0.84m deep, from the modern subsoil top and is thus broadly similar in size to the Roman ditch at Huntingtower, which averages

2.45m wide and 0.76m deep (Woolliscroft forthcoming a). The trench was extended roughly 1m into the site's interior but no surviving features were encountered and, given the degree of ploughing on the site, it seems likely that any positive features, such as the base of a normal Gask tower's internal rampart, would have been destroyed long ago.

The history of the ditch proved to be somewhat ambiguous. The bottommost layers (fig 6.3, L's 10,11 and 12) show a period of normal siltation, but the three layers have a combined thickness of only 0.24m and could have formed reasonably quickly. Above them, layer 9 was also made up of silty material, but layer 8 was a fairly loose deposit of red clay and gravel which appeared to have been dumped into place. The presence of a dump deposit over such a small amount of silt would suggest that the site was abandoned after only a fairly brief occupation, but it is rather hard to see from their shapes how layers 8 and 9 could have formed together. Layers 10 and 11 also appear somewhat truncated at their eastern ends and so it is probable that there has been some re-cutting here. It is possible that layer 9 represents a ditch recut that had silted for some time before being itself cut by layer 8, although on current evidence this can probably not be regarded as proven.

Higher still, layer 6 was made up entirely of degraded turfy material. This was remarkably homogenous and as it appeared to have entered the ditch from the interior, it seems probable that it might have derived from an internal turf bank or rampart. The shape of this layer, and the fact that it gives the impression of cutting layers 7, 8 and 9 also caused suspicion that it may represent the fill of a small re-cut, but again this cannot be regarded as proven, especially as the material did not lie on even the thinnest siltation deposit. Layer 6 did, however, yield the excavation's only small find: an Iron Age stone tool for burnishing pottery (see below).

Finally, layer 6 and its overlying loam layers (L's 4 and 5) had been cut by a small V shaped ditch, 0.45m wide and 0.3m deep which ran straight across the trench almost at right angles. No dating evidence was found associated with this feature but, as it was cut at a time when the ring ditch had been completely backfilled and as it also runs roughly at right angles to the nearby southern boundary of the modern field, it may represent part of a fairly recent field division.

Discussion

If identified as a Roman tower, the site would be the smallest currently known on the Gask. Indeed, at c.15.7m in diameter it is even slightly smaller than the inner ditches of some of the more southerly double ditched Gask towers (which average 15.75m). Nevertheless, it is only c. 0.5m smaller than its eastern neighbour, West Mains of Huntingtower, which is itself unusually small (diameter 16.2m), and, as its ditch dimensions and entrance break size, and the possible presence of an internal rampart, are also similar to Huntingtower, the site does appear consistent with the tower design of this particular part of the frontier. The lack of any central pit on the air photographs and resistivity plot would certainly make an identification as a barrow unlikely. Moreover, the ditch is V shaped and appears somewhat substantial for a round house, although the Gask Project's latest season of work at the Iron Age site of East Coldoch (Chap 4) found a round house inside the substantial (but flat bottomed) defensive enclosure ditch. The site is also almost exactly 1 1/3 Roman miles from Huntingtower and 2 2/3 Roman miles from Westmuir (the closest known tower to the west), which might suggest a 2/3 Roman mile spacing interval for the sites at this end of the line, in contrast to the 3/5 Roman mile spacing detected amongst the southernmost sites (Chap 1).

The presence of an Iron Age stone tool in the ditch fill does not necessarily conflict with a Roman date for the ring ditch, for it was found embedded in turf which may derive from the internal rampart. The tool could, thus have been inadvertently set into that rampart and so would already have been present in the turf when the Roman installation was built. It may, therefore have no dating implications whatever, for the ditch in which it was found, although it might add weight to the tentative native interpretation of the other possible ditches detected by resistivity just to the north. If so, and if it does derive from an Iron Age site based on these features, it would imply that this native activity also predated the Roman occupation and would add Peel to the growing list of Gask installations which overlie indigenous sites (Chap 1).

On present evidence the site does thus seem best interpreted as a Roman tower. The Gask Project's trenching and geophysical work has only strengthened the impression gained from aerial evidence and if this is the case it is interesting that the pollen data (see report below) suggests an intensification of agriculture here during the site's active life, perhaps in response to Roman logistical needs. Nevertheless, this cannot yet be regarded as fully proven, and only additional excavation will settle the matter for certain. Hopefully, the Project will be able to conduct further work on the site in the future, both within the ring ditch and amongst the possible ditch features to the north. In particular, if the site is Roman, it would be useful to get a clearer picture of its likely length of occupation, given the contrast between the small amount of silt in the current ditch section and the more lengthy lives emerging for other Gask towers.

Acknowledgements

The writer would like to thank the Dupplin Estate, their factor Mr J.M.Smith and their tenant Mr A.Simpson for allowing access to the land.

Lithic report

by A C Finnegan.

Coarse stone tool. Context: Layer 6.

Worn polisher/rubbing quartzite cobble stone tool, 65mm long x 61mm wide, broken. Two adjacent faces have been worn by polishing and/or rubbing. Striations are evident running along both areas suggesting it could have been used for burnishing pottery. 'Polish' is visible. Polish can be the result of abrasion rather than being indicative of phytoliths, and on this artefact it appears as if the 'polish' is the result of the abrasion of the quartzite inclusions. The artefact was found in the fill of the Roman ditch and was probably residual. Its context and size support an Iron Age date (Gleeson, 1998).

Pollen Analysis from Peel Roman Tower.

By Susan Ramsay
Dept. of Archaeology, University of Glasgow

Introduction

During the excavation of a Roman tower on the Gask frontier at Peel, three samples were taken from the ditch section to provide material for pollen and plant macrofossil analyses. Samples 1 (Layer 10) and 2 (Layer 11) are thought to represent the primary silt at the base of the ditch while sample 3 (Layer 6) is from a turf deposit which was thought during excavation to have been derived from the tower's internal rampart. The base of the ditch was very damp and so looked to be promising for the recovery of botanical remains.

Method

The samples were first divided into two portions: one of $c.2cm^3$ for pollen analysis and the remainder of the sample for plant macrofossil analysis.

The samples for pollen analysis were treated using standard pollen preparation techniques as outlined in Moore, Webb & Collinson (1991), with a hydrofluoric acid treatment used to remove the mineral component. Slides were examined using a binocular microscope with a magnification of x400. A pollen count of greater than 500 grains was made for samples 1 and 2 but only 300 grains for sample 3 due to the low pollen concentration of this sample. Pollen identifications were made using the keys and photographs in Moore *et al* (1991) and the pollen reference collection held in the University of Glasgow. Vascular plant nomenclature follows Stace (1997). The term Coryloid covers both hazel (*Corylus*) and bog myrtle (*Myrica*) pollen. A sum of total identifiable pollen and spores was used to calculate the pollen percentages and unidentifiable pollen was also expressed as a percentage of this pollen sum, although not included within it.

The samples for plant macrofossil analysis were sieved through a mesh of 300μm and then examined using a low magnification (x5 - x40) binocular microscope. Unfortunately no identifiable plant macrofossils were recovered from these samples and so they will not be discussed further in this context.

Results

The results of the pollen analyses are shown in Table 1 below.

Discussion

The pollen recovered from the Peel tower ditch is representative of an open grassy landscape with very little woodland present in the vicinity of the site. Alder and hazel / bog myrtle are the only trees and tall shrubs present at more than 1% of the total pollen present. This indicates that the vast majority of the wildwood had been cleared in this area before the tower was built at Peel. This corresponds well with much of the published information on the woodland history of lowland Scotland in the pre-Roman Iron Age (Dumayne 1992, 1998; Ramsay & Dickson 1997; Whittington & Edwards 1993).

The pollen record shows that the grassland was probably extensively grazed with high levels of ribwort plantain (*Plantago lanceolata*) which is a strong indicator of pastoral agriculture. There are also high values for dandelion type (Lactuceae) pollen which can grow in grazed grassland but also contains many species which colonise areas of trampled ground perhaps around the tower itself. Although the pollen sample analysed from the turf deposit is very similar to that from the primary ditch silt it shows a slightly higher grass pollen value and a lower representation of ribwort plantain and dandelion type. This suggests that the grazing regime changed, and perhaps increased, in the area after the cutting of the turf for the construction of the tower's internal rampart.

There is some evidence for heathland in the area in the form of heather (*Calluna vulgaris*) but it was either restricted to small patches or was located some distance from the tower itself.

In summary it would appear that the tower at Peel was located in a very open landscape ideally suited to signalling purposes. The pollen spectra recovered from the Peel ditch are similar to that obtained from the neighbouring tower at Huntingtower, although the Peel samples show an even more treeless landscape. However, it is evident that this landscape was already cleared before the construction of the signalling towers and that significant areas of woodland did not need to be felled before the signalling system could be effective.

Table 1: Peel Roman tower - results of pollen analysis

		Sample	1	2	3
		Context	Layer 10	Layer 11	Layer 6
		Description	silt	silt	turf
Taxon			%	%	%
Trees & Shrubs					
Alnus	alder		2	3	3
Betula	birch		+	+	-
Coryloid	hazel / bog myrtle		+	2	2
Pinus	pine		-	-	1
Ulmus	elm		-	-	+
Heaths					
Calluna vulgaris	heather		4	5	2
Herbaceous					
Anthemis type	chamomile type		+	-	+
Apiaceae	carrot family		+	+	+
Aster type	daisy type		1	+	-
Caryophyllaceae	pink family		+	1	+
Cyperaceae	sedge family		+	+	+
Filipendula	meadowsweet		+	-	3
Galium type	bedstraw type		+	+	+
Lactuceae	dandelion type		11	8	4
Plantago lanceolata	ribwort plantain		16	17	6
Poaceae	grass		55	57	68
Ranunculus acris type	meadow buttercup type		2	2	2
Rosaceae	rose family		-	+	-
Rumex acetosa	sorrel		-	-	+
Sinapis type	mustard type		-	-	+
Succisa	devil's-bit scabious		3	2	+
Ferns & Moss					
Filicales	ferns		+	+	2
Polypodium	polypody fern		2	-	1
Pteridium	bracken		-	+	+
Sphagnum	bog moss		+	+	2
Unidentifiable					
Broken			+	-	-
Crumpled			2	3	-
Corroded			1	3	-
Obscured			-	+	-

(+) indicates less than 1%

7. The Roman Gask Series Tower At Shielhill North, Including Excavations By The Late Prof J K St.Joseph

D J Woolliscroft

The Site

The tower of Shielhill North was first recorded by Thomas Pennant (1774, 100) in a brief account of a trip along the Roman road from Kaims Castle to Ardoch in 1772. At the time, the site was still visible as a surface feature and Pennant describes it as "a small round area, like those on Gask moor, but considerably stronger, being surrounded by not fewer than three fosses". Since Pennant's day, however, all surface trace of the site has been obliterated and it was not rediscovered until 1972, when Prof J.K. St.Joseph took two remarkably clear air photographs (CUCAP BKE-50 & 51) which provided a view of its ditch system, the Roman road, which lies just to the south, and even its four internal post holes (fig 7.1). He immediately identified the site as a Roman tower and as part of the Gask frontier (St.Joseph 1973, 218 & 1976, 22).

The tower lies at NN 8561 1220 on a small flat topped knoll, just above the 190m contour. It is located c.90m to the southwest of a small burn, which should have

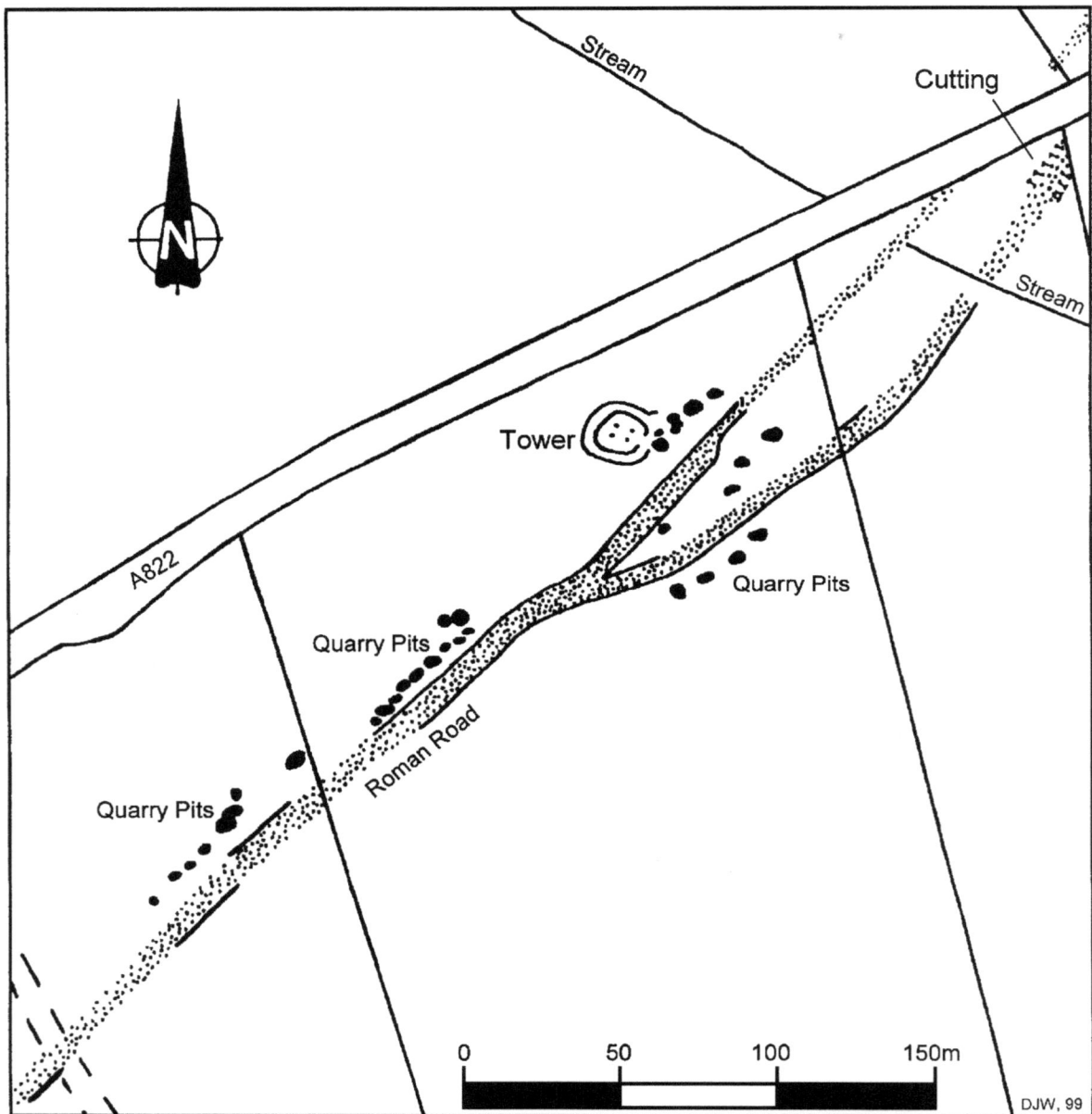

Fig 7.1. Shielhill North: the air photographic evidence.

provided a reasonably reliable water source, and near the top of the hill that carries Kaims Castle fortlet at its summit. The site is an excellent look out position for, as well as having a good command of its immediate vicinity, it enjoys superb longer range views in every direction except the north and northwest, where it still faces rising ground. Its view to the south is particularly impressive, stretching for many miles right across Strathallan to the Ochil Hills beyond, and taking in all of the known Gask installations to its south, from Shielhill South tower to the fortlet at Glenbank (fig 1.2). The fort of Ardoch, is in full view, at a range of c. 2.75km and even to the north, the site would have been intervisible with Kaims Castle from the full likely height of a Roman timber tower and, as Kaims is in turn intervisible with the fort of Strageath, the site would have been easily integrated into any frontier signaling system (Woolliscroft 1993, 297 & illus 3).

The Air Photographic Evidence

The Tower

Fig 7.1 provides a composite transcription of the two St.Joseph discovery air photographs, a later RCAHMS image (PT/11100) and Gask Project air photograph 00CN7#16. Together these show that the tower, like all of the Gask installations south of Kaims Castle, had a double ditch (instead of the usual one), with no sign of the third "fosse" reported by Pennant. Measurements taken from air photographs are always subject to a significant margin of error, but the inner ditch would appear to be sub-rectangular in plan and c.16m in external diameter. It surrounds an internal area of about 13m across. The outer ditch is c. 24m in diameter and is rather more circular in plan (if still distinctly irregular), which leaves an inter-ditch space which varies between 2m and a little over 3m wide.

Both ditches show a single entrance break oriented to the south-east, towards the Roman road. That of the inner ditch is c.3.3m wide, but the outer ditch only covers c. 290° of the full site circumference so that, although the southern butt end forms a neat line with that of the inner ditch, to the north of the entrance the outer ditch stops well short of the inner to leave a break of c.11m. This phenomenon is not unknown on Roman double ditched towers and a similar situation was encountered during the Gask Project's excavations at the southernmost Gask tower, Greenloaning (see fig 1.4), where once again the left hand side of the outer ditch entrance break, as seen from the tower interior, began noticeably short of the inner ditch break. Unusually, however, Shielhill North's outer ditch appears to make an outward turn of approximately 137° on this side of the entrance, to form an offset which runs for about another 3.5m before forming a butt end. So far as the writer is aware this is a unique feature for a Roman

tower and certainly no similar offset has been recorded elsewhere on the Gask. The post pits for the tower itself would suggest a structure of approximately 4.5m x 3.5m, which would give it an internal area of approximately $15.75m^2$ (see fig 1.11d).

The Road

The Roman road can be followed on air photographs running northeastwards from NN 8541 1198, past the tower to NN 8575 1234. Unusually for the Gask, clear traces of side ditches are visible as crop marks, albeit intermittently, as are the ubiquitous quarry pits which are the usual mark of the road on this system. The latter appear in distinct groupings at about 50m intervals, most (but not all) of which lie on the northern side of the road. One of these groups lies immediately to the south and east of the tower and it is noteworthy that one fairly large pit is located directly in front of its entrance.

For the most part the road is more or less what one would expect on the Gask, at about 7m wide between its ditches, and throughout most of this sector it follows the line mapped by the Ordnance Survey almost exactly. It does, however, show one highly unusual feature in that at NN 8559 1215, c. 40m south-west of the tower, it appears to swerve a few metres to the south and then forks. One line then continues along much the same heading as before. It gradually returns to the O.S. line and passes just to the south of the tower entrance, coming to within c. 9.7m of the outer ditch at its closest approach. Immediately to the east of the tower, however, this branch narrows abruptly (with an inturn of its southern side) to leave it about 4m wide within the side ditches. It crosses the small stream, mentioned above, immediately to the south of the modern A822 and there are surface and air photographic indications that it may have done so on a small embankment, although without excavation it is difficult to separate the ancient works from the modern road crossing, which has involved the construction of an arched stone built tunnel to canalise the burn. It then crosses the modern road and continues on the same course, apparently heading for Kaims Castle.

The second branch appears to maintain the original width throughout and follows a slightly more southerly track to reach a maximum separation from the northern branch of c.28m. Until August 2000, air photographic evidence only allowed it to be traced as far as the southern side of the stream, but Gask Project air photograph 00CN7#16, taken that month, showed clear indications of a linear feature continuing up the northern side of the burn valley until it disappeared at the modern dry stone wall at the northern edge of the field. A surface examination at this spot located faint signs of the road running northeast from the burn on a low mound or agger, and on exactly the course indicated by the air

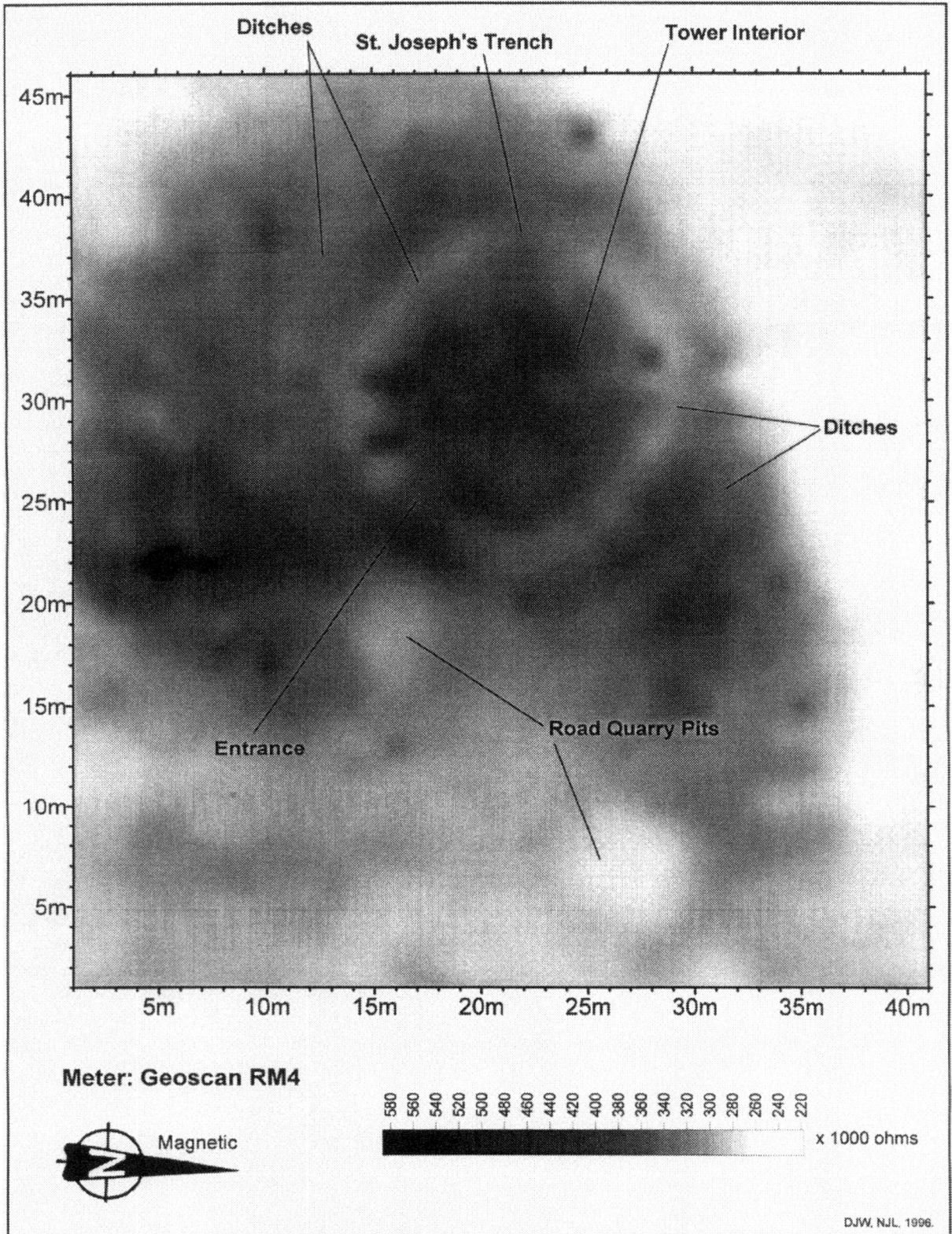

Fig 7.2. Shielhill North: resistivity.

photographic indications. More interestingly, however, the road encounters a low (c. 1m high), almost vertically sided knoll c. 20m south of the field wall and from here to the edge of the field it runs in a slight, but still clearly defined, cutting which does not appear to have been noticed before. This feature is reminiscent of a similar (and long known) embankment and cutting still visible about 1km further to the south, where the road crosses a similar burn valley immediately to the east of the tower at Shielhill South and is a sign of the attention to detail in the engineering of this most northerly of Roman roads.

All surface trace of the road has been ploughed out in the next field to the north, but this short extra road segment was still enough to provide another surprise. For its course, if extrapolated, would suggest that the road fork has begun to turn northwards again, as if it was intending to loop back to rejoin the northern branch.

The Geophysical Survey

In 1996, the Roman Gask Project conducted a resistivity survey of the site to act as a control to settle differences between the air photographic evidence and the J K St.Joseph excavation data discussed below. The results, as shown by fig 7.2, correspond well with the picture gained from the air, for they provide a clear trace of a sub-rectangular inner ditch and almost exactly confirm the dimensions given above. The outer ditch is considerably less well defined, however, which would suggest that it may have been rather less substantial. In particular, the offset at the northern outer ditch entrance could not be detected and the ditch's overall shape cannot be plotted with any confidence. Again, there was no sign of Pennant's third ditch, which thus seems unlikely to have existed, but intermittent areas of high resistance immediately outside the ditch system may represent the ploughed out remains of an upcast mound. A similar feature was detected by the Gask Project's resistivity survey of Greenloaning in 1995 (Woolliscroft and Hoffmann 1997, 565 and illus 3) and others are clearly visible outside a number of the best preserved tower ditches on the Gask Ridge itself: notably Kirkhill. The interior area shows a number of areas of high resistance, but there are no clear anomalies which could be taken as indications of either a rampart base or of the tower posts visible from the air.

St.Joseph's Excavations

In October 1972, shortly after rediscovering the tower, Prof J K St.Joseph undertook a limited program of trenching, which still represents the only excavation conducted on the site. This work was accompanied by rather larger scale excavations at the neighboring sites of Shielhill South and Blackhill Wood (fig 1.2), which

were at the time the only other members of the Gask's southern, double ditched, tower group known. Sadly, although some notes appeared in print shortly thereafter (St.Joseph 1973, 218 & 1976, 22), these latter sites are only now being fully published (for Shielhill South: Woolliscroft & Hoffmann 1998, for Blackhill Wood: Glendinning & Dunwell 2000) and the present chapter will attempt to do the same for the work at Shielhill North.

The excavation consisted of just two trenches. The first was a long (22m x 0.8m) slot running from east to west across the site (fig 7.3). This sectioned both ditches on the western side of the tower and explored one of the four internal post holes, before bending a little towards the south to reveal the inner ditch on the eastern side, this time, apparently, only in plan. The second was a much smaller (3.1m x 0.8m) cut and exposed just the inner ditch on the southern side of the tower, again, apparently, only in plan. No attempt was made to search for Pennant's third ditch outside the two visible through air photography.

St.Joseph's drawn plan (fig 7.3) is probably best regarded as a schematic representation of the site (albeit more or less to scale) to show its essential anatomy and the relationship of the excavation trenches to it, rather than as a strictly accurate representation. Both ditches are shown as perfectly circular which, as St.Joseph's own air photographs had already demonstrated, is clearly not the case, and the tower is shown as a perfect (3.34m) square, which again contradicts the aerial evidence. This was St.Joseph's usual practice on the Gask, for the ring ditches at Shielhill South (Woolliscroft & Hoffmann 1998, illus 2) and Blackhill Wood (Dunwell & Glendinning, 2000, 260) were also shown as perfect circles in his plans, even though more recent excavations have shown that again both are clearly sub-rectangular or sub-circular. Shielhill North had produced by far the best aerial evidence of the three towers studied and so this approach might be thought to be rather more surprising here, but it is probably understandable given the fact that St.Joseph's excavations were on such a small scale when compared to his work at the other two sites.

Nevertheless, despite the limitations of the site plan and a complete lack of datable finds, valuable data was produced by the excavation. The section (fig 7.4) produced two shallow "V" shaped ditches, with no visible "ankle breaker" bottom slots. In confirmation of the resistivity data, the outer ditch was extremely slight, at just 1.31m wide. The drawn section shows it as being just 0.2m deep, below the modern plough soil base, but St.Joseph's notes record a maximum depth of 0.37m so the bottom may have varied within the trench. The inner ditch was slightly more substantial at 1.9m wide and 0.43m deep, and the inter-ditch spacing, as measured between the ditch lips, was 2.4m. No signs of palisading

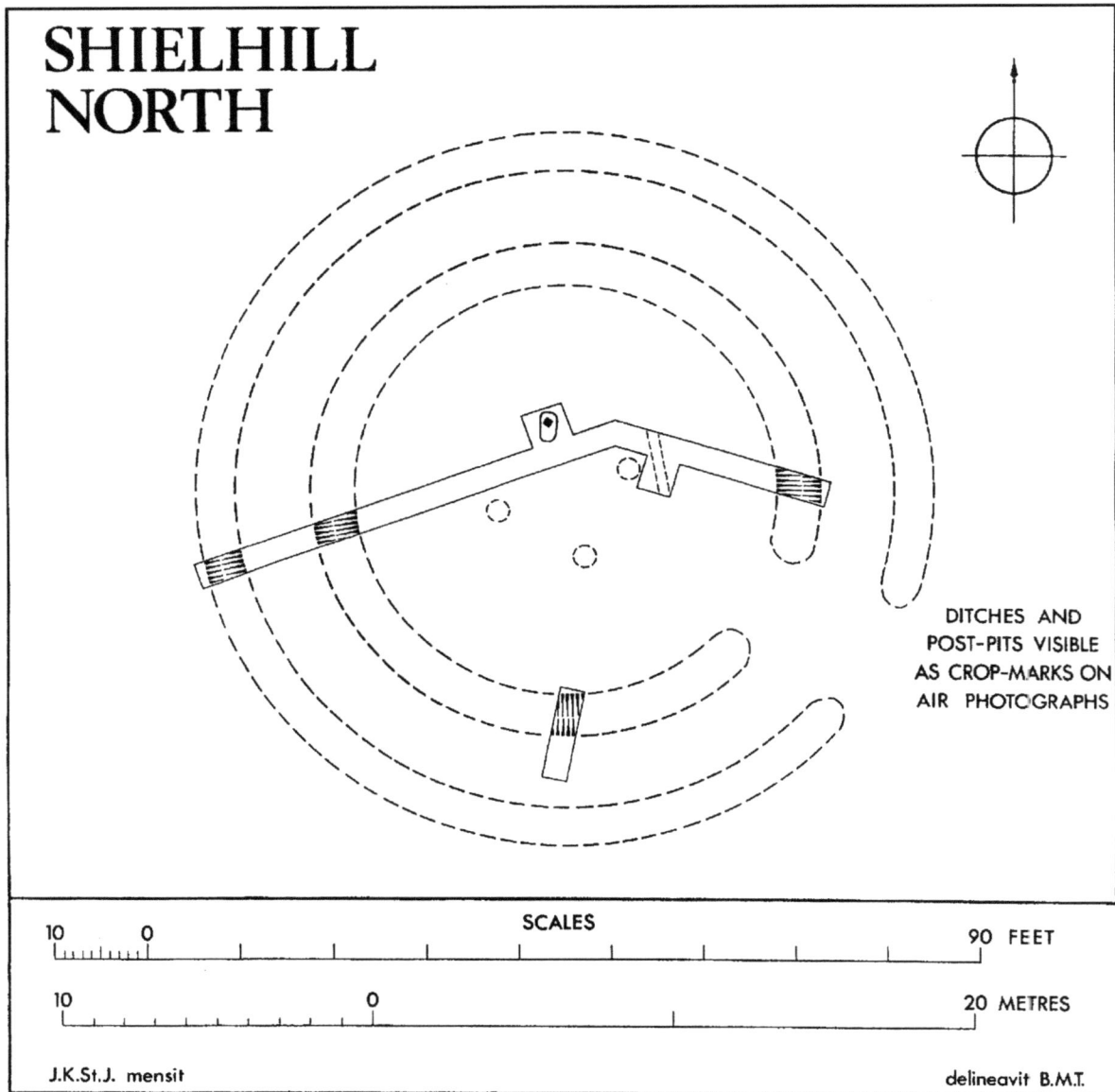

SHIELHILL NORTH

DITCHES AND POST-PITS VISIBLE AS CROP-MARKS ON AIR PHOTOGRAPHS

SCALES

10   0   90   FEET

10   0   20   METRES

J.K.St.J. mensit   delineavit B.M.T.

Fig 7.3. St.Joseph's site plan.

were uncovered either inside, outside or between the ditches. St.Joseph's notes offer no detailed description of the outer ditch fills, but his section drawing marks it as being filled with peat. The inner ditch contained a number of small boulders at its bottom and the ditch fills were otherwise described in St.Joseph's field notes as follows:

"The inner ditch revealed up to 10" (254mm) of ash, burnt clay and possibly daub, with a whitish, even textured silty earth (possibly turf) filling the rest of the ditch, rather as if the fill had been thrown in in shovelfuls. There was no silt beneath this. The fill for the last 2' (0.6m) on the interior side of the ditch consisted of more contaminated burnt clay/ash, etc as if this represented a throwing in of scrapings or tailings from the backfilling process. This mixed fill overlaps the inner lip, suggesting that it was thrown in from the

interior of the enclosure, and was overlain by a band of peaty soil of a dull matte colour, possibly an in situ natural growth of peat".

In the interior, the northeastern post pit was drawn in section and recorded in plan (Fig 7.5) at a depth of 0.37m below its surviving top, at which point the post pipe itself became visible, showing that the tower here had stood on a rectangular sectioned timber of 0.3 x 0.27m. A 0.44m depth of post pipe had survived, suggesting that the timber had originally extended to a full depth of at least 0.72m below the modern plough soil. The uppermost 0.28m had, however, been destroyed by a pit, presumably a demolition feature, dug to allow the timber to be removed when the site was abandoned. The post pit measured 0.97m x 0.8m at the depth at which it was planned. The post had been chocked with a fill of clean gravel (fig 7.5, Layer a),

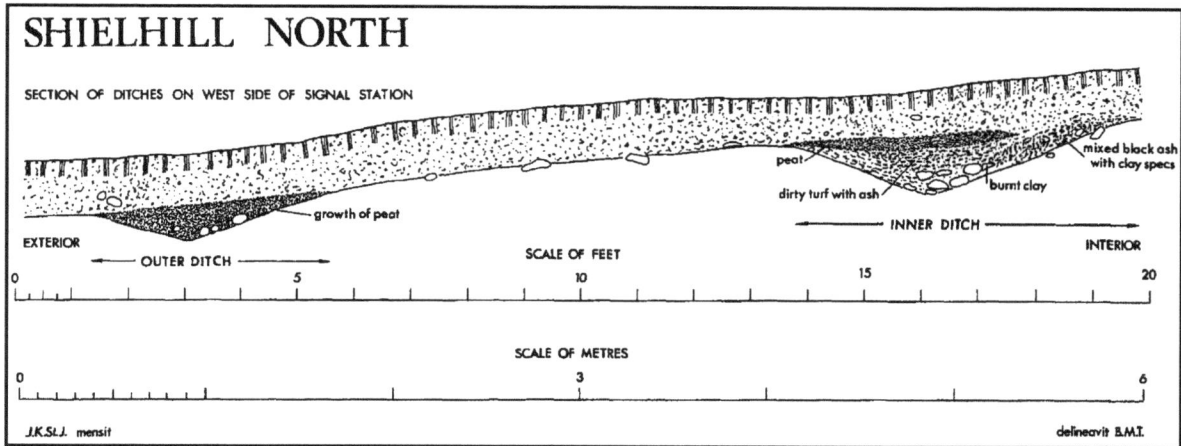

SHIELHILL NORTH

SECTION OF DITCHES ON WEST SIDE OF SIGNAL STATION

Fig 7.4. St.Joseph's ditch section.

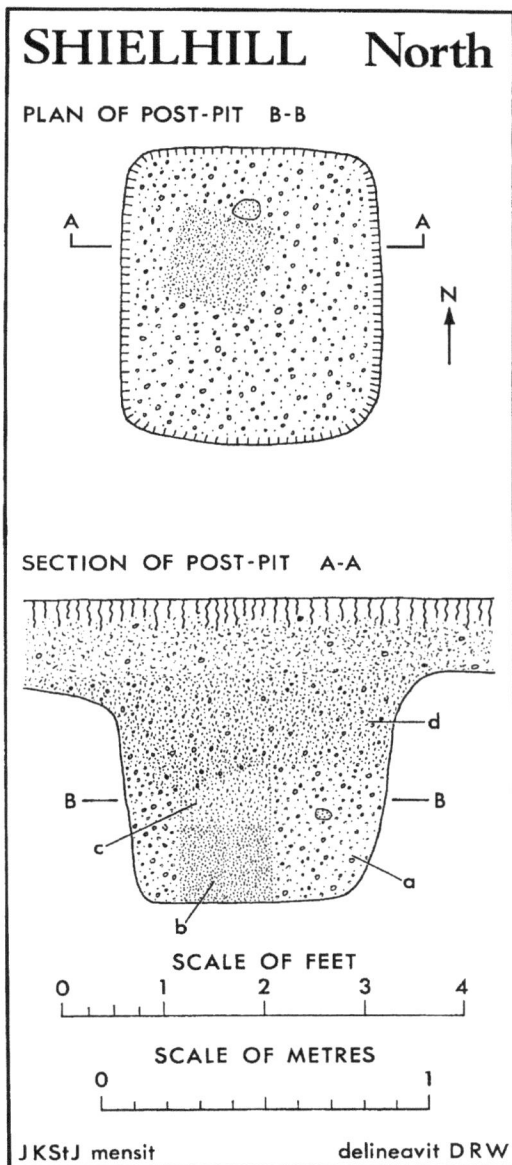

SHIELHILL North

PLAN OF POST-PIT B-B

SECTION OF POST-PIT A-A

Fig 7.5. St.Joseph's NW posthole section.

rather than with larger stones as might have been expected. The post pipe itself had filled with layers of fine silty earth (L's b and c), whilst the demolition pit (L'd) was filled with gravel similar to that of L'a but mixed with "dark earth", charcoal and daub specks. No other internal structures were located except for a narrow linear feature, which was probably a modern land drain and, in particular, St.Joseph's records make no mention of any trace of metalling in the interior, or of any surviving trace of an internal rampart. No attempt was made to look for a gate structure at the entrance, but these are anyway, so far, universally absent on the Gask towers despite deliberate searches, not least on the Gask Project's own excavations.

Discussion

The Tower

Despite the absence of dating evidence there seems to be no reason to doubt St.Joseph's original identification of the site as one of the Roman Gask series towers. As such, it is broadly consistent with the other three known double ditched towers at the southern end of the line: Shielhill South (Woolliscroft & Hoffmann 1998), Blackhill Wood (Glendinning & Dunwell, 2000) and Greenloaning (Woolliscroft & Hoffmann 1997). For example, the slight nature of the ditches can now be paralleled at all four southern towers. The average inner ditch width and depth amongst these sites is 1.83m x 0.51m, as compared to Shielhill North's 1.9m x 0.43, whilst the group's outer ditches average 1.67m wide x 0.36m deep, which compares well with Shielhill North's 1.31m x 0.2 - 0.37m. The closest parallel, not surprisingly, is the site's nearest neighbor, Shielhill South, whose inner and outer ditches average 1.16m x 0.47m and 0.99 x 0.36m respectively.

73

The overall diameters of the site's two ditches are also comparable with the rest of the southern tower group, as is the shallow "V" shaped profile. Whilst the lack of an "ankle breaker" sump is also a frequent (although not universal) feature of the minor Gask sites. St.Joseph's single ditch section does not show the unusual flared top profile recorded in the ditches of all three of the other southern Gask towers (e.g. Woolliscroft & Hoffmann 1997, 569, illus 5) but, as this feature appears only somewhat intermittently within the other sites' ditch circuits, it remains possible that further work might find it at Shielhill North as well. The asymmetrical outer ditch entrance break can, as already mentioned, be paralleled at Greenloaning (Woolliscroft & Hoffmann 1997, 568, illus 4), although no comparable offset was uncovered there. The apparent absence of silt in the ditches can also be seen elsewhere on the Gask and need not necessarily imply an unusually brief occupation, since the fortlet of Midgate appears to have been abandoned part way through a ditch re-cut (Woolliscroft 1993, 305ff); many other Gask sites show signs of similar re-cutting and Shielhill North may have passed through the process shortly before it was abandoned. The lack of palisading has so far proved to be universal on the Gask, although palisades are known from Roman towers elsewhere, both inside and between the ditches (e.g. Woolliscroft & Swain 1991), and the markedly sub-rectangular/sub-circular site plan has now been proved on all of the southern Gask tower group except Greenloaning, which does appear to be roughly circular.

In the interior, the shape and dimensions of the tower itself are also comparable with the rest of the southern group and, although square towers are known elsewhere on the system, all four double ditched sites are now known to have rectangular towers. The tower's ground area of roughly 15.75m^2 compares well with the group's average of 15.8m^2 and, although this figure does conceal a fairly broad range for the group, from 12m^2 at Shielhill South, to c.22.6m^2 at Greenloaning (one of the largest Roman timber towers known anywhere), these sites are almost universally larger than the towers on the much longer, northern, single ditched Gask sector, which average just 9.74m^2.

St.Joseph records no signs of metalling in the interior and, as this contrasts markedly with the other three towers on the southern sector, it might be a hint that a certain amount of the original surface has been ploughed away. Given the similarity of the ditch depths at all four towers, however, and the fact that Shielhill North's tower post holes are slightly deeper than the average for the group, the loss has probably not been significant. Whatever the case, some additional evidence for the interior can probably be inferred from the ditch contents. For example, St.Joseph does not record any signs of an internal turf rampart to parallel those long known further north on the towers of the Gask Ridge proper (Christison 1901 and Robertson 1974). But the

probable turf found in what is clearly a demolition deposit in the inner ditch fill may well have come from such a structure, all in situ trace of which may have been removed by a combination of Roman demolition and modern ploughing. In the past, (e.g. Woolliscroft & Hoffmann 1997, 573) the writer has tended to doubt whether the small interiors of the southern, double ditched Gask towers would have had enough room to contain such ramparts, despite the presence of a certain amount of, albeit less clearly stratified, turf in the inner ditch fills at Greenloaning and Shielhill South, but the recent discovery of surviving rampart remains at Blackhill Wood (Glendinning & Dunwell 2000, 269)) has obviously rendered this view untenable. Another objection to internal ramparts, the fact that the southern corner posts of the tower at Greenloaning were set so close to the inner ditch lip that again there would not have been room for a rampart (Woolliscroft & Hoffmann 1997, 571, illus 6), has also now been answered. For the northernmost and most recently excavated Gask tower, West Mains of Huntingtower (Woolliscroft forthcoming, a), proved to have a similar configuration, but with clear surviving evidence that the tower posts had been set into the rampart body, thus removing the space problem. This is a rare configuration in Roman towers, but it is common enough in forts and, given the evidence from Shielhill North, it is probably not unlikely now that all four southern group towers had ramparts, making them a universal feature on the frontier.

Likewise, the presence of daub in both the ditch fill and the demolition layers of the excavated post pit (which might suggest that the tower was fitted with wattle and daub side cladding) is also consistent with the rest of the southern group (and especially with Shielhill South, which also yielded carbonised hazel twigs which might have derived from wattling (Woolliscroft & Hoffmann 1998)), as is the evidence for systematic demolition and the in situ burning of demolition materials. Indeed, the entire Gask line has shown a similar picture of careful demolition (e.g. Woolliscroft 1993, 307 and Woolliscroft & Hoffmann 1997, 573) with or without signs of burning.

Finally, recent excavations at the four Gask towers of Greenloaning (Woolliscroft & Hoffmann 1997), Shielhill South (Woolliscroft & Hoffmann 1998), Huntingtower (Woolliscroft forthcoming, a) and Blackhill Wood (Glendinning & Dunwell 2000), have all produced signs of multiple structural phases in the towers themselves and, occasionally of ditch re-cutting. Work in the 1980's at the tower of Westerton (Hanson & Friell 1995, 504ff) also produced (albeit more equivocal) evidence for the same process and this general pattern of rebuilding has begun to make it seem likely that the Gask Frontier may have remained in use for appreciably longer than the brief, season or two, span that had previously been envisaged (e.g. Breeze

1982, 65). St.Joseph's Shielhill North excavations record evidence for only one tower and ditch phase, however, but for a number of reasons this cannot, by itself, be regarded as conclusive. For a start, it does have to be said that the same excavator did not recognise evidence for phasing at both Shielhill South and Blackhill Wood, which has now been deciphered by recent more extensive work. Moreover, St.Joseph's excavation at Shielhill North took in only a small sample of the site and it is perfectly possible, in this one ditch section and post hole, that secondary features may have completely destroyed any earlier evidence. Under the circumstances, therefore, whilst bearing in mind the possibility that this site really may have had just a single structural phase, it might be best to allow the matter to remain open, at least until more extensive work can be conducted to confirm or confound the picture presented by the limited data available so far.

The Road

The aerial evidence for the Roman road at Shielhill North raises two matters, both of which ultimately concern dating. The first is the fork immediately to the southwest of the tower. This occurs as the road nears a small stream crossing and it is, of course, far from rare for such crossings to migrate over time, especially where a Roman road has remained in use into later times. For these users may have lacked the ability and/or inclination to maintain Roman bridges, culverts or fords and so sought easier ground. Alternatively, riverine changes, differing usage patterns or damage caused by simple weight of traffic may have rendered the original crossing unusable or at least less ideal. On this occasion, however, both prongs of the fork do seem likely to be Roman, since both appear to be of similar size (at least initially) and construction and, in particular, both show their own sets of the associated quarry pits, which form such a strong diagnostic feature of the Roman road on the Gask. Of course this does not necessarily mean that both branches are exactly contemporary and there may well have been modifications made either within or even between the three main known Roman incursions into the area. But, even so, the branch does appear more likely to be a Roman, rather than a post-Roman feature. Certainly, there is one, albeit tenuous, piece of evidence that neither branch remained in use into at least relatively modern times. For, although Pennant was able to follow the line in 1772, and although the road was still marked, albeit as a dotted line, on Stobie's map of Perthshire in 1783, the only gate in the dry stone field wall at the northeastern side of the tower field lies well to the south of both road branches, whereas elsewhere on the Gask the field gates often lie right on the line of the road, reflecting its frequent later use as a field track. This is only of moderate help, however, and it is quite possible

that the road may have stayed in use for centuries before the present field system came into being.

It remains unproven, at present, that the southern branch does loop all the way back to the northern, as suggested above, although this does currently appear very likely, and the answer to this question must await excavation and/or better air photographic coverage. If it does, however, it might be thought to form a by-pass loop. This is a common enough feature at Roman forts, notably on the nearby Antonine Wall (e.g. MacDonald 1934, figs 17, 31 and 42) but, as far as the writer is aware, it is unprecedented at a tower, where it would seem to serve little purpose, since the main road line at the towers does not pass through the installation as it does at the forts, which means that there should really be little to bypass.

The second issue raised by the road is the presence of what are assumed to be quarry pits (although, as St.Joseph's excavation records do not mention the nature of the subsoil we cannot be sure what there was available to quarry) immediately outside the tower's outer ring ditch, including one that actually blocks the entrance. It is perfectly possible that this pit may have been backfilled to allow access to the tower, perhaps using spoil dug from its ditches, although this might have led to subsidence problems and would require excavation to test. But, at the very least, the positioning of this pit does seem rather odd for if it had been open during any part of the tower's occupation, it would have been inconvenient to say the least and would certainly have made the site's interior inaccessible to wheeled traffic. An alternative might be to suggest that this particular feature is actually a demolition pit dug to conceal abandoned materials from an enemy, albeit such a feature would be unprecedented on a Gask tower. But, although this could be tested by excavation, it would appear to require a certain amount of special pleading especially as elsewhere on the site so much obvious demolition material was found dumped indiscriminately into the ditches. For the pit seems to form such a natural part of a whole series of what do seem to be perfectly normal quarry pits along the road side. Of course the pit might have been retained as an additional defense, but it does raise the possibility that the road, at least in its final well surfaced form, might not have been contemporary with the towers. If so, the pit's position would suggest that the road as we have it might have been significantly later than the tower's occupation for, if the road was built first, it would have been perfectly easy to build the tower a few meters further to the west to avoid (or avoid the need to backfill) any preexisting pits. Alternatively, had the tower been in occupation, or at least planned, at the time the final version of the road was constructed, it would have been a simple matter to have dug the pit in a slightly different position. Indeed, it might even be argued that if the tower and road had been exactly contemporary there would have been no need for separate quarry pits at this point because the act of digging the ring ditches should have yielded adequate material. It might thus be worth speculating whether the road as we have it might be Antonine or even Severan. Against this hypothesis, however, is the fact that there is no evidence that any of the quarry pits cut (or were cut by) the tower ditches, although it is worth noting that, at Greenloaning, the tower's outer ditch was cut by a running feature which may have been a later side ditch for the road (Woolliscroft & Hoffmann 1997, 570 & 576). It also has to be said that elsewhere, road quarry pits have been found underlying structures built very shortly afterwards, probably as part of the same scheme (for example beneath the Antonine Wall expansion of Bonnyside East (Steer 1957, 164ff)) and we should not always, perhaps, expect Roman soldiers to show too much consideration to their fellows when building. Indeed, the wide outer ditch entrance break could be interpreted as an attempt to avoid a number of quarry pits, which might thus predate the tower. Moreover, the possible by-pass loop seems even more difficult to explain in the absence of the tower. It could be argued that the narrow stretch of road to the east of the site might represent an original Flavian track, with the broader road of the southern branch being later, but this would not explain why the southwesternmost section of the northern branch was also built at the same broad gauge. Under such a scenario, this would imply that the tower was returned to use in a later period, perhaps manned from Ardoch (which does lie to the southwest), but there is absolutely no evidence for such a reoccupation either at Shielhill North or at any other minor Gask Installation. It is also worth noting that no sign of an earlier trackway has ever been found in any section cut through the Gask road (e.g. Chap 5), although admittedly it is possible that such a feature could have been utterly destroyed by later, more substantial, road building. At the very least, however, this situation does act to highlight the fact that, at present, we still have no dating evidence whatever for the construction and history of the Roman Gask road and so a Flavian date exactly contemporary with the towers cannot simply be taken for granted.

Acknowledgements

The writer would like to thank Ardoch Farming Co Ltd, their then factor, Mr R.D. Baird, and their tenant Mrs M. Rimmer for allowing the resistivity survey. Thanks are also due to Mr G.S. Maxwell and the RCAHMS for allowing access to Prof St.Joseph's field records and for providing copies of his drawings.

8. A Geophysical Survey in the Annexes of the Roman Fort of Strageath.

By N J Lockett

The author and the Roman Gask Project have, for some years, been interested in the extent of extra-mural activity associated with the Gask frontier forts. To this end an extensive geophysical survey was undertaken to search for such activity, whether military or civilian, outside the fort of Strageath.

The site lies nearly five miles to the north of the well known fort at Ardoch, on the line of the Gask Roman road. Its position is significant, for it stands at both a river crossing and a major change in the alignment of the frontier. The road from Ardoch runs approximately northwards towards the fort but at Strageath it swings abruptly to the east to cross the Earn and climb the Gask Ridge. While the exact course of parts of the Roman road are disputed in this area, the attention of the author was attracted by the significance of the change in

alignment and the considerable extra-mural activity which has been noted from the early antiquaries onwards (e.g. Roy 1793, pl 32).

In recent years the interior of the fort has received considerable attention, mainly through the work carried out by Professors S. S. Frere and J. J. Wilkes (1989) on behalf of the Scottish Field School of Archaeology, which investigated almost the whole of the interior in excavations between 1973 and 1986. However, despite the existence of considerable numbers of aerial photographs which show features to the west of the fort platform, no field work has, hitherto, been carried out in that area. The brief of the present survey was, therefore, to conduct a large geophysical survey to the west of the fort in order to ascertain the extent of remains within this extra-mural area.

In recent years fieldwork and desk-based assessments by the Roman Gask Project have revealed a more complex picture of the occupation and life-span of the Gask frontier. In particular, the excavations have shown that the orthodox view that the Gask was a briefly occupied

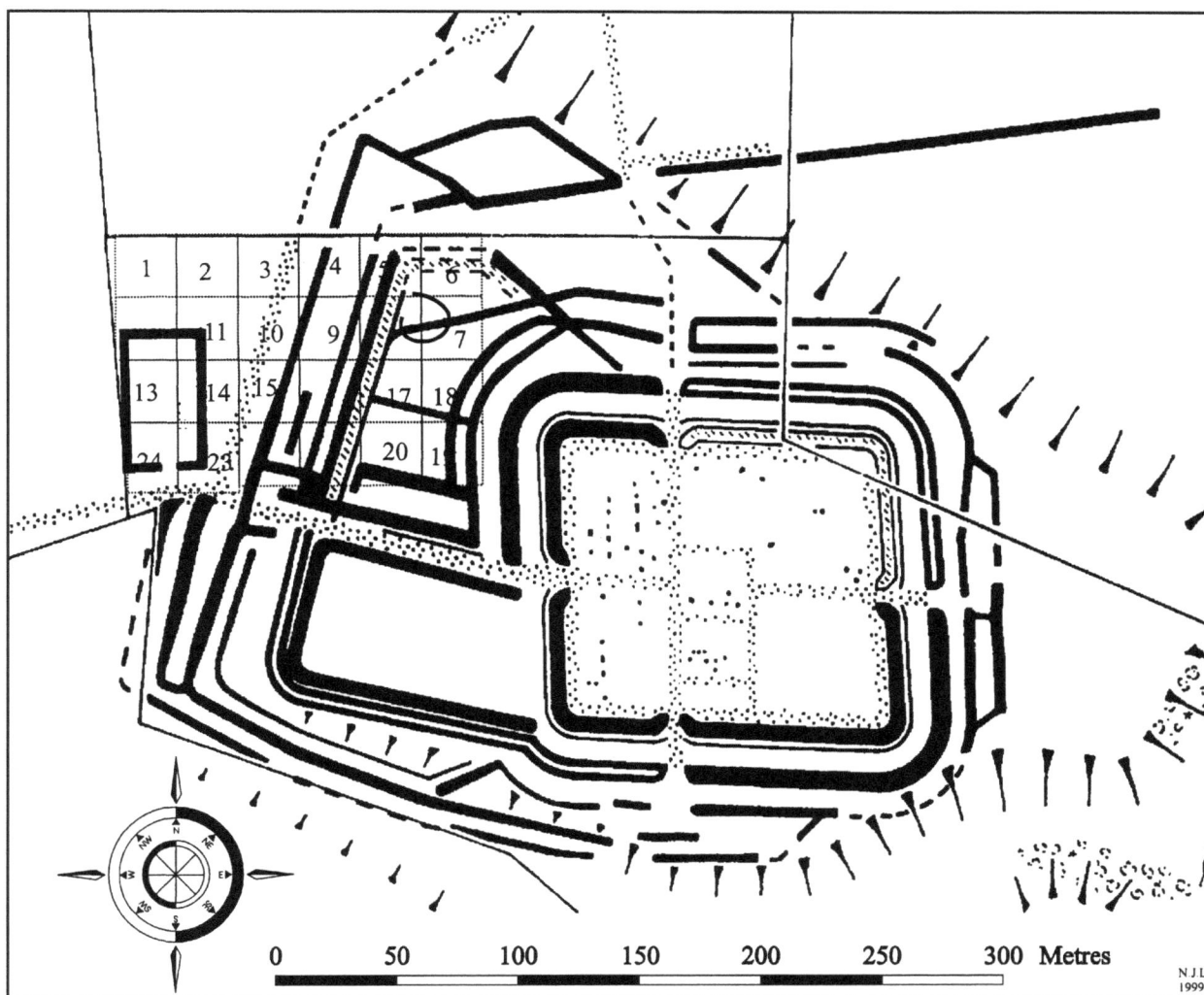

Fig 8.1. Strageath and its environs, showing the position of the resistivity grids (base plan after Frere and Wilkes).

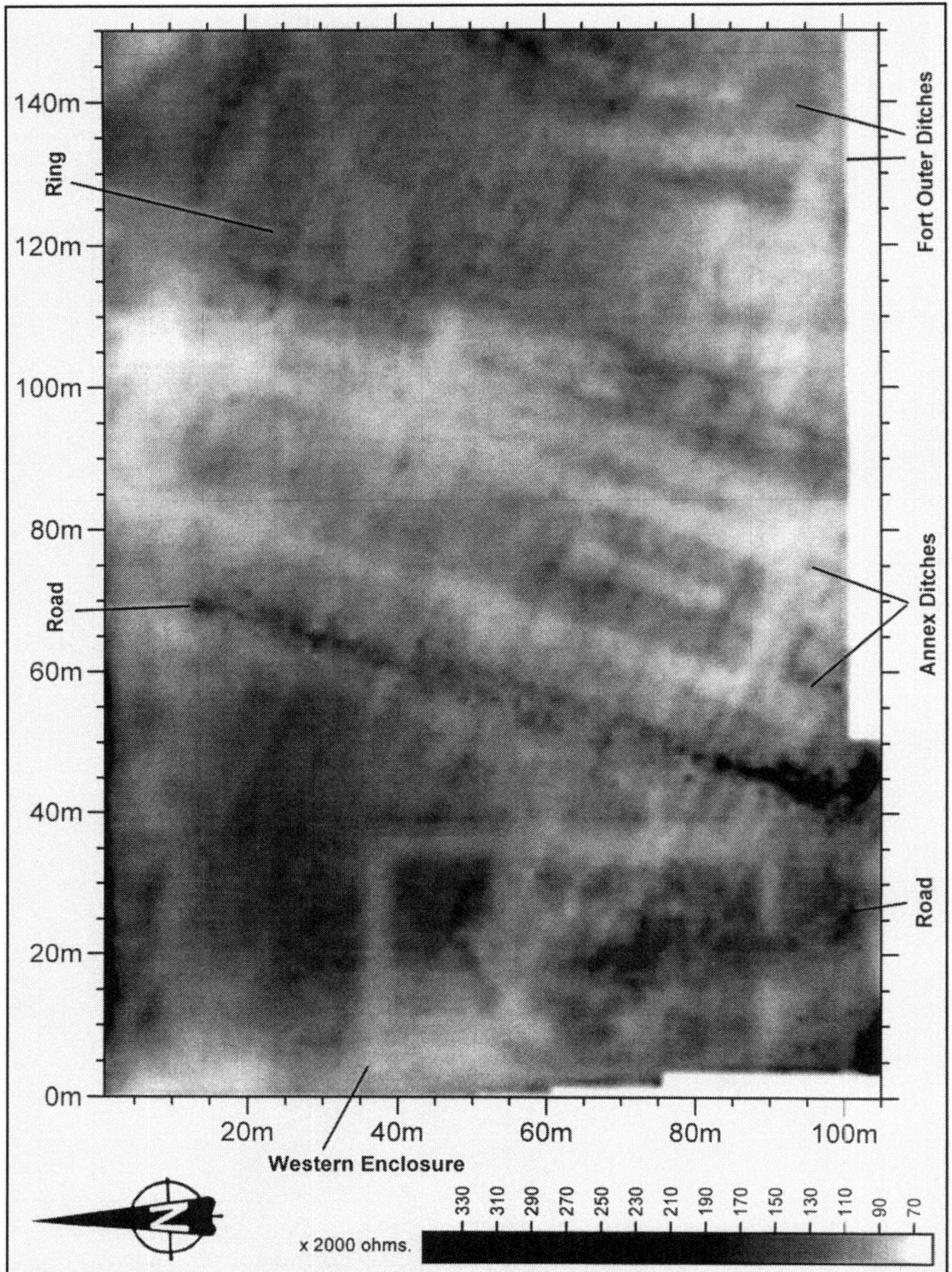

Fig 8.2. Strageath: resistivity survey.

system may now be considered untenable. It has also long been known that Strageath is one of two forts on this system that have two first century and two second century phases (Chap 1), all of which suggests that the Roman army was present in Perthshire for longer than any had imagined. Under these circumstances the system acquired potential significance for the author's research into the extra-mural settlements of forts in the north-western provinces of the Roman Empire, which has been carried out towards the award of the degree of PhD at the University of Nottingham. Part of this research has involved the examination of all forms of Roman extra-mural activity in order to assess the extent to which these settlements grew during the lifetime of the host fort. Unfortunately, for the majority of Roman forts, the situation is complicated by poor pre-excavation survey and by complex occupation patterns within the fort. However, with the Gask frontier we have the opportunity to investigate extra-mural activity within closely-defined time periods, as well as the ability to look at settlement which may have got little further than its initial phase of construction. This is particularly true at Strageath where the extra-mural remains are of some complexity, particularly to the west of the fort.

The geophysical survey was carried out using a Geoscan RM4 resistivity meter set to a 2000Ω resolution setting. The survey was laid out in $(25 \text{ m})^2$ grids from the north western corner of the field in which the fort is situated (fig 8.1) and readings were taken at 1m intervals. The resulting data were processed using the "Surfer" surface mapping suite and then plotted out, both as individual grids and as a composite image of the whole survey (fig 8.2).

The results confirm the extensive nature of the extra-mural remains at Strageath and reveal more information about several enigmatic features to the west of the fort area. Firstly, it has long been known that there were two annexed enclosures to the west of the fort, one of which was studied by the present survey. The other lies further to the south and is expected to form a primary target for further geophysical surveys at the site. Within the northern annexed enclosure aerial photographs have shown possible subdivisions of unknown date. These show clearly in the resistivity plot, but the limitations of geophysical survey mean that little further can be said about their date and it is possible that at least some of them may relate to later agricultural use of the field. Additional evidence may be gained from General Roy's (1793, pl 32) survey of the fort and its environs c.1760, in which the fort is shown under cultivation.

We can add little firm evidence for civilian usage of the extra-mural area. However, any division of the western annexed area during the Roman period is of potential significance towards postulating some form of contemporary civilian presence. It has long been known

that the fort at Strageath was occupied on successive occasions during the Roman advancement into Scotland and, as with other sites in both England and Scotland, extended occupation is likely to have attracted civilian traders and settlers. Whilst the occupation at Strageath is unlikely to have been long enough for extra-mural structures to have warranted costly replacement in stone, the presence of, as yet undetected, Roman period structures seems not improbable. It is unfortunate that the present survey was only able to use soil resistance surveying, which typically does not reveal timber features. However, the survey has, at least, shown areas – particularly within the northern annexed area – which may reward future work.

The survey did produced some startling results. Firstly, within grids 7 and 8 (fig 8.3), a rounded band of higher resistance, c. 20m in diameter, was observed amongst the defences of the northern annexed enclosure. The significance of this feature is considerable, as no trace of the feature can be located on any of the existing air photographs of the site. The feature's identity remains somewhat uncertain, but the fact that the resistivity plot shows it as an area of higher resistance may suggest that it is a rounded stone platform, or a stone foundation wall for a native dwelling, similar to that found in 2000 at the round house at East Coldoch (D J Woolliscroft pers com). The presence of high resistance bands which extend from the feature may offer the possibility that it was surrounded by a field system, although interpretation at this level is inevitably somewhat risky.

The relationship of this rounded feature with the fort and annexed defences is also somewhat ambiguous, although it does appear that part of an annex ditch may truncate the feature, as a lower resistance band is visible crossing it. This would suggest that the rounded feature pre-dates the fort, but more definite relationships are only likely to be understood through excavation.

One further discovery made by the survey, was to establish the extent of the separate ditched enclosure to the west of the annexes. This was first identified by Frere and St. Joseph (Frere and Wilkes 1989, 11) during their preliminary survey of the site. However, nothing was known of the western extent of this structure. The survey has, finally, been able to confirm that its western ditch lies just within the fort field, thus making the enclosure dimensions c. 55m (n-s), by c. 35m (e- w) over the ditches. This is an exceptional size, with an internal area of ¾ that of the southern annexed enclosure. No date is known for this feature, although it is clear that it post dates the east-to-west road running into the fort from Ardoch, as its entrance faces the road and the whole structure is aligned at right angles to it. Within this enclosure, air photographs (e.g. RCAHMS neg: PT15126) have revealed two parallel lines of pits, which may represent the post holes of a timber building and the survey located slight high resistance traces

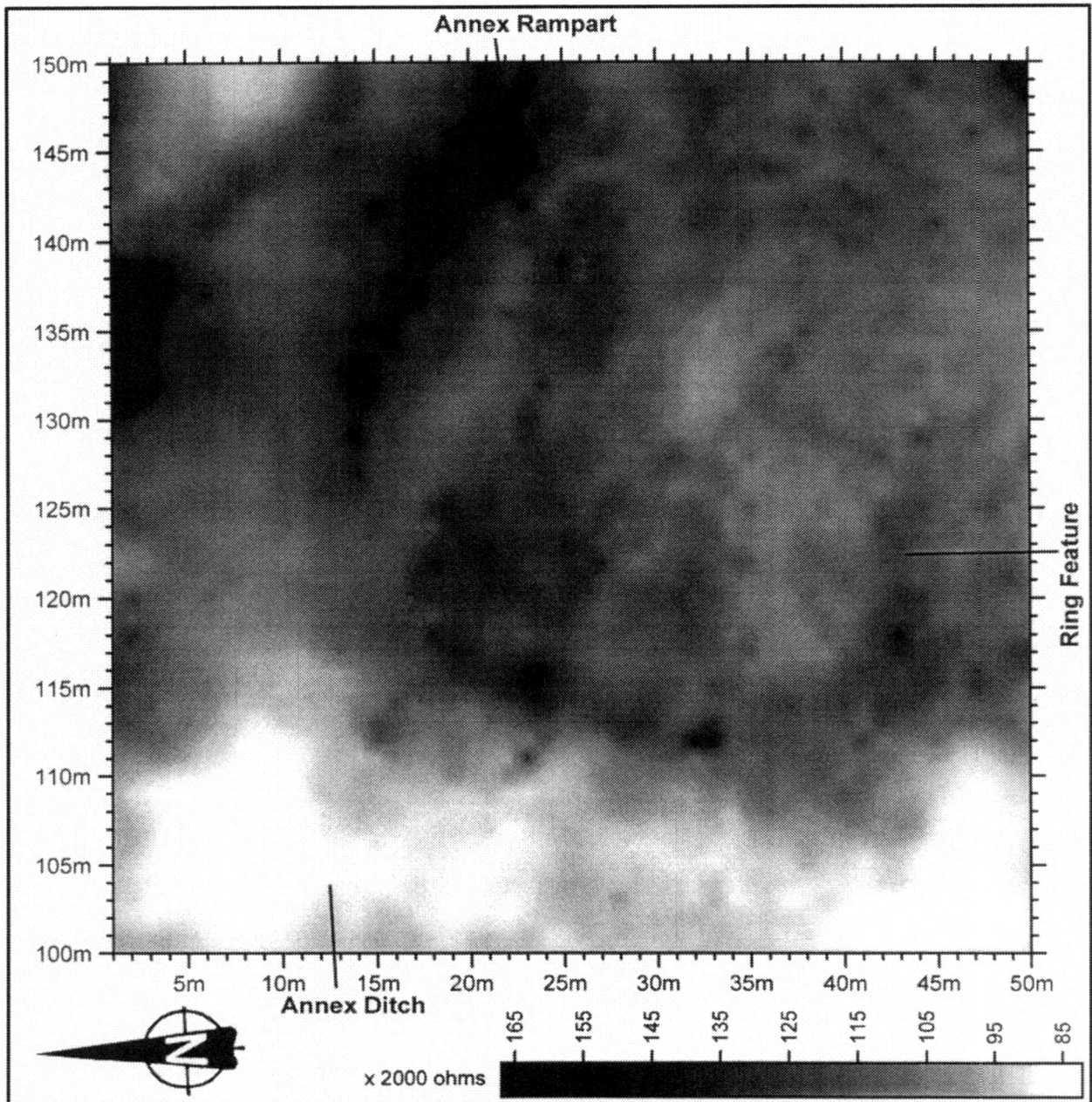

Fig 8.3. Strageath: resistivity, NW corner.

which may be the metalling of some form of hard-standing or courtyard relating to this structure. However, little more was offered by the survey as to the purpose of the enclosure.

In conclusion, the present survey has achieved most of the aims set out earlier. In particular, a more accurate picture has been obtained of the western extra-mural area of the fort, although no absolute date can be attributed to many of the features surveyed. Of the features located, perhaps the most interesting is the rectangular enclosure to the west of the annexes, which presents many difficulties in interpretation and is unparalleled at forts elsewhere in Britain. The location

of this enclosure and its likely internal structures may seem odd when one considers the extensive areas annexed to the fort. However, assuming that this feature is Roman in date, one may be able to suggest that it enclosed a *mansio* or related facility of the *cursus publicus*. Whilst it has to be admitted that many of the structures identified as *mansiones* are located within the annexed enclosures of other forts in Britain, the situation at Strageath during the Roman occupations may have precluded the inclusion of such a facility within the annexed area. An alternative might be that the feature represents a post-Roman moated enclosure similar to that at nearby Hallyards (Coleman and Perry 1997, Illus 5), but this might seem unlikely as one would have expected a medieval defended site to lie inside the fort, which is on higher ground and which might still, at the time, have had usable defenses. Despite the continued temptation to identify this feature as a *mansio*, however, the present survey does not provide enough information to be more definite and so further speculation is of limited use.

The confirmation of the road alignments to the west of the fort offers us further tantalising hints of, as yet undiscovered, extra-mural structures. In particular the north-south aligned road, after passing the enclosure mentioned above, may offer further opportunities for the search. All that can be said at present is that whilst no individual structures were located during the survey, the features which have been traced do suggest further activity which was not detectable by resistance surveying.

9. A Pair of Denarii from Findo Gask, Strathearn, Perthshire

By M A Hall

Two denarii of the late 2nd century (one of the Emperor Commodus and the other of his mother, Faustina) were found in circa 1955. The finder was a road-mender, working on the stretch of minor road between Lawrencefield and Findo Gask School, approximately 13 km or 8 miles WSW of Perth. This gives a notional NGR centring on NO 04440 1968. The circumstances of the discovery are not recorded and the finder is now deceased. The current owner was given the coins (by the finder) when a small boy and recently brought them into Perth Museum & Art Gallery for identification.

The find spot is effectively on the line of the Gask Ridge (it is no more than one mile from the Moss Side Signal Tower) and its road running north to Bertha. The question of late second century coin finds from Eastern Scotland has most recently been reviewed by Bateson & Hall (forthcoming). There Bateson linked the find of a hoard of 6 denarii from Inchyra, on the river Tay, to 5

other known hoards, all from the reign of Commodus. Two of these were found in Lanarkshire and one each was found in Perthshire, Kinross-shire and Fife (see Robertson 1978, 190-2 & 201-4). The cumulative picture these give is most likely to be one of Roman political bribery or subsidy in support of maintaining the peace on the British frontier. The date range of the two denarii in question, circa 175/80 – 191 is close enough for the coins to have been associated prior to their deposition or loss (particularly as they are from back-to-back reigns – Marcus Aurelius to his son Commodus). Given the occurrence and distribution of the Commodan hoards mentioned above the possibility of a dispersed hoard in the Findo Gask area has to be considered. In this context it is also worth bearing in mind the historically documented but now lost hoards from the vicinities of Strageath and Drummond Castle, including silver denarii of Marcus Aurelius, Diva Faustina and Commodus (and probably no later issues). These are fully described and appraised with due caution in Macdonald (1918, 231 & 263). That said we cannot discount the possibility of these two coins being isolated losses which arrived in the area as part of the pattern of trade. It should though be noted that the denarius of

Fig 9.1. The Findo Gask coins.

Commodus (cat 2 below) bears the title "Britannicus". This was added to the Emperor's titles after the supposed victory of Ulpius Marcellus (Governor of Britain) on the British frontier (Maxwell 1989, 33). Maxwell (1989, 33) also notes the possibility of re-occupation north of Hadrian's Wall at the time of Commodus – with the telling proviso that there was yet no firm evidence for this. This is a theme that John Casey has covered in recent lectures with some persuasion (pers comm D Woolliscroft). The generally accepted view of the political situation in the late second-early third century is well summarised by Armit (1999, 590-2). There, such matters are discussed in the context of souterrain closure and there is no suggestion of a late second century re-occupation beyond the Antonine Wall.

The two denarii are not particularly worn. The obverse portraits are relatively clear and sharp, as are the reverse deities, and the inscriptions are all clear. A degree of difference is discernible between the two coins however, with the Faustina Junior coin (see cat 1 below) being marginally more worn than the Commodan piece, consistent with a slightly longer circulation life. There is minor edge cracking and possible clipping on both coins. The denarius of Commodus is noticeable in having a substantial break – the upper sixth portion of the coin (taking of the top off the head of Commodus but appearing to respect the figure of Apollo on the reverse) is absent. The break appears to be of some antiquity: the break-line is uneven and pitted and shows signs of copper alloy corrosion in the middle of the coin and there is a stress fracture evident on both sides of the coin running down from the mid-point of the break. However this is comparatively recent damage, probably due to the impact of a tool at the time of discovery. The owner recalls that when given the coin (shortly after discovery) the now lost fragment was still loosely attached but broke off and was lost sometime in the 1950s. Otherwise, the wear of the coins is consistent with loss or deposition in the second century.

CATALOGUE

1. Denarius, Marcus Aurelius, commemorating Faustina Junior. Issued AD 175-80.
   Diam: 18.3mm; Weight: 3.17gms; *RIC*: 347
   Obv: DIVA FAUSTINA
   Bust of Faustina, right.
   Rev: AETER NITAS
   Aeternitas (Eternity) standing left, holding phoenix in her right hand and raising her skirt with her left.

1. Denarius, Commodus. Issued AD 190-91
   Diam: 17.6mm; Weight: 1.92gms; *RIC*: 218.
   Obv: M COMM ANT [P FEL] AUG BRIT PP
   Laureate bust of Commodus, right.
   Rev: APOL PA[L PM TR] P XVI COS VI
   Apollo standing front, head right, holding plectrum in his right hand and with his left hand holding a lyre on a column. (This is the statue of the Palatine Apollo or "Apollo of the Palatine", used as the model for coins struck to mark the 15th anniversary of Commodus's reign in 189, though the bulk of the denarii with this type belong to 191).

Acknowledgements

Thanks must go to Donal Bateson (Hunterian Museum) for chasing up RIC references on my behalf and for making some valuable comments; to Paul Adair (Perth Museum) for taking the photographs and to David Woolliscroft for bringing John Casey's comments to my attention. Particular thanks must go to the owner of the coins, who willingly brought them into Perth Museum & Art Gallery for identification and research.

10. Roman and Post-Roman Glassware Found in the Vicinity of the Gask Ridge

By Birgitta Hoffmann

Introduction

During the work of the Roman Gask Project, various items of glass have been picked up, whilst other items have been brought to the attention of Mark Hall of Perth Museum and Art Gallery. As these seem to represent a fair cross-section of the history of the Gask Ridge and this part of Perthshire, from antiquity to the modern period, and in the hope of encouraging the reporting of glass material found in the future, it was thought appropriate to present them here, in chronological order.

A Roman bottle fragment from Cargill Roman fort, Perthshire

1 fragment, shoulder of a blue-green bottle. Shoulder with vertical scratches. Small bubbles. No weathering. Dimensions: 38 mm x 20 mm Thickness: 5 mm.

Surface find, September 2000, found in the south-west corner of the field (area of the fort interior).

The fragment is part of a Roman cylindrical or rectangular bottle. These bottles are frequent finds on most sites of the late first to early third century and are the most common glass vessel found on military sites of that period.

Depending on the diameter of the neck they could be used as storage and transport vessels for liquids and some small food stuffs, such as pickles and have, most commonly, volumes of about 0.6 - 1.3 l (c. 1-3 pints), although much larger vessels also exist (Hoffmann (forthcoming).

A Roman Glass Vessel from Muirton, Perthshire: NO 105 255

Two joining fragments, rim and neck, of a colourless jug or flask; blown. Short funnel mouth, edge rolled in. Small bubbles. Milky layer of weathering.
Diameter (rim): 42 mm Diameter (neck): 22 mm. Thickness: 1 mm.
Perth Museum Inv. No: 292 ROM/18 (fig. 10.1).

Similar flaring rims with a rolled-in lip can be found on a number of Roman glass vessels. They are particularly frequent in the second and third centuries, when this form becomes the most common rim type for

Fig. 10.1. The Glass vessel from Muirton. Scale 1:1.

the numerous small jug shapes in circulation and is usually associated with the tablewares of the period.

Vessel glass is comparatively rare north of the Antonine wall (see Table 1). The best known items are the complete, or near complete, vessels from the graves at Airlie (a cylindrical beaker) and Turiff (a long-necked conical jug) (both: Curle 1932, 291). Apart from these two, glass vessels are usually found as fragments and very little can usually be said about their original shape.

Glass material from the Roman forts is quite common and usually reflects the periods of occupation of the fort, with the Flavian occupation particularly well represented. The glass assemblage from the Roman sites is usually dominated by utilitarian vessel shapes, such as bottles, with only a small percentage usually being attributable to table wares. On the native sites there seems to be a differentiation as to the vessels used, while the southern brochs such as Leckie and Fairy Knowe, Buchlyvie, favour first century cylindrical bottles, native sites in Perthshire and Angus appear to contain predominately tablewares of the second century. It is however, dangerous to assume that the usage differentiations (storage/table ware) of the Romans can be directly transferred onto the indigenous society and it cannot be ruled out that all vessel types had the same standing: as 'Roman imports' (see Table 1).

It is currently impossible to provide any further information as to the site type the vessel from Muirton came from, as it was found as a stray find. Whilst the fort at Bertha is not too far away, it has to be stressed that of all the Roman installations north of the Antonine Wall only Ardoch has so far produced firm evidence of non-defensive structures outside the fort ditches. The tombstone of Ammonius, centurion of the Coh I Hispanorum (RIB 2213) suggests that we have to expect Roman style burials outside the forts, but it is probably true that Muirton is too far away from Bertha to be a likely site for a fort cemetery.

On the other hand we also know of at least one indigenous site from the area of Perth city: a souterrain at Barnhill (NO 125 226) on the opposite bank of the Tay, which was found in the early 20th century during road construction (Hutcheson 1904, 541-7). In the same area a small statuette of Mercury was found c.30 years later (Anon, PSAS 71, 1936-7, 93f fig. 2) and, although this is far from proven, it seems likely that both relate to the same settlement. Also from Perth, but without any further information as to its origin, is a small copper-alloy bell, which is now in the National Museum of Scotland in Edinburgh (Clarke 1971, 228-230 and fig. 3,3).

At Muirton itself a Romano-Celtic head with ram-horns was discovered on a stone pile in 1965, whose closest parallel comes from the Roman fort of Netherby (Ross 1965, 36 pl. III,2). Prof Anne Robertson discussed the head, in a paper on Roman finds from non-Roman sites, as possible plunder (Robertson 1970, 205). Given the proximity of a Roman fort site, as well as the finds of Roman imports in the area of Perth, it is, however, equally possible that both items, the glass vessel and the head, were either brought in antiquity from the fort, which has now produced material from the second century AD (see chapter 3), or even from some indigenous site with strong Roman influences.

Table 1: Roman glass vessels found in North Stirlingshire, Perthshire and Angus

Site:	Vessel Type:
Roman sites:	
Cardean Roman fort (Hoffmann in preparation):	extensive range.
Inchtuthil Roman fortress (Price in: Pitts and St.Joseph 1989):	extensive range.
Cargill, Roman fort (see above):	bottle.
Strageath Roman fort (Price in: Frere and Wilkes 1989):	extensive range.
Shielhill South Roman watch tower (Woolliscroft and Hoffmann 1998):	bottle.
Ardoch Roman fort (Anderson in: Christison 1898, 453):	drinking vessels, bottle.
Carpow Roman fortress (Price in: Dore & Wilkes 1999, 561):	bottle.
Native sites and stray finds:	
Constantine's Cave, Fife (NO 632 100) (Curle 1932, 290):	bottle.
Camelon native site (NS 863 812) (Proudfoot 1978, 127f.):	jug or flask.
Keir Hill, Gargunnock (NS 706942) (McLaren 1958, 83):	?
Fairy Knowe, Buchlyvie, Stirlingshire (NS 585942) (Ingemark 1998, 335-7):	cylindrical bottle.
Leckie Broch, Stirlingshire (NS 692940) (Ingemark 1998, 336):	cylindrical bottle.
Castlehill, Stirlingshire (NS 751908) (Robertson 1970, Table III):	bowl, bottle.
Muirton, Perthshire (NO 105 255), see above:	jug or flask.
Hurly Hawkin, Angus (NO 332328) (Taylor 1982, 232, No. 57):	?
Tealing, Angus (NO 412381) (Robertson, 1970, 198-217):	bowl.
Airlie, Angus (NO 315502) (Curle 1932, 387):	cup.
Kingoldrum, Angus (NO 339554) (Curle 1932, 387):	?

Report on two glass beads found at Dunning

1. Blue, peacock blue to sky blue translucent annular glass bead. D-section. Translucency due to the presence of many very small bubbles. Wound bead. White layer of iridescence.

Outer diameter: 6 mm Inner Diameter: 2 mm Height: 3 mm.

2. Opaque white spherical bead. Pottery? Surface soft and slightly flaking. Very small drilled hole. Outer diameter: c. 6 mm Inner diameter: 1 mm Height: 6 mm.

Both found at Ashgrove, Quarry Road , Newton of Pitcairns, Dunning in 1999, now in Perth Museum & Art Gallery.

Medium blue annular glass beads are a common feature, both in the British Iron Age and Roman periods. In particular, small examples with diameters of under 1.5 cm can be found all over Britain and examples from Scotland include pieces from the Culbin Sands, and several examples from the Lowlands and the west of Scotland (Guido 1978,155-162). The dated examples span the whole period from the Iron Age to the Viking era, as well as some examples which appear to be Victorian (Guido 1978, 18). Given the pitted surface of this bead, the latter can probably be ruled out in this context. Roman examples of this type include beads from South Shields, as well as examples from Corbridge, Chester and Great Chesters (Allason-Jones and Miket 1984, 279 no's 4.35 - 4.37).

The second bead has a very carefully drilled small perforation which is only rarely encountered in Roman or prehistoric beads and it seems likely, therefore, that this is a modern example, perhaps early 20th century.

An early modern bead found in the River Almond near Bertha

The following assessment is based on three 35mm colour slides, 2 black and white photographs and a drawing of the object (Showing different aspects of it), which were send to the writer by Mr M.A. Hall of Perth Museum & Art Gallery.

The bead appears to be biconical; pentagonal cross-section; colourless with blue shimmer. The bead appears to be wound. So-called "Pentagonal bead".
Size (according to drawing): Greatest diameter: 13 mm
Inner Diameter: 3 mm Height: 8 mm.
Perth Museum Inv. No: PERGM 1998.121 (fig. 10.2)

Although initially believed to be Romano-Egyptian (Beck 1928, 17: twisted square bead), it has since been shown that this type is not usually found either in Romano-British or early Medieval contexts, with the only possible exception being a dark green, multifaceted bead from South Shields (Allason- Jones and Miket 1984, 280, fig. 4.51), which is, however, too dissimilar to be a parallel for the Bertha bead.

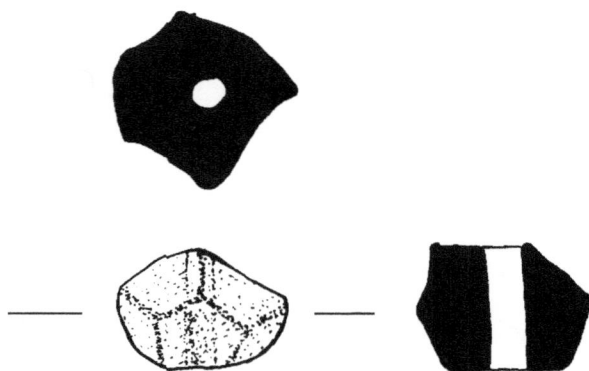

Fig 10.2: The Pentagonal bead from Bertha (Drawn by M.A.Hall, Perth Museum & Art Gallery). Scale 2:1.

In the late 1960's production debris and half finished beads of this type were found in large quantities in Amsterdam, together with tobacco pipes dating to the 17th and 18th centuries (Van der Sleen 1973, 98; 110f. Fig. 104 and frontispiece). Bead and glass production is historically attested in Amsterdam from 1602 to 1679, when production was moved to Haarlem (Karklins 1982, 113). These early 'trade beads' which are found in amber, colourless, blue and white glass, were originally produced in vast quantities and exported from the Netherlands mainly as objects for barter in Africa, Asia and America. Their occurrence in the vicinity of Perth is slightly unusual, but not entirely surprising, as we know from historical documents that Dutch beads were ordered by British entrepreneurs of the time, for trade in America up to 1727 (Karklins 1982, 113-4).

A modern glass fragment from Peel Roman tower, Perthshire

Glass trail, bright green. Thick blob of glass with drawn out trail, broken off. One large bubble in the centre of the blob. No weathering.
Peel 2000, surface find by gamekeeper.

Although glass easily deforms under the influence of heat, finds of glass trails such as this are comparatively rare, and it shows relatively little evidence of having been in contact with a surface before cooling or of preserving any trace of an original shape. As the colour, a bright green, is unusual for older glass, it is likely that this is the remains of a recent piece. In glass production similar blobs and trails occur when the temperature and texture of a batch of glass is tested and given the fact that glass was produced in Perth from 1836 onwards, it seems not impossible that this may be a translocated remnant of this glass production (Perth Museum & Art Gallery 1994).

A Modern Glass Clay pigeon from Ardoch.

8 body fragments, some joining. Mid blue. Mould-blown. Globular body with regular raised ribs in lattice work. In the centre a horizontal band with lettering which is linked and obscured by three horizontal lines. The letters KS and NOR? survive. No weathering.

Dimensions: 30 mm x 23 mm b)14 mm x 28 mm c) 23 mm x 34 mm d) 29 mm x 25 mm e) 24 mm x 26 mm f) 9 mm x 40 mm g) 13 mm x 19 mm h) 6 mm x 23 mm
Thickness: 2 mm.

Found as a surface find on the rampart, near the NE-corner of the 52.6 ha (130 acre) temporary camp at Ardoch.

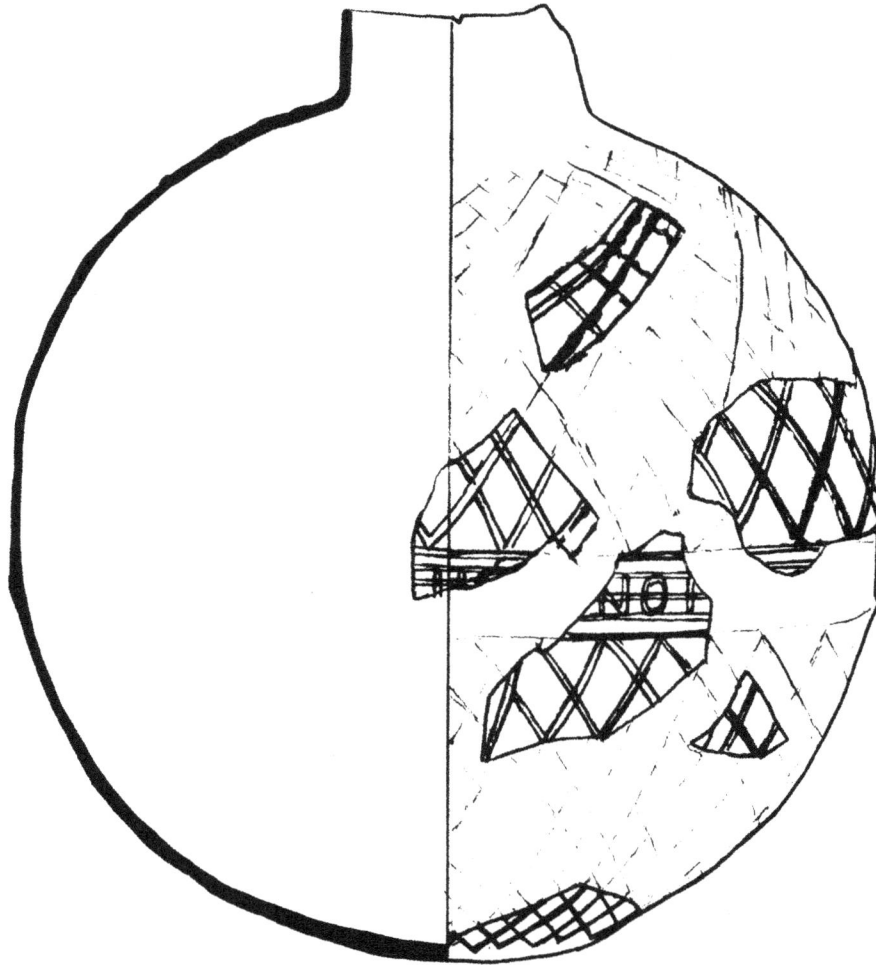

Fig. 10.3: Reconstruction of the target ball from Ardoch. Scale 1:1.

The above fragments belong to a small mould-blown glass ball, which was originally covered in evenly spaced lattice-work. In the centre of the ball, space was set apart for the inscription: NORTHERN BRITISH GLASSWORKS PERTH. The only recognisable letters on our fragments are the NOR suggesting that 'NORTHERN' was not abbreviated, as well as the upper half of the final 'KS' from the word 'GLASSWORKS'

These glass spheres were produced by John Moncrieff's Northern British Glassworks in Perth, and Perth Museum and Art Gallery has a complete example (Inv. No. 1992.243) on display. Its inscription reads "N.B.GLASSWORKS PERTH" with inverted 'S' throughout the inscription, showing that it was originally blown into a different mould from the Ardoch piece.

Similar fragments are sometimes found on archaeological sites, although rarely as concentrated, as at Birdoswald on Hadrian's Wall where the remains of c. 25 glass balls where found in the modern backfill of the haha in the garden, mostly also displaying the inscription "N.B.GLASSWORKS PERTH".

The glass balls appear to have been originally filled with feathers and used for clay pigeon shooting, although the shattering glass apparently quickly made these target balls unpopular (Lole 1997, 11). It is currently impossible to gauge the scale of production at any time, but we know from differences in the lettering that at least three different moulds must have been used. The target balls were produced in amber, blue and green glass and were last blown as a special consignment for use on board the Cunard liner Queen Mary after the Second World War (Lole 1997, 12 and pers. comm. Hildegard Berwick, Perth Museum & Art Gallery).

These glass balls appear to have been in use from the late 19th century onwards and, apart from the Northern British Glassworks, other examples were produced by Bogardus. Similar spheres from other manufacturers were filled with water, sodium bicarbonate or (of all things) carbon tetrachloride and were used as fire extinguishers (Lole 1997, 12).

People who used these target balls, explain the ribs as a means to prevent ricochets off the target and so ensure that it would break when hit. They also record that after the shoot the broken fragments of the target balls had to be collected (newspaper clipping (unsourced, c. 1970s) by Q.C.Gurney, Bawdeswell Hall, Norfolk). To judge from our fragments (which were all found close together), this did not always take place and the shattered glass must have provided a hazard to animals and unsuspecting passers-by.

Acknowledgements

My thanks to Mr M.A. Hall of Perth Museum and Art Gallery for providing access to some of the material covered and to Peter Lole (Manchester) and Hildegard Berwick (Perth Museum & Art Gallery) for their help in the research on the Ardoch vessel. Thanks are also due to Mr Bill McIntosh for providing the Peel glass trail.

Appendix 1

Roman Sites North of the Antonine Wall: Map references and National Monuments Record (Scotland) Numbers

Permanent Military Sites

Site	Map Ref.	OS 1:10,000 sheet	NMRS No
Camelon Fort.	NS 863810	NS88SE	23
Doune Fort.	NN 727012	NN70SW	36
Glenbank Fortlet.	NN 812057	NN80NW	19
Greenloaning Tower.	NN 830071	NN80NW	38
Ardoch Fort.	NN 839099	NN80NW	10
Blackhill Wood Tower.	NN 845108	NN81SW	7
Shielhill South Tower.	NN 850115	NN81SW	9
Shielhill North Tower.	NN 856122	N81SE	8
Kaims Castle Fortlet.	NN 861129	NN81SE	1
Westerton Tower.	NN 873146	NN81SE	7
Strageath Fort.	NN 898180	NN81NE	2
Parkneuk Tower.	NN 917185	NN91NW	6
Raith Tower.	NN 932185	NN91NW	2
Ardunie Tower.	NN 947188	NN91NW	3
Roundlaw Tower.	NN 958189	NN91NE	2
Kirkhill Tower.	NN 968188	NN91NE	4
Muir O' Fauld Tower.	NN 982190	NN91NE	5
Gask House Tower.	NN 990192	NN91NE	3
Witch Knowe Tower.	NN 998195	NN91NE	6
Moss Side Tower.	NO 008199	NO01NW	14
Midgate Fortlet & ?Tower.	NO 021204	NO02SW	6
Westmuir Tower.	NO 029208	NO02SW	8
Peel Tower.	NO 060232	NO02SE	38
Huntingtower Tower.	NO 072247	NO02SE	65
Bertha Fort.	NO 097268	NO02NE	25
Carpow Fort.	NO 207179	NO21NW	24
Cargill Fortlet.	NO 163377	NO13NE	26
Cargill Fort.	NO 166379	NO13NE	27
Black Hill Tower.	NO 176392	NO13NE	7
Cardean Fort.	NO 289460	NO24NE	12
Drumquhassle Fort.	NS 484872	NS48NE	13
Malling/Menteith Fort.	NN 564000	NN50SE	6
Bochastle Fort.	NN 614079	NN60NW	17
Dalginross Fort.	NN 772210	NN72SE	2
Fendoch Fort.	NN 919283	NN92NW	2
Fendoch ? Tower.	NN 908284	NN92NW	1
Inchtuthil Fortress.	NO 125397	NO13NW	5
Inverquharity Fort.	NO 404581	NO45NW	10
Stracathro Fort.	NO 617657	NO66NW	18

Temporary Camps

Site	Map Ref.	OS 1:10,000 sheet	NMRS No
Auchinhove.	NJ 463516	NJ45SE	5
Muiryfold	NJ 489520	NJ45SE	2
Bellie.	NJ 355611	NJ36SE	8
Durno	NJ 697273	NJ62NE	31
Kintore Deer's Den.	NJ 786161	NJ71NE	28
Kintore II. ?camp	NJ 784175	NJ71NE	N/A

Site.	Map Ref.	OS 1:10,000 sheet	NMRS No
Glenmailen/Ythan Wells	NJ 655381	NJ63NE	2
Burnfield Rothiemay.	NJ 540476	NJ54NW	25
Innerpeffray West.	NN 907182	NN91NW	25
Innerpeffray East.	NN 916182	NN91NW	14
Shielhill South ?camp.	NN 852114	NN81SW	N/A
Ardoch Group	various	NN80NW	various
Aldonie Cottage, ? camp.	NN 855135	NN81SE	9
Strageath Group.	various	NN81NE	various
Raith.	NN 932185	NN91NW	N/A
Dalginross Group.	various	NN72SE	1 & 21
Callender (doubtful)	NN 632074	NN60NW	6
Bochastle	NN 611077	NN60NW	3
Gask House.	NN 990190	NN91NE	9
Malling	NN 564997	NN59NE	13
Lake of Menteith.	NN 560000	NN50SE	16
Auchterarder. ?camp.	NN 948136	NN91SW	N/A
Dunblane Hillside.	NN 775006	NN70SE	11
Netherton ? camp.	NN 743020	NN70SW	21
Dornock.	NN 878190	NN81NE	14
Inverquharity.	NN 406580	NO45NW	24
Eassie.	NO 351466	NO34NE	26
Finavon.	NO 496574	NO45NE	21
Longforgan.	NO 298304	NO23SE	18
Cardean.	NO 299463	NO24NE	15
Invergowrie.	NO 344299	NO32NW	26
Edenwood.	NO 357116	NO31SE	39
Gagie.	NO 448383	NO43NW	23
Lunanhead.	NO 468521	NO45SE	11
Marcus	NO 511580	NO55NW	37
Dun.	NO 689595	NO65NE	21
Carpow.	NO 210175	NO21NW	58
Carey/Abernethy.	NO 174165	NO11NE	27
Grassy Walls.	NO 105280	NO12NW	8
Kair House.	NO 767767	NO77NE	1
Balmakewan.	NO 665666	NO66NE	5
Kirkbuddo.	NO 490442	NO44SE	15
Keithock.	NO 610639	NO66SW	1
Raedykes.	NO 841902	NO89SW	2
Normandykes.	NO 829993	NO89NW	1
Kinnell.	NO 613505	NO65SW	26
St.Madoes/Nether Mains.	NO 209196	NO21NW	39
Lintrose/Campmuir.	NO 220376	NO23NW	5
Auchtermuchty.	NO 242118	NO21SW	17
Bonnytown.	NO 546127	NO51SW	14
Battledykes/Oathlaw.	NO 458555	NO45NE	12
Dunning.	NO 024150	NO01NW	7
Forteviot.	NO 039175	NO01NW	1
Inchtuthil Group.	NO 1139	NO13NW	5
Easter Powside.	NO 056245	NO02SE	52
Steed Stalls.	NO 115427	NO14SW	15
Scone Palace.	NO 104271	NO12NW	14
Stracathro.	NO 613656	NO66NW	13
East Mid Lamberkine.	NO 074225	NO02SE	10
Craigarnhall.	NS 756985	NS79NE	20
Ochtertyre.	NS 745982	NS79NW	51
Dunipace/Househill.	NS 843825	NS88SW	9
Lochlands I, Camelon.	NS 856817	NS88SE	7
Lochlands II, Camelon.	NS 853819	NS88SE	96

Site.	Map Ref.	OS 1:10,000 sheet.	NMRS No
Carmuirs D-F/Three Bridges.	NS 857808	NS88SE	22
Wester Carmuirs, Camelon.	NS 851805	NS88SE	27
Carmuirs E.Junction, ?camp	NS 859810	NS88SE	35
Carmuirs, Lochlands.	NS 853816	NS88SE	66
Bogton.	NS 854812	NS88SE	67
Waterside Mains/Alva.	NS 869968	NS89NE	N/A
Carberry/Dunnikier ?camp.	NT 284947	NT29SE	28

Other Sites Mentioned.

Site.	Map Ref.	OS 1:10,000 sheet.	NMRS No
Upper Quoigs.	NN 822063	NN80NW	36
Cuiltburn.	NN 89231765	NN81NE	19
Dornock.	NN 882188	NN81NE	25
Upper Cairnie.	NO 038192	NO01NW	4 & 17
East Coldoch	NS 703986	NS79NW	35

Appendix 2

Gask Tower Data and Dimensions

Greenloaning

Distance from western neighbour (Glenbank fortlet): 2,300m, 2750m from NE neighbour, Ardoch fort.
Height above OD: 121m.
Distance from road: c. 11m.
Direction from road: South-east.
Number of ditches: 2.
Ditch shape in plan: Both circular.
Signs of outer upcast mound: Resistivity.
Ditch entrance width: Inner, 3.6m. Outer, 11.1m.
Ditch width and depth: Inner, 1.54 - 2.15m (Av, 1.91m) wide x 0.54 - 0.46m (Av 0.54m) deep. Outer, 1.03 - 1.74m (Av, 1.45m) wide x 0.28 - 0.49m (Av, 0.4m) deep.
Ditch external diameter: Inner, 15.54m. Outer, 24.7m.
Inter-ditch spacing: 3.2m.
Interior diameter: 12.5m.
Entrance orientation: NW, towards road.
Tower shape and size: Rectangular, only three posts located but c. 5.25m (n-s) x 4.25m (e-w), or 22.31m².
Tower orientation: Short axis faces entrance.
Evidence for internal rampart: ?turf in ditch.
Dating evidence: Possible Roman coarse ware.
Other features: 2-3 tower phases. Rear tower uprights very close to ditch lip and so may be set in rampart.
Current condition: Crop mark
Refs: Woolliscroft and Hoffmann, 1997.

Blackhill Wood

Distance from W neighbour (Ardoch fort): 900m.
Height above OD: 140m.
Distance from road: 15m.
Direction from road: North-west.
Number of ditches: 2.
Ditch shape in plan: Both sub-circular.
Signs of outer upcast mound: Excavation.
Ditch entrance width: Unknown (area damaged by later temporary camp).
Ditch width and depth: Inner, 2.0 - 2.75m (Av, 2.38m) wide x 0.5 - 1.2m (Av, c. 0.72m) deep. Outer, 2.5 - 3.4m (Av, c. 2.45m) wide x 0.4 - 0.55m (Av, c. 0.48m) deep.
Ditch external diameter: Inner, Av, 16.94m. Outer, Av, 25.75m
Inter-ditch spacing: 1.6 - 2.5m.
Interior diameter: 11.2 - 12.3m.
Entrance orientation: SE towards road.
Tower shape and size: Roughly Square , only 3 posts were located but c. (3.6m)² or 12.96m².
Tower orientation: N/A, square.
Evidence for internal rampart: Rampart base.

Dating evidence: None except site morphology.
Other features: 2 tower phases. Oven set in outer ditch, but may derive from later temporary camp.
Current condition: Invisible at surface in wood.
Refs: Glendinning and Dunwell, 2000.

Shielhill South

Distance from western neighbour: 875m.
Height above OD: 155m.
Distance from road: c. 15m.
Direction from road: North-west.
Number of ditches: 2.
Ditch shape in plan: Inner, sub-rectangular. Outer sub-circular.
Signs of outer upcast mound: None.
Ditch entrance width: Inner, 2.76m. Outer, unknown.
Ditch width and depth: Inner, 1.1 - 1.3m (Av, 1.16m) wide x 0.33 - 0.64m (Av 0.47m) deep. Outer, 0.54 - 1.64m (Av, 0.99m) wide x 0.24 - 0.47m (Av 0.36m) deep.
Ditch external diameter: Inner, 15.6m. Outer, 24.3m.
Inter-ditch spacing: 3.5m.
Interior diameter: 13.3m.
Entrance orientation: South-east, towards road.
Tower shape and size: Irregular rectangle with sides 3.45m (W), 3.6m (N), 3.7m (E) and 3.1m (S), or approx 12m².
Tower orientation: No real long axis.
Evidence for internal rampart: ?turf slip in ditch.
Dating evidence: Late 1st century Roman glass. St.Joseph claimed to have found native Iron Age pottery although no detail was given. This find has recently been relocated in the National Museum of Scotland and its identity has been confirmed by the Gask Project's Prehistorian: Ms C. McGill.
Other features: 2-3 tower phases. Burning including burnt daub from demolition.
Current condition: Crop mark
Refs: St.Joseph, 1976, 22 and Woolliscroft and Hoffmann 1998.

Shielhill North

Distance from western neighbour: 950m., 875m to E neighbour Kaims Castle fortlet.
Height above OD: 193m.
Distance from road: 10m.
Direction from road: North-west.
Number of ditches: 2.
Ditch shape in plan: Inner, sub-rectangular. Outer, sub-circular.
Signs of outer upcast mound: Resistivity.
Ditch entrance width: Inner c. 3.3m, c. 11m.
Ditch width and depth: Inner 1.9m x 0.43m. Outer 1.31 x 0.2 - 0.37m
Ditch external diameter: Inner, c. 16m. Outer, c.24m.

Inter-ditch spacing: c. 2.4m.
Interior diameter: c. 13m.
Entrance orientation: South-east towards road.
Tower shape and size: Rectangular, c. 4.5m (e-w) x 3.5m (n-s), or 15.75m^2.
Tower orientation: Short axis faces entrance.
Evidence for internal rampart: Turf in ditch.
Dating evidence: None except site morphology.
Other features: Road quarry pit in entrance. Loop in Roman road by-passes site. Burnt daub from demolition.
Current condition: Crop mark
Refs: St.Joseph, 1976, 22 and Chapter 7.

Westerton

Distance from Western neighbour (Kaims Castle): 2,300m, 4,200m, from NE neighbour, Strageath.
Height above OD: 140m.
Distance from road: 10m.
Direction from road: North-west.
Number of ditches: 1.
Ditch shape in plan: Circular.
Signs of outer upcast mound: None.
Ditch entrance width: 1.2m.
Ditch width and depth: 1.5 - 2.8m (Av c. 2.1m) wide x 0.6 - 0.98m (Av 0.77m) deep.
Ditch external diameter: 18.44m.
Interior diameter: 13.9m
Entrance orientation: South-east towards road.
Tower shape and size: Rectangle, 2.5m (n-s) x 3.8m (e-w), or 9.5m^2.
Tower orientation: Short axis faces entrance.
Evidence for internal rampart: Turf in ditch.
Dating evidence: Possible Flavian pottery from ditch fill.
Other features: Probably 2 tower phases. Possible external ladder base on road side of tower. Ditch is of the asymmetrical 'fossa punica' type with a near vertical outer face.
Current condition: Cropmark
Refs: Hanson and Friell 1995.

Parkneuk

Distance from W neighbour (Strageath): 1,750m.
Height above OD: 56m.
Distance from road: c. 25m.
Direction from road: South.
Number of ditches: 1.
Ditch shape in plan: Sub-circular.
Signs of outer upcast mound: Slight earthwork.
Ditch entrance width: 2.44m.
Ditch width and depth: 3.66 wide x uncertain, but probably 0.9 - 1.2m deep.
Ditch external diameter: 22.5m.
Interior diameter: 15.9m.

Entrance orientation: North, towards road.
Tower shape and size: Rectangular, c. 3.05m (e-w) x 3.35m (n-s) or 10.22m^2, but only 3 posts excavated.
Tower orientation: Short axis faces entrance.
Evidence for internal rampart: Earthwork. and excavation.
Dating evidence: None except site morphology.
Other features: Unusually large for this area of the system.
Current condition: Well preserved earthwork
Refs: Robertson 1974, 21ff

Raith

Distance from western neighbour: 1,520m.
Height above OD: 91m.
Distance from road: c. 170m.
Direction from road: South.
Number of ditches: None found.
Ditch shape in plan: Unknown.
Signs of outer upcast mound: None.
Ditch entrance width: Unknown.
Ditch width and depth: Unknown.
Ditch external diameter: Unknown.
Interior diameter: Unknown.
Entrance orientation: Unknown.
Tower shape and size: Square, (approx 2.74m)^2 or c. 7.51m^2.
Tower orientation: No long axis.
Evidence for internal rampart: None.
Dating evidence: None except site morphology. Pottery was found, but has disappeared without analysis.
Other features: Large oak fragments were found, in a post hole along with remains of small hazel and willow branches and a barley grain. Site identity uncertain. May be tower or fortlet.
Current condition: Cropmark
Refs: Christison 1901, 28f.

Ardunie

Distance from western neighbour: 1,510m.
Height above OD: 65m.
Distance from road: c. 10m.
Direction from road: South.
Number of ditches: 1.
Ditch shape in plan: Sub-circular.
Signs of outer upcast mound: Slight earthwork.
Ditch entrance width: c. 2.5m.
Ditch width and depth: c. 2.4m wide as surface feature. Depth unknown.
Ditch external diameter: 19.2m.
Interior diameter: 14.4m.
Entrance orientation: North towards road.
Tower shape and size: Unknown (unexcavated).
Tower orientation: Unknown.
Evidence for internal rampart: Slight earthwork.

Dating evidence: None except site morphology.
Other features: None No excavation has taken place here.
Current condition: Well preserved earthwork.
Refs: Crawford 1949, 52 and 136.

Roundlaw

Distance from western neighbour: 1,110m.
Height above OD: c. 83m.
Distance from road: c. 20m.
Direction from road: North.
Number of ditches: 1.
Ditch shape in plan: Circular.
Signs of outer upcast mound: None.
Ditch entrance width: 1.83m.
Ditch width and depth: 2.13 wide x 0.61 - 1.22m (Av 0.92m) deep.
Ditch external diameter: 18.76m.
Interior diameter: 14.5m.
Entrance orientation: South towards road.
Tower shape and size: Rectangular, 3.05m (e-w) x 4.25m (n-s), or 12.96m^2.
Tower orientation: Short axis faces entrance.
Evidence for internal rampart: Turf in ditch.
Dating evidence: None except site morphology.
Other features: The ditch is of the "fossa punica" type with a near vertical outer face (although no section drawings are known). Oak fragments and Iron nails were found in the northern post holes.
Current condition: Cropmark.
Refs: Robertson 1974, 24ff. For Oak identification, Woolliscroft forthcoming (a).

Kirkhill

Distance from western neighbour: 960m.
Height above OD: 91m.
Distance from road: c. 40m.
Direction from road: South.
Number of ditches: 1.
Ditch shape in plan: Circular.
Signs of outer upcast mound: Earthwork.
Ditch entrance width: Roughly 1.4m.
Ditch width and depth: Roughly 3.66 wide x 1.22m deep.
Ditch external diameter: c. 21.34m.
Interior diameter: c. 14.02m.
Entrance orientation: North towards road.
Tower shape and size: Square, (2.9m)^2 or 8.41m^2.
Tower orientation: No long axis.
Evidence for internal rampart: Faint earthwork.
Dating evidence: None except site morphology.
Other features: None.
Current condition: Well preserved earthwork.
Refs: Christison 1901, 28.

Muir O' Fauld

Distance from western neighbour: 1,440m.
Height above OD: 110m.
Distance from road: c. 15m.
Direction from road: South.
Number of ditches: 1.
Ditch shape in plan: Circular.
Signs of outer upcast mound: Earthwork.
Ditch entrance width: c. 2.59m.
Ditch width and depth: c. 3.25 wide as earthwork. Depth unknown.
Ditch external diameter: 22.2m.
Interior diameter: 15.7m.
Entrance orientation: North towards road.
Tower shape and size: Unknown.
Tower orientation: Unknown.
Evidence for internal rampart: Slight earthwork.
Dating evidence: None except site morphology.
Other features: None.
Current condition: Well preserved earthwork. *Refs:* Christison 1901, 27.

Gask House

Distance from western neighbour: 870m.
Height above OD: 115m.
Distance from road: c. 10m.
Direction from road: South.
Number of ditches: 1.
Ditch shape in plan: Sub-circular.
Signs of outer upcast mound: Earthwork.
Ditch entrance width: Less than 2.7m.
Ditch width and depth: 2.7 - 3.35m (Av c. 3.03m) wide x 0.9m deep.
Ditch external diameter: 22.12m.
Interior diameter: 16.97m.
Entrance orientation: NNW towards road.
Tower shape and size: Rectangular, 3.05m (e-w) x 2.44m (n-s) or 7.44m^2.
Tower orientation: Long axis faces entrance.
Evidence for internal rampart: Earthwork and excavation.
Dating evidence: Flavian mortarium fragment from ditch fill.
Other features: Tower slightly to rear of centre. Small temporary camp to immediate South.
Current condition: Well preserved earthwork. *Refs:* Christison 1901, 26f and Robertson 1974, 18ff.

Witch Knowe

Distance from western neighbour: 800m.
Height above OD: 127m.
Distance from road: c. 70m.
Direction from road: North.
Number of ditches: 1.

Ditch shape in plan: Sub-circular.
Signs of outer upcast mound: Earthwork.
Ditch entrance width: 1.83m.
Ditch width and depth: 4.27m wide x 1.83m deep.
Ditch external diameter: 21.95m.
Interior diameter: 13.41m.
Entrance orientation: South towards road.
Tower shape and size: Rectangular, 3.35m x 2.74m, or 9.18m^2.
Tower orientation: Long axis probably faces entrance. No plan is provided and Christison is not specific, but elsewhere he generally gives dimensions in the order e-w before n-s.
Evidence for internal rampart: None.
Dating evidence: None except site morphology.
Other features: None.
Current condition: Well preserved earthwork. *Refs:* Christison 1901, 26.

Moss Side

Distance from western neighbour: 1,120m.
Height above OD: 134m.
Distance from road: c. 60m.
Direction from road: North.
Number of ditches: 1.
Ditch shape in plan: Circular.
Signs of outer upcast mound: None.
Ditch entrance width: c. 3m from air photographs.
Ditch width and depth: Width approx 2.9m from air photographs. Depth unknown.
Ditch external diameter: Approx 21m from Air photographs.
Interior diameter: c. 15.24m.
Entrance orientation: South towards road.
Tower shape and size: Square, (3.35m)^2 or 11.23m^2.
Tower orientation: No long axis.
Evidence for internal rampart: Excavation.
Dating evidence: None except site morphology.
Other features: Tower uprights replaced by sleeper beams, which may thus represent 2nd phase.
Current condition: Cropmark
Refs: Christison 1901, 29f.

Midgate/Thorney Hill.

Distance from western neighbour: 1,400m.
Height above OD: 147m.
Distance from road: c. 30m.
Direction from road: North.
Number of ditches: 1.
Ditch shape in plan: Oval to fit narrow knoll.
Signs of outer upcast mound: None.
Ditch entrance width: 1.45m.
Ditch width and depth: 3.05m wide x 1.52m deep.
Ditch external diameter: Oval, 21.34m (e-w) x 15.5m (n-s).

Interior diameter: 15.24m (e-w) x 9.4m (n-s)
Entrance orientation: South towards road.
Tower shape and size: Unknown, no posts found.
Tower orientation: Unknown.
Evidence for internal rampart: None.
Dating evidence: None except site morphology.
Other features: Very close (c. 13m) to E neighbour, Midgate fortlet. Identity as a tower has been questioned.
Current condition: Very faint surface feature.
Refs: Christison 1901, 32ff, Woolliscroft 1993, 304ff and Hanson and Friell 1995, 514.

Westmuir

Distance from western neighbour: 915m.
Height above OD: 145m.
Distance from road: c. 40m.
Direction from road: North.
Number of ditches: 1.
Ditch shape in plan: Circular.
Signs of outer upcast mound: None.
Ditch entrance width: Approx 1.5m from air photograph.
Ditch width and depth: Width approx 2m from Air photograph. Depth unknown.
Ditch external diameter: Approx 15m from Air photograph.
Interior diameter: Approx 11m from air photograph.
Entrance orientation: South towards road.
Tower shape and size: Faint indications of post holes on RCAHMS air photo, neg B5100, suggest a rectangular structure roughly 4.07m (e-w) x 3.01m (n-s), or 12.25m^2.
Tower orientation: Air photo indications suggest that the long axis faces the entrance.
Evidence for internal rampart: None.
Dating evidence: None except site morphology.
Other features: None.
Current condition: Cropmark
Refs: St.Joseph 1965, 82.

Peel

Distance from western neighbour: 3975m
Height above OD: 65m.
Distance from road: Exact road uncertain here, but c. 50m
Direction from road: South.
Number of ditches: 1
Ditch shape in plan: Circular.
Signs of outer upcast mound: None.
Ditch entrance width: c. 3m.
Ditch width and depth: 2.05m wide x 0.84m deep.
Ditch external diameter: 15.7m
Interior diameter: 11.6m
Entrance orientation: N, towards road.
Tower shape and size: Unknown.

Tower orientation: Unknown.
Evidence for internal rampart: Turf in ditch.
Dating evidence: None except site morphology.
Other features: Iron Age tool found in turf deposit in ditch, probably from internal rampart.
Current condition: Crop mark
Refs: Chapter 6

West Mains of Huntingtower

Distance from western neighbour: 1,940m, 3,175m from NE neighbour, Bertha fort.
Height above OD: 46m.
Distance from road: Approx 30m (road's exact position somewhat uncertain).
Direction from road: South-east.
Number of ditches: 1.
Ditch shape in plan: Circular.
Signs of outer upcast mound: None.
Ditch entrance width: 3.22m.
Ditch width and depth: 2.14 - 2.88m (Av 2.45m) wide x 0.64 - 0.92 (Av 0.76m) deep.
Ditch external diameter: 16.44m (e-w) x 15.87m (n-s), Av 16.16m.
Interior diameter: 12.1m (e-w) x 10.96m (n-s), Av 11.53m.
Entrance orientation: North-west towards road.
Tower shape and size: Irregular, sides are 4.3m (N), 3.1m (S) and 3.2m (E&W), area c. 12m^2.
Tower orientation: Longest side faces entrance.
Evidence for internal rampart: Rampart base.
Dating evidence: Roman coarse pottery.
Other features: Tower built at rear of enclosure with

rear uprights set in rampart.
Current condition: Cropmark
Refs: Woolliscroft forthcoming (a).

Black Hill.

Distance from western neighbour: N/A. On current evidence the site appears to be an independent tower and not part of the Gask line, but the possibility of the Gask towers extending north of the Tay cannot be ruled out.
Height above OD: 63m.
Distance from road: None known.
Direction from road: None known.
Number of ditches: 1.
Ditch shape in plan: Sub-rectangular.
Signs of outer upcast mound: Earthwork and excavation.
Ditch entrance width: 1.91m.
Ditch width and depth: Both excavations reports are very vague on this and Richmond published no section, but approx 3m wide x 0.92m deep.
Ditch external diameter: Approx 24m.
Interior diameter: c. 15.63m.
Entrance orientation: North.
Tower shape and size: Square, (4.27m)^2, or 18.23m^2.
Tower orientation: No long axis.
Evidence for internal rampart: Earthwork and excavation.
Dating evidence: Site morphology and possible Roman glass, nails and fibula pin.
Other features: Founded on at least five posts, rather than the four of the whole of the Gask series.
Current condition: Earthwork
Refs: Abercromby 1904 and Richmond 1940.

Bibliography

Abbreviations

RIB = Collingwood, R G and Wright, R P 1965, *The Roman Inscriptions of Britain*, Oxford.

Ancient Writers

Frontinus, *Strategematon*, Loeb edition, 1969, Trans: Bennett, C E.

Pliny the Elder, *Naturalis Historia*, Loeb edition, Trans: H Rackham.

Statius, Silvae, V,II, Laudes Crispini Vetti Bolani Filii. Loeb edition, 1955, Trans: Mozley, J H.

Tacitus, *De Vita et Moribus Iulii Agrigolae*, Loeb edition, 1914, Trans: Peterson, W.

Modern Writers

Abercromby, J 1904 'Excavations Made on the Estate of Meikleour Perthshire in May 1903', *Proc Soc Antiq Scot*, 38, 82-96.

Adamson, H C 1979 'The Roman Fort at Bertha', in Breeze D J (ed) *Roman Scotland Some Recent Excavations*, Edinburgh, 33ff.

Adamson, H C and Gallagher, D B 1986. 'The Roman Fort at Bertha: the 1973 Excavation', *Proc Soc Antiq Scot*, 116, 195ff.

Allason-Jones, L & Miket, R 1984 *The Catalogue of the Small Finds from South Shields Roman Fort*, Newcastle.

Anderson, W A 1956 'The Roman Fort at Bochastle', *Trans Glasgow Arch Soc* (New ser 14), 35-,63.

Armit, I 1999 'The Abandonment of Souterrains: Evolution, Catastrophe or Dislocation?', *Proc Soc Antiq Scot* 129, 577-96.

Barclay, G J 1983 'Sites of the Third Millennium bc to the First Millennium ad at North Mains, Strathallan, Perthshire', *Proc Soc Antiq Scot*, 113, 122-281.

Bateson, D & Hall, M forthcoming, 'Inchyra, Perthshire', in *Coin Hoards From Roman Britain* XI. (London).

Beck, H C 1928 'Classification and Nomenclature of Beads and Pendants', *Archaeologia* 77, 1-76.

Bellhouse, R L 1952 'A Newly Discovered Roman Road from Drumburgh to Kirkbride', *CW*(2), 52, 41-45.

Birley, A R 1976 'The Date of Mons Groupius', *Liverpool Class Monthly*, 1.2, 179-90.

Birley, E 1953 *Roman Britain and the Roman Army*, Kendal.

Boyd, W E 1984. 'Environmental Change and Iron Age Land Management in the Area of the Antonine Wall, Central Scotland: a Summary', *GAJ*, 11, 75-81.

Breeze, D J 1982 *The Northern Frontiers of Roman Britain*, London.

Breeze, D J 1983 'The Roman Forts at Ardoch', in O'Connor, A and Clarke, D V *From the Stone Age to the Forty Five*, Edinburgh, 224ff.

Breeze, D J 1988 'Why Did the Romans Fail to Conquer Scotland?', *Proc Soc Antiq Scot*, 118, 3-22.

Breeze, D J 2000 'The Romans in Perthshire' in Perthshire Society of Natural Science, Archaeological and Historical Section (ed) *Dirt, Dust and Development, 50 Years of Perthshire Archaeology*, Perth.

Butler, S 1989 'Pollen Analysis From the West Rampart' in Frere, S S & Wilkes, J J 1989 *Strageath, Excavations Within the Roman Fort 1973-86*. Britannia Monograph Series No.9, London, 272-274.

Caprino, C 1955 *La Colonna Di Marco Aurelio*, Rome.

Caruana, I D 1997 'Maryport and the Flavian Conquest of North Britain', in Wilson, R J A (ed) *Roman Maryport and its Setting*, Nottingham 40 -51.

Caruana, I D forthcoming *The Roman Forts at Carlisle: excavations at Annetwell Street, 1973-84*.

Christison, D J 1901 'Excavations Undertaken by the Society of Antiquaries of Scotland of Earthworks Adjoining the "Roman Road" Between Ardoch and Dupplin Perthshire', *Proc Soc Antiq Scot*, 35, 16-43.

Christison, D J and Cunningham, J H 1898. 'Account of the Excavation of the Roman Station at Ardoch, Perthshire Undertaken by the Society of Antiquaries of Scotland in 1896-97', *Proc Soc Antiq Scot*, 32, 399ff.

Clarke, D V 1971 'Four Roman Bells from Scotland', *Proc Soc Antiq Scot* 103, 228-231.

Coleman, R and Perry, D 1997 'Moated Sites in Tayside and Fife' *Tayside and Fife Archaeol J*, 3, 176-187.

Cool, H E M and Price, J 1995 *Roman vessel glass from excavations in Colchester, 1971-85*. Colchester Archaeological Report 8.

Crawford, O G S 1949 *Topography of Roman Scotland North of the Antonine Wall*, Cambridge.

Curle, J 1932 'An Inventory of Objects of Roman and Provincial Roman Origin Found on Sites in Scotland Not Definitely Associated With Roman Constructions'. *Proc Soc Antiq Scot* 66, 277-397.

Dumayne, L 1992 *Late Holocene Palaeoecology and Human Impact on the Environment of North Britain*. Unpublished Ph.D. Thesis, University of Southampton.

Dumayne, L (1998). 'Human impact on the environment during the Iron Age and Romano-British times: palynological evidence from three sites near the Antonine Wall, Great Britain', *Journal of Archaeological Science* 25, 203-214.

Dunwell, A J and Keppie, L J F 1995 'The Roman Temporary Camp at Dunning, Perthshire: Evidence From Two Recent Excavations', *Britannia*, 26, 51-62.

Frere, S S 1980 'The Flavian Frontier in Scotland', *S.A.F.*, 12, 89-97.

Frere, S S 1987 *Britannia*, (3rd ed), London.

Frere, S S & Wilkes, J J 1989 *Strageath, Excavations Within the Roman Fort 1973-86*. *Britannia* Monograph Series No.9, London.

Gleeson, A C 1998 'Coarse Stone', in Alexander, D and Watkins, T 'St Germains, Tranent, East Lothian: the Excavation of Early Bronze Age remains and Iron Age Enclosed and Unenclosed Settlements', *Proc Soc Antiq Scot*, 128, 240-242.

Glendinning, B and Dunwell, A 2000, 'Excavations of the Gask Frontier Tower and Temporary Camp at Blackhill Wood, Ardoch, Perth & Kinross', *Britannia*, 31, 255-290.

Groenman van Waateringe, W 1980 'Urbanisation and the North-West Frontier of the Roman Empire', in Hanson, W S and Keppie L J F (ed) *Roman Frontier Studies 1979*, Oxford (Brit Arch Rep Int Ser, 71, vol 3), 1037-44.

Groves, C 1990 *Tree-ring Analysis and Dating of Timbers From Annetwell Street, Carlisle, Cumbria, 1981-84*, A.M. Lab Report 49/90, London.

Gudea, N 1997 ' Die Verteidigung der Provinz Dacia Porolissensis Zwischen Mauersperre und Verteidigung in der Tiefe', in Groenman van Waaterings, W et al,

Roman Frontier Studies 1995, Proceedings of the 16th International Congress of Roman Frontier Studies, Oxford, 13-24.

Guido, M 1978 *The Glass Beads of the Prehistoric and Roman Periods in Britain and Ireland*, London.

Hanson, W S 1978 'The Roman Military Timber Supply', *Britannia*, 9, 293-306.

Hanson, W S 1987 *Agricola and the Conquest of the North*, London.

Hanson, W S & Friell, J P G 1995, 'Westerton: a Roman Watchtower on the Gask Frontier', *Proc Soc Antiq Scot*, 125, 499-520.

Hartley, B R 1972 'The Roman Occupations of Scotland: The Evidence of Samian Ware', *Britannia*, 3, 1-55.

Hingley, R C 1992 'Society in Scotland From 700BC to AD200', *Proc Soc Antiq Scot*, 122, 7-53.

Hobley, A S 1989 'The Numismatic Evidence for the Post-Agricolan Abandonment of the Roman Frontier in Northern Scotland', *Britannia*, 20, 69-74.

Hoffmann, B. (forthcoming), *The Roman and native Glass from Newstead*, Edinburgh: NMS.

Holder, P A *The Roman Army in Britain*, London.

Hutcheson, A 1904 'Notice of the Discovery of the Remains of an Earth-House at Barnhill, Perth', *Proc Soc Antiq Scot* 38, 541-547.

Ingemark, D 1998 'Roman Glass'. in: Main, L 'Excavation of a timber Round-house and Broch at the Fairy Knowe, Buchlyvie, Stirlingshire, 1975-8', *Proc Soc Antiq Scot*, 128, 335-337.

Jarrett, M G 1994, 'Non-Legionary Troops in Roman Britain', *Britannia*, 25, 35-78.

Jones, G D B & Woolliscroft, D J 2001 *Hadrian's Wall from the Air*, Stroud.

Karklins, K 1982 'Dutch Trade Beads in North America' in Hayes, C F *Proceedings of the 1982 Glass Beads Conference*, Research Records of the Rochester Museum of Arts and Science 16, Rochester, 111-115.

Keppie, L J F 1983 'Roman Inscriptions From Scotland: Some Additions and Corrections to RIB I', *Proc Soc Antiq Scot*, 113, 391ff.

Keppie, L J F 1996 'Roman Britain in 1995, Scotland', *Britannia*, 27, 396-405.

Keppie L J F 1998 *Scotland's Roman Remains (2nd ed)*, Edinburgh.

Klee, M 1989 *Der Limes Zwischen Rhein und Main*, Aalen.

Körtüm, K 1998 'Zur Datierung der römischen Militäranlagen im obergermanisch-rätischen Limes gebiet, Chronologische Untersuchungen anhand der Münzfunde', *Saalburg Jahrbuch*, 49, 5-65.

Lole, P 1997 'Limpid Reflections', *Glass Circle News* 70, January 1997, 11-12.

Luttwak, E N 1976 *The Grand Strategy of the Roman Empire*, Baltimore.

Macdonald, G 1918 'Roman Coins Found in Scotland', *Proc Soc Antiq Scot*, 52, 203-76.

Macdonald, G 1919 'The Agricolan Occupation of North Britain', *JRS*, 9, 112-138.

Macdonald, G 1924 'Roman Coins Found in Scotland II', *Proc Soc Antiq Scot*, 58, 325-329.

Macdonald, G 1934 *The Roman Wall in Scotland*, (2nd ed), Oxford.

Maxwell, G S 1981 'Agricola's Campaigns: the Evidence of the Temporary Camps', *Scot Archaeol Forum*, 12, 25-54.

Maxwell, G S 1983 'Recent Aerial Discoveries in Roman Scotland: Drumquhassle, Elginhaugh and Woodhead', *Britannia*, 14, 167-182.

Maxwell, G S 1984 'New Frontiers: The Roman Fort at Doune and its Possible Significance', *Britannia*, 15, 217ff.

Maxwell, G S 1989 *The Romans in Scotland*, Edinburgh.

Maxwell, G S 1990 'Flavian Frontiers in Caledonia', in Vetters, H and Kandler, M (ed) *Akten des 14. Internationalen Limeskongresses 1986 in Carnuntum*, Vienna, 353ff.

Maxwell, G S and Wilson, D R 1987 'Air Reconnaissance in Roman Britain 1977-1984', *Britannia*, 18, 1-48.

McLaren, A 1958 'Excavations at Keir Hill, Gargunnock'. *Proc Soc Antiq Scot* 91, 78-83.

Millett, M 1990 *The Romanization of Britain*, Cambridge.

Moore, P D, Webb, J A & Collinson, M E 1991 *Pollen Analysis*, (2nd ed), Oxford.

Ogilvie, R M and Richmond, I A 1967 *Cornelii Taciti de Vita Agricolae*, Oxford.

Peacock, D P S and Williams, D F 1991 *Amphorae and the Roman economy: an introductory guide*, London.

Pennant, T 1774 *A Tour in Scotland: 1772*.

Perth Museum & Art Gallery 1994 *Perth Glass*, Perth.

Pitts, L F and St.Joseph, J K 1985 *Inchtuthil, The Roman Legionary Fortress*, Britannia Monograph Series, No.6, London.

Price, J 1985 'The Roman Glass'. in: Pitts, L F and St Joseph, J K *Inchtuthil. The Roman Legionary Fortress*, Britannia Monograph Series No 6. London, 303-312.

Price, J 1989 'The Roman Glass'. in: Frere, S S and Wilkes, J J *Strageath, Excavations within the Roman fort 1973-1986*, Britannia Monograph Series No 9, London. 192-203.

Price, J 1999 'Bottle fragment', in: Dore, J N and Wilkes, J J 'Excavations directed by J D Leach and J J Wilkes on the Site of a Roman Fortress at Carpow, Perthshire, 1964-79. *Proc Soc Antiq Scot* 129, 481-575.

Proudfoot, V W 1978 'Camelon Native Site'. *Proc Soc Antiq Scot* 109, 112-128.

Ramsay, S 1995 Woodland Clearance in West-Central Scotland During the Past 3000 Years. University of Glasgow, unpublished Ph.D. Thesis.

Ramsay, S & Dickson, J H (1997) 'Vegetational History of Central Scotland' *Botanical Journal of Scotland*, 49(2), 141-150.

Richmond, I A 1940 'Excavations on the Estate of Meikleour Perthshire 1939', *Proc Soc Antiq Scot*, 74, 37ff.

Richmond, I A and McIntyre, J 1936 'The Roman Fort at Fendoch in Glen Almond', *Proc Soc Antiq Scot*, 70, 400ff.

Richmond, I A and McIntyre, J 1939 'The Agricolan Fort at Fendoch', *Proc Soc Antiq Scot*, 73, 110ff.

Rivet, A L F 1964 'Gask Signal Stations', *Arch J*, 121, 196-198.

Robertson, A S 1964 'Miscellanea Romano-Caledonica', *Proc Soc Antiq Scot*, 97, 180-201.

Robertson, A S 1970 'Roman Finds From Non-Roman Sites in Scotland', *Britannia* 1, 198-227.

Robertson, A S 1974 'Roman "Signal Stations" on the Gask Ridge', *Trans Perthshire Society of Natural Science,* (Special Issue), 14-29.

Robertson, A S 1978 'The circulation of Roman coins in North Britain: the evidence of hoards and site-finds from Scotland' 186-216 in Carson, R A G and Kraay, C M *Scripta Nummaria Romana.* (London).

Robertson, A S 1979 'The Roman Fort at Cardean', in D.J.Breeze (ed) *Roman Scotland Some Recent Excavations*, Edinburgh, 42ff.

Robertson, A S 1983 'Roman Coins Found in Scotland, 1971-82', *Proc Soc Antiq Scot*, 113, 405-448.

Rogers, G 1974 *Poteries sigillées de la Gaule Centrale. Les motifs non figurés*, Gallia Suppl, 28, Paris.

Rogers, I M 1993 'Dalginross and Dun: excavations at two Roman camps', *Proc Soc Antiq Scot*, 123, 277-290.

Roman Gask Project (The). World Wide Web Site, www.morgue.demon.co.uk/Pages/Gask/ index.html

Romans, J C C and Robertson, L 1983 'The General Effects of Early Agriculture on the Soil Profile', in Maxwell, G S (ed) *The Impact of Aerial Reconnaissance on Archaeology*, CBA Res Report 49.

Ross, A 1965 'A Celtic (?) Stone Head From Perthshire', *Transactions and Proceedings of the Perthshire Society of Natural Science* 11, 31-37.

Roy, W 1793 *Military Antiquities of the Romans in North Britain.*

St.Joseph, J K 1951 'Air Reconnaissance in North Britain', *JRS*, 41, 52-65.

St.Joseph, J K 1955 'Air Reconnaissance in Britain, 1951-5', *JRS*, 45, 82-91.

St.Joseph J K 1958 'Air Reconnaissance in Britain, 1955-7', *JRS*, 58, 86-101.

St.Joseph J K 1965 'Air Reconnaissance in Britain, 1961-64', *JRS*, 55, 74ff

St.Joseph, J K 1969 'Air Reconnaissance in Britain, 1965-68', *JRS*, 59, 104ff.

St.Joseph, J K 1970 'The Camps at Ardoch, Stracathro and Ythan Wells: Recent Excavations', *Britannia*, 1, 163ff.

St.Joseph, J K 1973 'Air Reconnaissance in Britain, 1969-1972', *JRS*, 63, 214-46.

St Joseph, J K 1976 'Air Reconnaissance of Roman Scotland 1939-75', *G.A.J.*, 4, 1ff.

St.Joseph, J K 1977 'Air Reconnaissance in Britain, 1973-76', *JRS.*, 67, 125ff.

St.Joseph, J K 1978 'The Camp at Durno, Aberdeenshire and the Site of Mons Graupius', *Britannia*, 9, 271ff.

Shotter D C A 1996 *The Roman Frontier in Britain*, Preston.

Shotter, D C A 2000a 'Petillius Cerialis in Northern Britain'. Northern History, 36:2, 189-198.

Shotter, D C A 2000b 'The Roman Conquest of the North-West', CW(2), 100, 33-54.

Snape, M E and Speak, S C 1995 'An excavation on Dere Street at Riding Mill', *The Arbeia Journal*, 4, 21-34.

Stace, C 1997 *New Flora of the British Isles*, (2nd ed), Cambridge.

Steer, K A 1957 'The Nature and Purpose of the Expansions on the Antonine Wall', *Proc Soc Antiq Scot*, 90, 161-169.

Steer, K A 1964 'Ardoch Fort', *Arch J*, 121, 196ff.

Syme, R 1958 *Tacitus*, Oxford.

Taylor, D B 1982 'Excavation of a Promontory Fort, Broch and Souterrain at Hurly Hawkin, Angus', *Proc Soc Antiq Scot* 112, 215-253.

Turner, I 1997 'Closure of the Northern British Glassworks', *The Glass Cone* No. 43, Autumn 1997, 4.

Van der Sleen, W G N 1973 *A Handbook on Beads*, Liège.

Welfare, H and Swan, V 1995, *Roman Camps in England, the Field Archaeology*, London.

Whittington, G & Edwards, K J 1993 'Ubi solitudinem faciunt pacem appellant: the Romans in Scotland, a palaeoenvironmental contribution', *Britannia*, 24, 13-25.

Wilkes, J J   1974   'The Antonine Wall Fortlet at Wilderness Plantation, Lanarkshire', *G.A.J*, 3, 51-65.

Woolliscroft, D J   1988   'The Outpost System of Hadrian's Wall', *CW(2)*, 88, 23-8.

Woolliscroft, D J   1989   'Signalling and the Design of Hadrian's Wall', *Archaeologia Aeliana*, ser 5, 17, 5-19.

Woolliscroft, D J   1993   'Signalling and the Design of the Gask Ridge System', *Proc Soc Antiq Scot*, 123, 291-314.

Woolliscroft, D J   1994   'Signalling and the Design of the Cumberland Coast', *CW(2)*, 94, 55-64.

Woolliscroft, D J   1996   'Signalling and the Design of the Antonine Wall', *Britannia*, 27, 153-178.

Woolliscroft, D J   1999   'The Roman Gask Project' in Gudea, N   (ed),   Roman Frontier Studies 1997, *Proceedings of the XVIIth International Congress of Roman Frontier Studies*, Zalau, 293-301.

Woolliscroft, D J   2000   'More Thoughts on Why the Romans Failed to Conquer Scotland' *Scot Archaeol J*, Vol 22.2, 111 - 122.

Woolliscroft, D J   2001   *Roman Military Signalling*, Stroud.

Woolliscroft, D J   forthcoming (a) 'The Roman Gask Series Tower at West Mains of Huntingtower, Perth & Kinross', *Proc Soc Antiq Scot*, 130.

Woolliscroft, D J   forthcoming (b) 'Excavations at Cuiltburn on the Roman Gask System', *Proc Soc Antiq Scot*, 131.

Woolliscroft, D J & Hoffmann, B   1991   'Zum Signalsystem und Aufbau des Wetterau-Limes', *Fundberichte aus Baden-Württemberg*, 16, 531-543.

Woolliscroft, D J & Hoffmann, B   1997   'The Roman Gask System Tower at Greenloaning, Perth & Kinross', *Proc Soc Antiq Scot*, 127, 563-576.

Woolliscroft, D J & Hoffmann, B   1998   'The Roman Gask Series Tower at Shielhill South, Perth & Kinross. Excavations in 1973 and 1996', *Proc Soc Antiq Scot*, 128, 441-460.

Woolliscroft, D J & Hoffmann, B   1999   ' Zum Signalsystem und Aufbau des rätischen Limes', *Germania*, 77, 163-183.

Woolliscroft, D J and Hoffmann, B   forthcoming, 'Sites on the Line of the Antonine Wall at Garnhall, Cumbernauld', *Proc Soc Antiq Scot*.

Woolliscroft, D J and Swain, S A M   1991   'The Roman "Signal" Tower at Johnson's Plain, Cumbria', *C&W(2)*, 91, 19-30.